ROUTLEDGE LIBRARY EDITIONS:
DEVELOPMENT

POWER AND INDEPENDENCE

POWER AND INDEPENDENCE

Urban Africans' perception of social inequality

P. C. LLOYD

Volume 92

Routledge
Taylor & Francis Group

LONDON AND NEW YORK

First published in 1974

This edition first published in 2011
by Routledge
2 Park Square, Milton Park, Abingdon, Oxon, OX14 4RN

Simultaneously published in the USA and Canada
by Routledge
711 Third Avenue, New York, NY 10017

Routledge is an imprint of the Taylor & Francis Group, an informa business

First issued in paperback 2013

© 1974 P. C. Lloyd

British Library Cataloguing in Publication Data
A catalogue record for this book is available from the British Library

ISBN 13: 978-0-415-58414-2 (Set)
ISBN 13: 978-0-415-60190-0 (Volume 92 hbk)
ISBN 13: 978-0-415-85012-4 (Volume 92 pbk)

Publisher's Note
The publisher has gone to great lengths to ensure the quality of this reprint but
points out that some imperfections in the original copies may be apparent.

Disclaimer
The publisher has made every effort to trace copyright holders and welcomes
correspondence from those they have been unable to contact.

Power and independence

Urban Africans' perception of social inequality

P. C. Lloyd

School of Social Sciences,
University of Sussex

Routledge & Kegan Paul
London and Boston

First published in 1974
by Routledge & Kegan Paul Ltd
Broadway House, 68–74 Carter Lane,
London EC4V 5EL and
9 Park Street,
Boston, Mass. 02108, USA
Set in 10 on 12 Times Roman
and printed in Great Britain by
Butler & Tanner Ltd, Frome and London
© P. C. Lloyd 1974
ISBN 0 7100 7973 7

Contents

Illustrations

Tables

Preface

Everywhere in the Third World men and women are flocking to the cities. The capitals, especially if they are also ports and industrial centres, now contain a high proportion of the nations' populations, living in their peripheral shanty towns. The rural areas, often lacking much exploitable wealth and even, in some locations, facing land shortage due to a rapidly rising population, offer few opportunities to the school leaver. The patterns of migration too are changing; fewer come to the cities seeking work for a few months only, more expect to spend the whole of their working lives there. With the rapid growth of the state bureaucracies and of the manufacturing sector there are indeed more skilled and well-paid jobs. But the total number of new jobs created each year falls far below that of primary school leavers or of urban migrants. Thus an ever-growing proportion find work in the 'informal' economy as artisans, petty traders and in personal service occupations; some prosper, many are grossly under-employed. The few in the skilled and well-paid jobs are affluent in comparison with the urban masses who live on incomes well below the declared minima necessary for subsistence. Their poverty contrasts with the wealth of the top professional and mercantile élite, who enjoy a living style commensurate with that of the middle classes of Western industrial nations.

In this situation social tension is anticipated. The indigenous property owners fear the violence of the mob which so clearly surrounds them. The expatriate radical looks to the urban workers and the poor to provide, variously, the leadership, the support or the spark for the revolution. Yet those who have lived in these shanty towns report neither the active radicalism nor the abject apathy and violence associated with the sub-culture of poverty. Instead they describe what we would call *petit bourgeois* attitudes of hope, hard work and achievement. This study is an attempt to explore such attitudes, showing both their genesis and the type of action, particularly organised protest, which they engender.

My association with the Yoruba of the south-west of Nigeria has now lasted for twenty-five years. From 1949 to 1956 I was a research fellow of the West African Institute of Social and Economic Research at, as it then was, University College, Ibadan. In my first two tours, spent in Iwo, Shaki and Ado-Ekiti, my studies were primarily ethnographic, with a focus upon the traditional political structure. In the next tour, spent in Ijebu Ode, I examined the relationship between the traditional polity and the newly created local government system. After an interlude among the neighbouring Itsekiri I returned to the Yoruba and, as a land research officer in the Western Region Ministry of Lands and Labour, prepared a report on customary land law, based upon two areas which I already knew—Ekiti and Ijebu—and two new ones—Egba and Ondo. These three years as a senior civil servant (in status, though hardly in mode of work), together with the five succeeding years, 1959-64, when I taught in the University of Ibadan, brought me into close contact with the upper echelons of Yoruba society. This culminated in my organisation of the sixth International African Institute seminar on the New Elites in Tropical Africa, held in Ibadan in July 1964. Class formation and class consciousness were dominant themes in the seminar. In the ensuing years my own interests have continued to be directed towards the emergent patterns of social stratification but with a growing emphasis on the position of the urban, usually immigrant, worker.

Since returning to England in 1964 my visits to Nigeria have been frequent. In the summer of 1968 I carried out a pilot project, generously financed by the Nuffield Foundation, in which an interview schedule with open-ended questions was administered to thirty Ibadan men whose occupations ranged from farmer to senior civil servant. The success of this led to the design of a much more ambitious project which was financed by the Social Science Research Council. In this two research fellows—Gavin Williams and Adrian Peace—participated. Each spent eighteen months in Nigeria, July 1970–December 1971, living and working substantially in the manner associated with social anthropologists. Gavin Williams worked in Oje, a traditional quarter of Ibadan, which my wife had previously studied (B. B. Lloyd, 1967; Mabogunje, 1968); here the majority of men were living in their natal compounds though engaged in urban occupations. Ties with the rural area remain close, for each descent group holds its own farm land. A rural rebellion, the Agbekoya movement, had reached its apogee a few months earlier, and though largely confined to farmers, had had a considerable impact on the town. Adrian Peace worked in Agege, a town twenty miles north of Lagos which began to grow in the early years of this century with the settlement there of leaders of the African Church and their establishment of cocoa plantations; it has subsequently become a busy commercial centre on the outskirts of Lagos. Its growth and development have rapidly increased with the establishment, on its margins, of the Ikeja Industrial Estate. The population of Agege is of course overwhelmingly of recent immigration. Peace focused his study upon the workers in some of the factories, examining trade union activity at the grass-roots level; fortuitously, widespread strikes occurred during his research. But he saw the workers as members, too, of a thriving commercial community in which the values of independent employment and entrepreneurship were strongly stressed.

In examining Yoruba perceptions of social inequality we had originally intended to contrast the native population of Oje with the migrant population of Agege. But it seems that possible differences along this variable are obscured by the greater contrast between the stagnation of Oje and the prosperity of Agege, and by the presence of factory employment in the latter area, its absence in the former. Both before our arrival in Nigeria and repeatedly thereafter we discussed our common objectives. But, as is inevitable, we each brought slightly different theoretical viewpoints to the research; variations in field situations, in dominant events and in close rapport with different categories of persons all conspire to make a strictly comparative approach impossible. A questionnaire was administered to a similar sample in Oje and Agege but this yielded more valuable qualitative results in the answers to open-ended questions than in the quantitative comparison of the two locations. The results of this research project are presented therefore as complementary, rather than comparative, studies.

In the present monograph I present an overview of the patterns of stratification in Yoruba society. The material in chapters 2 to 5 comes from the totality of my research and experiences and cannot be assigned to any particular project. The data on attitudes in chapter 6 derives from the pilot study in 1968 and the questionnaire survey of 1971. I have not made specific use of the field data collected by Gavin

Williams or Adrian Peace, beyond their already published reports cited in my final chapter. A full list of their publications to date, reporting upon their own data, is given in the Bibliography.

It would be arrogant, and certainly false, to assume that my research answers most of the questions with which I started. The fieldwork itself, and even more so the subsequent analysis of material, raise new issues and suggest substantial changes in my theoretical orientations. The writing of this monograph has certainly had this effect. First, at the comparative level I feel that this type of study might be replicated elsewhere to explore in particular the relative determining effect on current Yoruba attitudes of their traditional open or egalitarian social structure and of the individual's experiences of education, subsequent migration and present employment in urban areas. Which in effect are more important—the values to which a man is socialised in his youth or the effect of his past and current experiences—in changing his image of his society? Second, and at a theoretical level, we should endeavour to develop our techniques for ascertaining and describing the image of the world, or some aspect of it such as social inequality, held by our subjects. Although I believe that I have progressed further than most in presenting, for any society, its members' perceptions of social inequality, my methods now seem to me to be rather crude—a combination of some hard data with a welter of impressions. To which I can but say, as would most social anthropologists, that my own impressions in this area are richer than those of most of my readers. Yet a model is hard to find. Philosophers urge the importance of studying the subjects' definition of a situation; psychologists describe experimental situations of minuscule scale, statisticians and economists describe decision-making in situations which are simple when compared with that which we seek to describe, using mathematical techniques which seem inappropriate in their complexity to the data which we can collect. I believe this is an area in which the social anthropologist may make a valuable contribution.

Acknowledgments

Inasmuch as this monograph reports research conducted over a very long period, it is impossible to name all of those who have assisted in one way or another both in making my sojourn in Nigeria long and pleasant and in stimulating the development of my ideas. My greatest debt must lie with the Yoruba people in whose towns I successively worked, and with my collagues in the Ministry of Lands and Labour, and the University of Ibadan. Next I must acknowledge the help given by those who at various periods worked with me as research assistants in Nigeria: Ben Orimolade, A. O. Shote, P. Dosummu and Paul Alabi, and Norman Roper and Robin Howard who analysed the questionnaire data. My debt to Gavin Williams and Adrian Peace, colleagues in my recent research project, will be evident in these pages; I could not have wished for two more able scholars, and the combined results of our research will, I hope, demonstrate the profitably of collective effort. At the many seminars at which since 1968 I have presented interim reports of this research, participants have offered stimulating suggestions. To the secretaries who have struggled with my handwriting—Molly Braxton, Adrienne Hirschfeld and Wendy Smith—I offer my heartfelt thanks.

I acknowledge the permission given by Pierre L. van den Berghe and Stanford University Press. to reprint extracts contained herein.

P. C. LLOYD

University of Sussex

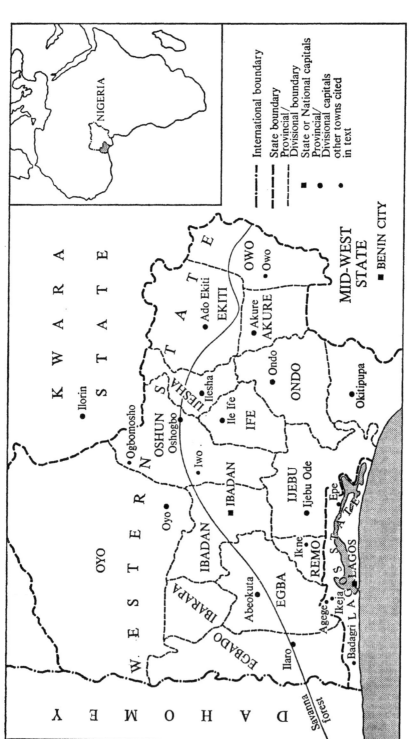

MAP 1 *South-western Nigeria*

1 Introduction

Barely a century separates the cession of Lagos to the British Crown from the granting of independence to Nigeria in that same city in 1960. For 350 years following the first contacts with Benin in 1498 European ships had traded on this part of the West African coast and their activities undoubtedly stimulated the growth of the Yoruba kingdoms. But it was not until 1901 that a British protectorate was declared over these kingdoms. In the second half of the nineteenth century British penetration was limited to missionary activity and the peregrinations of consular officials attempting to end local wars and open the country to peaceful trade. To assert that these sixty years of colonial rule wrought changes greater than had previously been experienced by most human societies is trite but nevertheless true.

British colonial administration united into the modern Nigeria not only the Yoruba kingdoms but many other ethnic groups as well. Bureaucratic in form, it contrasts markedly with traditional forms of government which were nevertheless overtly maintained as instruments of local rule. Administrative positions were filled by British officials whose salaries were equivalent to those paid in the United Kingdom; Nigerians appointed to executive posts received salaries/wages related to the incomes of local farmers and traders. Thus the best-paid clerk earned much less than the newly appointed administrative officer at the bottom of his salary scale. To train the executives, primary and secondary schools were established but a small number of men went further, obtaining a university education, becoming lawyers and doctors, and leading the nationalist movement. Nigerians now man the vastly expanded and increasingly centralised administration but the basic differentials in the salary structure still remain.

Much of Yoruba country, and notably the more populous forested zone, is well suited to cocoa growing and it is this crop which has provided the wealth which makes this part of Nigeria one of the more affluent regions of tropical Africa. (Cocoa yields a substantial income relative to the input of labour necessary for its cultivation.) It is however grown on small plots by a large proportion of the farming population, and few individuals have large incomes from this source. Marketing boards originally established to protect the farmer from the vagaries of price fluctuation on the world markets, are now the instrument whereby any excess over the fixed price paid to the farmers is channelled into government revenues constituting, for the Western State, a large proportion of its income and financing not only the social services widely enjoyed but also the salaries of the ever-growing number of civil servants. The wealth from cocoa has also stimulated the growth both of local craft industries and of wealthy entrepreneurs—the cocoa buyers and lorry owners.

Little was done during the colonial period to stimulate manufacturing industry; a tobacco factory was established in Ibadan, a brewery in Lagos. But since the mid-1950s this sector has expanded rapidly, though most new industries are located in the industrial estates on the outskirts of Lagos. Almost all the new factories have been established by the expatriate firms though in many there is some Nigerian participation. They tend to be capital—rather than labour—intensive. Conditions of employment and factory origination are substantially similar to those in Western countries—though a distinction may be made between those managed by British or American firms and those with Asian management. However, in industry as in administration, the same wide gap exists between the remuneration of the unskilled worker and of management personnel.

Today the primary school leaver might expect to earn little more than £100 a year in his first job and his ceiling is perhaps double. A secondary school leaver will earn between £200 and £500 a year while the university graduate or similarly qualified person will have an initial annual salary of £800 and may rise to over £3,000 as a senior civil servant or university professor. Farmers and most craftsmen are assumed to earn less than £100 a year. This is a situation typical of most developing countries—a situation in which an educated élite enjoys a style similar to that of the 'middle classes' of the industrial nations, whilst the poor, albeit benefiting variously from improved social services—piped water, electricity and radio—have seen little improvement in their material conditions over the past two decades. It is a situation which in Nigeria as elsewhere has not radically changed since independence.

The disparity described above is exacerbated by two other factors. First, to assuage the demands of their electorate the political leaders of Western Nigeria rapidly increased educational facilities in the 1950s and 1960s and a vast number of school leavers now flock annually to the towns in search of wage employment. The output of primary and secondary schools is ten times the number of places created by the growth of the civil service and of manufacturing industry. Many are absorbed into the private service sector; many are 'applicants'—the local term for unemployed; are all very poor. Second, the 1960s witnessed a declining growth rate in most developing countries and a reduction in foreign aid and investment—in other words, near-stagnation. In Nigeria the costs of the Civil War are now balanced by the large revenues from the oil industry which, although not located in Yoruba country, nevertheless bring indirect benefit to the whole country. Inflation in recent years has however brought considerable hardship to the Nigerian poor.

In Western Nigeria, as was fairly typical in colonial Africa, recruitment to the well-paid posts in the modern sector was from a wide social base. Many of those now holding doctoral degrees have come from poor rural homes, from families completely lacking in education. Yet it is becoming increasingly apparent that the well-educated are today able to ensure, by their wealth and their ability to understand and manipulate the school system, that their own children receive as good or a better education than themselves and that they will constitute the educated élite of the coming generation. Conversely the urban worker has the least chance of any social category that his son will enter secondary school. An open society is rapidly closing.

In this situation one might expect increasing protest from the peasant farmers, the factory workers, the urban craftsmen and petty traders, and the partially or totally unemployed school leavers against the gross inequalities in income and in frustration as their hopes for a better life, promised by the politicians in the 1950s, do not materialise. One might expect a growing consciousness of class among the underprivileged. Protests there have been, as my colleagues have described elsewhere—the Agbekoya peasant rising around Ibadan and elsewhere in the Western State, and widespread strikes in the industrial estates of Lagos (Peace, 1974; Williams, 1974). Yet all observers report the conspicuous absence of class terminology among even the English-speaking Nigerians and the virtual absence of an ideology proposing a radical restructuring of society in a more egalitarian form.

It is not difficult to explain this apparent conservatism. The Yoruba well fit Marx's classic description of the French peasantry as undifferentiated potatoes in a sack.

The industrial worker is a recent migrant to the towns, hopes to move eventually into self-employment as artisan or trader and to return to his home village; his commitment to industrial work is minimal. But whilst he is so employed his income is considerably more than that of most of his fellows. Nevertheless there is a growing volume of literature in which the African farmers are categorised as peasants, the urban workers as a proletariat (Allen, 1972; Amin, 1964; Cohen, 1972; Grundy, 1964; Heisler, 1970; Worsley, 1972). In the attempt to define these terms and apply them to Africans some useful insights into the economic position are stressed. But many of the articles then proceed to predict, on the basis of theories derived from Western or Asian experience, that the African peasant or proletariat will, according to the radical viewpoint adopted, constitute the revolutionary force in African society.

Whatever might be the validity of these predictions, conspicuous by absence from this literature is any discussion of the African's own view of his society. What does *he* think about the inequalities described above? How does *he* view his opportunities? His actions, in accepting his society or protesting, are founded upon his image of this society and we cannot understand or explain them satisfactorily save in terms of this image. Models which ignore this factor may well prove to have some predictive value—but they would surely be so much better were they to incorporate it. The focus of this monograph is the image which the Yoruba have of their society.

To start by looking for class consciousness among the Yoruba, by categorising the cocoa farmer as a peasant, the factory workers as a proletariat, betrays one's ethnocentrism. As Bohannan notes apropos of his study of Tivland, 'the anthropologist's chief danger is that he will change one of the folk systems of his own society into an analytical system, and try to give it wider application than its merit and usefulness allow' (1957, p. 5). This stricture applies with even greater force to those in other disciplines, for the social anthropologist, in relying on his informants as well as his own observation for his data, has always tended to produce a description of society which is a refinement but not a contradiction of that held by its members. For a long period the distinction between the observer's portrayal of the society and that of the actors was not stressed. In focusing upon the 'folk model' of the Tiv, Bohannan was reacting against Gluckman's (1955) earlier description of Barotse society in which he argued *inter alia* that Western legal concepts were quite applicable and that the Barotse could be said to have a legal system as we would understand it. More recently Lévi-Strauss, in differentiating between the conscious models or structures of the actors and the deep or unconscious models elucidated by the observer, has re-emphasised the distinction.

But how can the external observer describe the images of their society held not merely by one member of that society but by many? To record every utterance and action and subject the record to content analysis is a practical impossibility. He must use his own ideas of relevance in abstracting from all that he sees and hears, and he here injects his own bias. One solution adopted widely by social anthropologists has been to focus upon a single concept. Thus Bohannan opens his book (1957, p. 1):

> To understand the social relations of the Tiv, the cultural idiom in which they are conducted, and the terms in which both are imagined and valued, we need to know something about one concept that is fundamental. That concept is *tar*.

Similarly, Mediterranean studies have focused upon 'honour' and 'shame' (e.g. Peristiany, 1965). But these studies are open to the same objections as those which try to portray our own Western society in terms of 'class'; they imply an overriding and consensual concern with the one concept. How many of us would claim that a description of our own society in terms of class or some other such concept was but a highly subjective exercise; how therefore can the social anthropologist working in an alien culture defend himself against the accusation that his is but an impressionistic account of the society he studies?

In describing the Yoruba image of their society we must certainly eschew the use of such concepts as class or proletariat, at least until that late stage in our discussion when we compare the situation in Nigeria with that obtaining elsewhere in the world. Those concepts, as used by us, derive from our interpretation of our history and carry considerable overtones apart from being difficult to define, even minimally. We must endeavour to use terms which are culturally as neutral as possible against which to set those used by the Yoruba.

One last problem of interpretation remains. We try to present the Yoruba view of inequality in their society in as unbiased a manner as possible. But are the Yoruba as concerned with inequality as we are? Our own concern with Equality (with a capital 'E') may be said to originate in the eighteenth century; the peculiar stress placed on achievement may be a feature of industrial societies. A study of a primitive communistic settlement—a kibbutz or a hippy commune —solely in terms of the social inequality perceived by its members would be rightly criticised as missing the essential elements in the structure of the community. I can but assert, on the basis of long experience among the Yoruba, that the issues which feature in the following chapters are of concern to them.

Structures

Men seek order in their environment. To be able to manipulate it successfully they must be able to predict the outcome of their own actions, the responses of others and their impact on the physical world. They create in their minds an image of their environment which is but an approximation to reality; this image is continually being modified as predictions are disconfirmed and as actions transform reality. We can term this image a structure since it is a system of interrelated parts capable of transformation and is self-regulatory. Inasmuch as we are concerned with the image of the social environment, the constituent parts of the structure are social relationships. These can be described at two different analytical levels: first, in terms of observable behaviour as the statistical norms, i.e. what people actually do, or as the jural norms, i.e. what people say they ought to do, the values underlying their behaviour; second, at a much more abstract level, as in the deep or unconscious structures of contemporary 'structuralists'. In the process of structure-building the individual becomes depersonalised; he becomes a set of statuses or positions performing the expected roles and thus incorporated into the institutions which the sociologist or social anthropologist sees as constituting the society.

The structural approach is a method, not a theory. It does not posit *what* relationship might exist between its constituent parts. But it does assert that the relationships are determined and not random and that a finite number of transformations are possible. But since the structure is self-regulating towards equilibrium, the source of these changes lies outside the structure; the structure cannot change itself. The structural approach may help us to predict the direction of change; it cannot tell us how or by what process the changes occur. For this we must return to the individual.

Every individual has a structured image of the society in which he lives (see Kelvin, 1970, ch. 1; McHugh, 1968). This comprises a vast number of concepts and of propositions relating to them. These he derives from his childhood socialisation, from his family and peers; they are modified continually by his own experiences which may confirm or disconfirm his expectations, by the experiences of others and by the articulation of his own image. A further socialising force may be an ideology propounded by the political leaders of the society. In this image of his society the individual perceives the goals which he might seek, the routes by which he might attain these, his own opportunities and the constraints imposed by others. He can evaluate the benefits likely to accrue to himself against the possible costs in terms of the negative sanctions of others and the personal guilt experienced in flouting internalised values. His actions, and the values which he asserts in justifying or defending them, constitute a confirmation or rejection of the statistical and jural norms.

Every individual in a society has a different image of his society. Forces making for differentiation are the peculiar patterns of socialisation and the subsequent events in the life of each individual; forces making for congruence lie in peer interaction, the impact of ideologies and the fact that each image must approximate to the reality of events. Again individuals vary in their ability to relate the various propositions which they hold, to draw inferences from events in their lives, to modify their image in face of disconfirmation of the predictions. Furthermore, in different situations an individual may use different concepts and propositions; they may seem to us to be mutually incompatible yet nevertheless appear to serve his ends. The observer's task is to recognise this diversity yet to generalise either within specific social groups or categories or across the whole society.

Studies of the 'folk' image of society have hitherto presented this as a single model. I think that an understanding of this image is enhanced if we delineate two distinct models; but I would emphasise that this is a heuristic device and that we should not imagine that

the individual himself makes this clear distinction or that he consciously applies one model in one situation, the other in a different
one. I shall term the two models the externalised analytic structure
and the ego-centred cognitive map—or analytic structure and cognitive map for short, although admitting that all four words here used
are equally applicable to either model. I shall discuss more fully
below the nature of these two models; here I outline their essential
differences.

In using an analytical structure the individual stands outside his
society—though noting his own place within it. He sees his society
as an integrated whole and is concerned with the interrelationship
between the constituent parts. In the cognitive map the individual is
placed at the centre; surrounding him is his personal network of
relationships; the map specifies the goals available to him, the routes
by which he can attain them. It is the cognitive map which is the
individual's guide to action, though as I shall argue later the two
models are not to be seen in isolation. To some extent the distinction
between the models which I have drawn parallels a dichotomy
between a national (or worldwide) view of society and the view of the
local community. Certainly the individual's cognitive map is focused
upon the local community. But the distinction which I wish to
emphasise is that between the externalised image and the ego-centred
image of society.

Studies of folk images in peasant society have in fact stressed many
of the elements of my cognitive map in emphasising local relationships and largely ignoring the relationship between the rural community and the nation or its capital. In studies of industrial society,
surprise has been expressed that workers do not seem to hold the
class-conflict images usually attributed to them. I suspect here that the
questions upon which the data were based probed issues concerned
more with the cognitive map than with the analytical structure.

At this point it becomes pertinent for me to distinguish my own
approach from the objective–subjective dichotomy which is so
ubiquitous in social stratification studies. The objective description
of a stratification system is based upon scientific measurement of
certain qualities—the results are supposedly free from personal
bias and prejudice. The concepts used are supposed to be of some
degree of abstraction and to have near-universal validity. But we
are in fact biased in what we choose to measure and there is no in-
trinsic reason why the choice of the external observer, scholar though

he may be, is more valid than that of the individual member of the society. The models of each exist to be judged useful or not in prediction. Conversely the subjective view, as described, tends to emphasise the homespun nature of the concepts used, the paucity of information available to the individual, his inability to draw correct inferences from his experiences and the possibility that he may develop a false consciousness—being lulled into internalising values which are incompatible with his *real* interests, as interpreted by the external observer. Understressed is the rationality exercised by the individual in constructing his image of his society and in deciding his courses of action. Bohannan, as cited above, makes a distinction between the analytical system and the folk system. In each of these dichotomies the external observer is the highly trained sociologist, whilst the member of the society tends to be portrayed as being of average or below-average wealth, status and intelligence. What of the folk system or subjective view of society of one of its highly educated and articulate members?

Every individual has his cognitive map, but it needs some level of intellectual skill to construct an externalised view of society. (In the same way, Lerner (1958) emphasises the significance of empathy— the ability to conceive roles other than one's own.) But I would hold that in some measure most individuals have this capacity and they can therefore construct an analytic structure of their society as I shall outline. Nevertheless they may not use this analytic structure as frequently as they employ their cognitive map. I repeat that I distinguish between these two models both of which are used by the individual member of the society. The observer, completely external to the society, constructs his own analytical structure on similar principles, but he has no cognitive map relating to that society. (If, in studying the society, he lives among its members, he will of course have his own cognitive map emphasising his special status in the society, the means of obtaining information and so on.) One further point merits repetition. The external observer constructs a single model of the society, simplified as far as is consonant with its predictive value. The individual member of the society operates, as I have outlined above, different types of models and partial models for specific situations; these again vary from one individual to another.

Social inequality

In the preceding paragraph I have introduced some thoughts about the nature of the individual's image of his society, stressing the multiplicity and diversity of the models used by members of a society. In this monograph I am not concerned with the total view of society held by its members but only with a specific aspect of it—that pertaining to social inequality. I have accepted that a description given by an external observer will inevitably be biased by his own prejudices but argued that he should attempt to find culturally neutral concepts with which to work. At one extreme lies the danger of imposing one's own 'folk' image on the society studied. Yet simply to organise one's data around one key concept has its dangers too. Members of a society do not provide the observer with a neat framework of analysis; he must provide his own. In the following paragraphs I shall indicate what I understand by social inequality, both so that my own prejudices should be seen and so that the relevance of the material presented in later chapters is explicable. The outline is crude in the extreme. I make no pretence of acknowledging the source of all the ideas I present; nor do I contrast these with other, rival, viewpoints. To do so would necessitate another, much larger book.

Members of any society are not merely differentiated according to the roles which they perform (necessitated by a division of labour) but they are ranked hierarchically. This ranking is marked by many deferential acts of behaviour which indicate superiority/inferiority. I term this social inequality and not social stratification—for it is a matter of empirical investigation whether people of similar rank do form recognisable strata in the society. As a corollary I assert that it is the natural desire of individuals to rise in rank. To the comment that many individuals in society seem perfectly happy with their position and evince no desire to rise, I would reply that their overt attitude is a response to their inability to rise (through lack of opportunity, constraints) and the underlying attitude is still displayed in the deference paid to those above them in rank. But, in terms of what are men unequal? What are the criteria of ranking?

In the literature on stratification, three elements are ubiquitously cited—power, wealth and prestige—and these do in fact seem to be a convenient starting-point for my own purposes. Runciman (1966) has argued that these three concepts are not irreducible in terms of one another; thus one has three ranking scales, though empirical study may well disclose a high degree of congruence. However, I will define these concepts in such a way as to indicate a substantial interdependence between them.

Paramount is the concept of power; that is to say, individuals are ranked in terms of power. Power I would define broadly as the ability of one actor to determine that another behaves in such a manner as he would not otherwise have done, and perhaps against his will. It is an element of every interpersonal relationship. But, thus defined, power is a concept extremely difficult to operationalise. At the micro level interaction between two individuals is rarely a zero-sum game and thus it is possible for each to consider that he had the best of an exchange. In many structures the individual cannot say whether he is more or less powerful than another. At the macro level we find it very difficult to describe the exact means by which the 'power élite', the ruling class, or the 'establishment', exerts its will and dominance. Yet few would deny the reality of power and we must continue to use it however loosely or ambiguously it might be defined.

Power exists in all social relationships; yet we are here concerned only with a certain constellation, that concerning social inequality. Power is here exercised in the maintenance of the existing pattern of inequality or in its deliberate modification, in the mode and control of allocation of rewards to individuals. Power can be exercised impersonally—through the making of laws or the decision to invest in new factories and thus create employment; or personally—the hiring and firing of individual workers. Power may thus be located in specific offices, conferring political or economic authority, in other modes of control of scarce resources, in the ability to apply sanctions and in the ability to influence others without recourse to sanctions. Whilst it is impossible, save in the most general manner, to rank individuals in terms of power, it is the ability to control one's destiny rather than have it determined by others, which is a dominant human motive.

The distinction between power, wealth and prestige parallels a division of human activity into political, economic and social spheres. I have used 'power' to embrace what others might term both political and economic power. So, as my next concept, I take not wealth but rewards, and consider the varied ways in which an individual may be rewarded for his efforts in his society.

Rewards may be material or non-material. In the former category are all forms of income whether in monetary form or in kind. Such income is easily quantified and can thus be scaled; but in addition to the mere amount of income one must consider a number of other factors: What is its stability from year to year and the prospects of future growth or decline? Are trading profits likely to rise or fall? Is a job permanent, secure, incremental, as in a career? The characteristics of an income may be objectively measured, but between individuals in any one society and between the consensus in two or more societies the attributes of income—amount, stability—may be differently valued. In some societies, and the Yoruba are an example, an income from land or other property is valued above income from trade; the stability of the former is one possible factor but equally important is perhaps the possession of power implied in property ownership. In considering rewards I exclude property control or ownership, usually considered within the concept 'wealth', save in the extent to which it yields an income.

Non-material or symbolic rewards include honours—titles, medals and the like (presuming that these do not affect the power of the individual)—and leisure. Here too a ranking is possible: titles are graded, leisure can be measured in time. But a problem arises here in evaluating, let us say, income against leisure: which is more desired—an extra week's holiday or a £100 pay increase?

Power has been defined as the control over rewards; it is not necessary that the possessor of power ranks equally highly in the reward scale. In fact the powerful man may seek to live modestly in order not to draw too much attention to his power and thus engender opposition. Thus we have postulated one ranking in terms of power, and another set in terms of the varied forms of reward. Logically power is superior to reward but rewards are more easily observed; furthermore it is to be assumed that an individual who cannot rise on one scale will try to rise on another. In contemplating a course of action a rational individual is assumed to maximise. If by maximise we mean 'get the highest possible income', then the assumption is not valid because power and other types of reward may be more highly valued. But we go too far if we dismiss the assumption as tautological on the grounds that we cannot prove or deny the claim that whatever the individual in fact gains is what he most valued. For any society or for any social group or category in society we may evaluate power and various forms of reward and predict that most individuals will display a certain order of preference. Again, we might assume that the individual adopts the mini-max principle—that he seeks a course which will maximise his chance of gain whilst minimising his chances of loss; the degree of risk tolerated by an individual is determined by his personality, but this too can be allowed for in making predictions within broad limits.

The third element cited in social ranking is prestige, a concept which is grossly overloaded with divergent meanings. Inasmuch as the existence of social ranking is demonstrated in interpersonal behaviour, prestige is an important concept. We should be far less concerned with the unequal distribution of rewards were it not for the fact that to have more is seen to be 'good', to have less as 'bad'. But I would hold that prestige derives from power and reward, as I have defined them. In fact I would suggest that different terms be used for different ranking criteria: thus deference as the correlate of power, admiration of reward. (Esteem might be accorded to membership of social groups to be described below.) The allocation of these words is somewhat arbitrary. My main concern is that these forms of prestige are seen as correlates of the rankings already described and do not form an alternative mode of ranking.

One form of prestige, which I would term respect, is concerned only marginally with social inequality. Respect is given to those whose performance meets the highest standards expected—the good husband, the skilled craftsman, the generous employer. These qualities are recognised but are not accorded the deference or admiration given to power and reward. How can people be scaled in terms of respect—how can a good husband be compared with a skilled craftsman? Nevertheless respect is related to social inequality in two ways. First, a respected man can use this quality to gain power or reward; he may be elected to office, selected among competitors for a job. Second, respect can be used to counter social ranking. Those who fail to achieve power or rewards assert that the successful have not observed the moral code of their society whilst they themselves have maintained it—perhaps failing to achieve just because they have maintained it. This is the 'poor but honest' syndrome.

Implicit in much of the literature on social stratification is the notion that there is, or ought to be, a simple scale of social ranking. To the external observer it is neater to have one combined ranking than three separate ones; the task of correlating that vast range of attributes—from voting behaviour to taste in newspapers—with social rank would be immeasurably more difficult if one recognised a multiplicity of ranks. From the point of view of the individual actor a multiplicity of ranking scales is awkward to say the least, for how does he behave towards a man who ranks above him in power, below him in reward? In practice, the context of the situation provides a solution on many occasions. But an actor is assumed to desire status congruence, this frequently referring to an equivalence in rank on wealth and prestige scales.

I believe that I have reached a simplified model of the structure of social inequality by excluding a separate prestige scale and stressing a relationship between power and reward scales. However, these remain distinct, though power is ill-defined and reward scales embrace several unrelated criteria. The inconsistencies and incongruities in these scales feature on the cognitive map of the individual, directing his action and often determining his goals.

Social mobility

To describe the ranking of individuals in a society is to present a static picture; its dynamic aspect is the manner by which the positions in the ranking scale are allocated to individuals and the degree to which they can rise or fall in rank, either within a lifetime or between generations—in other words, the degree to which the ranking of individuals or families is perpetuated.

Inequality exists in social ranking in two ways. First is the range between the top and the bottom of the scales. On the power scale this is largely the function of the scale of the society. Whilst ranking in terms of power is inevitable in a society, ranking in terms of rewards is not—individuals could be rewarded with absolute equality. Though absolute equality exists in no known society, the range of rewards does vary—from the wide range in Nigeria and other developing countries, to the relatively narrow range in east European countries. Second, a society may be open (upward and downward movement in rank is frequent) or closed (individuals tend to hold the same social position in terms of rank as their parents, grandparents and so on). Four types of society are thus theoretically possible— wide range of rewards/open; wide range/closed; narrow range/open; narrow range/closed. The term 'egalitarian' society is conventionally used to describe both a society with a narrow range of rewards and an open society; changes in the structure of a society may be described in a like manner.

The measurement of social mobility is conceptually simple but fraught with practical difficulties. It is easy for us to understand that a man is higher in social rank than was his father. But, for instance, what point in the lives of father and son does one take for comparison? How does one relate different reward scales—traditional versus modern, rural versus urban, present versus past? To simplify the problem, we may for example divide a population into blue- and white-collar workers and calculate the inter-generational movement between these two categories; but are we sure that these are relevant categories? In simplifying the statistical issues we raise more serious problems in the realm of concepts.

We are interested not only in the amount or degree of social mobility, but also in the manner by which it is achieved. By what routes does the individual rise, or fall, in rank? What are the necessary qualifications or resources—technical skills, education, age, social skills? What are the accepted modes—by examination or by patronage?

In describing the pattern of social mobility in a society we are often apt to seize upon very generalised statistical data and to describe the mobility routes as if they were open to almost all. It is essential however that we should examine social mobility from the point of view of those at different positions in the social ranking. How do the routes available to those at the bottom differ from those used in the middle? Are there, in fact, barriers within an ostensibly open system which are nevertheless difficult to surmount?

Social mobility was described above as the dynamic element in the pattern of ranking. If seen exclusively in structural terms it too can become a static study. The pattern is not immutable—it is the outcome of individual actions and is maintained or altered by such action. Those who maintain or alter the pattern according to their own wishes and against the attempts of others acting in a contrary direction, are, by our definition given above, the powerful in the society. In examining social mobility we must not only ask how those in power do in practice maintain the structure of inequality in society and preserve their own privileged position within it, but ask also under what conditions the structure is altered.

Social groups

In the previous pages I have described the terms in which I think
social ranking should be viewed. Since I hold that individuals seek
to rise in rank or at least demonstrate the superiority of those above
them, it follows that they do recognise the ranking system. But it
does not follow that the social groups which are recognised are
constituted on the basis of social rank. We are apt to presume on the
basis of our own experience that minimum social distance exists
between persons of similar rank, maximum distance between persons
of very dissimilar rank. But it is possible for a society to exist in
which minimum social distance exists between members of the same
ethnic group—a descent group, caste, religious category—irrespective of power or reward status; maximum distance between persons
of similar rank but of different ethnic affiliation.

There are two aspects to the study of social groups—reference
groups and units of interaction. The individual in a society perceives
its members as falling into one or other of a small number of broadly
defined categories. These constitute reference points for his own
behaviour and for that of others. He may wish to be included within
a category or he may simply wish to emulate or denigrate characteristics displayed by those within it. Such a reference group need not
exist save in the minds of individuals. Members of the category
named may not interact with more than random frequency or
intensity.

Alternatively, social groups exist when people interact believing
that there is a minimum social distance between them. In much
social interaction disparity in social ranking is openly acknowledged
—it is often the basis of the interaction inasmuch as one actor seeks
to benefit from the other's power or reward status. Again many
associations are formed for the common pursuit of a specific and
limited interest; the social inequality among members is apparently
recognised in the selection of the high-ranking as leaders and office
holders. I am concerned here with such interaction and associations
as are created because the individual sees others as 'people like me'
sharing common values and a common culture. With such individuals he is prepared to contemplate what he regards as the more
intimate modes of interaction—marriage, eating together, shared
recreation (though what a society regards as intimate may well vary,
e.g. as where hypergamy rather than homogamy is the rule). Between

such individuals we may say there is a minimum social distance. It is a matter of empirical observation to discover which individuals interact in this manner and what is the category that embraces them —whether rank, ethnic affiliation or some other characteristic. Where, however, social rank is not the basis of social grouping as perceived by members of the group (or by others in the society) we should nevertheless examine the degree of correspondence between social rank and social grouping in ethnic terms—for the world is full of examples of societies in which the correspondence is so marked as to make ethnicity a mere mask for class.

We might scale the solidarity of social groups along two dimensions. On one we measure the degree to which such interaction leads to the emergence of a distinct sub-culture in the society, differentiated from others by style of life, speech and dress habits, values and to the perpetuation of such a sub-culture through generations. Along the other we measure the awareness of the members of their distinctiveness, moving towards a recognition of common interests, the articulation of these interests and, through leadership, towards action to preserve these interests.

So far I have done little more than list a number of topics which are embraced within the concept of social inequality. In doing so I have stated what *I* think one should be looking for, that is to say the variables which one should use in constructing one's own observer's model. But the same leads are equally useful in a study of the image or model which the Yoruba have of society. For each topic stated I would ask: 'How do the Yoruba see this issue—what concepts and propositions do they employ?' This method is crude in the extreme when compared with many exercises in ethnoscience—but these latter concern the most minute problems. Yet it is I believe an advance on the selection of a 'key concept' and the apparent distillation from the entirety of one's observation with nothing but intuition as the basis of selection.

Actors' models

I suggested above that one might portray the individual's view of his society not in terms of one model but of two—and I termed these the analytical structure and the cognitive map. For the first model the individual views society from the outside, as it were, seeing it as a whole and concentrating upon the relationship between the constituent parts. The degree to which any individual can project himself in this way will of course vary from one to another. The cognitive map is ego-centred; every individual must have such a map, for without it he could make no choices.

For both the analytical structure and the cognitive map used by any individual we must discover empirically two sets of data: the concepts and propositions which he has learned and the information available to him as a result of his experiences. These will differ at least slightly between one individual in society and another, though there may be a consensus at a more general level. They may differ greatly from the concepts and information used by the external observer.

The external observer *qua* observer is concerned solely with the question: 'How does this society work?' The member of the society asks this too; but he also asks: 'How might it work better or how ought it to work?' In other words, he sees the structure of his society as either legitimate or illegitimate. In the former case he accepts the patterns of distinction of power and reward as fair, he accepts the rules or principles which determine social mobility and he endeavours to manipulate these to his own advantage. In the latter case he variously rejects the pattern of distribution—it ought to be more or less wide in range; or the rules of mobility—upward movement should be easier for some or all categories of people. The reactions to this viewpoint will range from active attempts to change the structure of social inequality in the desired direction, to apathy, with the recognition that either one is powerless to change the structure or the costs of doing so seem unlikely to balance the likely rewards. The individual does not see his cognitive map in static terms; some relationships are held to be more important than others, some need to be strengthened, others reduced in intensity if the individual is to achieve his goals.

The analytical structure

I have outlined the elements which constitute the analytic structure— the nature and range of power and rewards and the values variously attaching to them, the rate and routes of social mobility, the social groups perceived in society. These elements provide a relatively static picture of the society (mobility describes the movement of the individual within the structure but not necessarily the process by which the structure is maintained or altered). As we asked earlier: 'How is the structure maintained or altered?' The answer lies in considering the relationship perceived between different hierarchical parts of the structure. I use the vague word 'parts' for whilst a society may on one hand be seen as a series of rigidly defined strata; the social groups of which the individual is aware may, on the other hand, not be arranged hierarchically, though he will be aware of a hierarchy of positions of power and reward.

Ossowski (1963, p. 19) has provided us with 'three spatial metaphors of the vertical stratification of social classes, which represents a society as an aggregate of people, of whom some are above, others below'. First is the dichotomic conception—the division of society into opposed categories, the 'haves' and the 'have-nots'. The emphasis here is on the power of the 'haves' in maintaining the structure and their position in it. This view of social inequality is more likely to be held by the 'have-nots', rebelling against their underprivileged position, than by the 'haves' who might be unwise to boast of their own status. Second is the system in which the relationship between the strata is seen not in terms of dependence but as an ordering relation. The strata form a ladder up and down which people can move. This conception parallels the view of a society as open—rather than as closed as in the case of the dichotomic conception. It is a view to be favoured by those who have experienced upward mobility. In the third, functional conception the relationship between the perceived groups or categories in society is seen 'in accordance with the functions which they fulfil in social life'; they are 'mutually essential to each other', even though their interests may be incompatible— 'in either case, whether the emphasis is on harmony in the performance of tasks or on conflict of interests, we may in the functional scheme discern a network of reciprocal relationships' (1963, p. 58). Whilst the dichotomic scheme usually implies rejection of the perceived structure of inequality, adherence to the gradation scheme is more likely to be associated with acceptance of it. Functional dependence seems to me to be more a quality of the cognitive map which I shall describe below.

The individual sees his society as a structure of interrelated parts; he must also see himself as a part of that structure, locating himself with reference to one or the other part. On one hand he sees himself as a member of a social category or group—but more than that, he assesses his own position within that group and in relation to others.

He may be either a solid member of the group, accepting his own position within it and accepted by others; or he may be a marginal member either striving to enter the group and gain acceptance or to leave it for a group more highly ranked. The individual may see himself placed not with respect to social groups or categories but simply at some point in the social hierarchy. He measures his position, expressed in terms of power, and, more usually, reward, both absolutely and relative to that of others. And he may see himself as deprived relative either to his own expectations of his achievements, and to others' expectations of his achievements, or to his evaluation of what others in a similar position to himself seem to have achieved. The term 'relative deprivation' is thus used in two senses—the first in terms of absolute power or rewards, the second of achievements relative to others.

The cognitive map

The concept of the world-view or folk image, in its several forms, has been used by anthropologists; but its use has usually been restricted to peasant or primitive societies, thus facilitating the contrast between the perceptions of the members of the society studied and the anthropologist studying them. Wallace (1961, pp. 16–17) developed the concept of the mazeway:

> Mazeway is to the individual what culture is to the group. Just as every group's history is unique, so every human individual's course of experience is unique. Every human brain contains, at a given point of time, as a product of this experience, a unique mental image of a complex system of objects, dynamically inter-related, which includes the body in which the brain is housed, various other surrounding things, and sometimes even the brain itself. This complex mental image is the mazeway. Its content consists of an extremely large number of assemblages, or cognitive residues of perception. It is used, by its holder, as a true and more or less complete representation of the operating characteristics of the 'real' world.
>
> The mazeway may be compared to a map of a gigantic maze, with an elaborate key or legend and many insets. On this map are represented three types of assemblage: (1) goals and pitfalls (values, or desirable or undesirable end-states); (2) the 'self' and other objects (people and things); and (3) ways (plans, processes

or techniques) which may be circumvented or used, according to their characteristics, to facilitate the self's attainment or avoidance of values. For heuristic purposes, let us crudely categorise the content of the mazeway, recognising that these categories (like the categories represented by different colours, shading, shapes, or thicknesses of line on a map) do not represent the only possible analytical divisions and relationships.

Elsewhere (1965) Wallace describes the mazeway as the sum of all cognitive maps. As an example he outlines his cognitive map of his drive from home to office. This map comprises the route—the corners, traffic lights, etc.; rules about driving; driving operations; the monitoring of information received and processed. He concludes by doubting whether this framework of analysis can be applied to the much more complex processes of social organisation. The difficulties are undoubtedly great but I feel that the attempt needs to be made even though our results, at this stage, may be crude in the extreme. Some simplification is indeed achieved by restricting one's interest, as is attempted here, to the pattern of social inequality and by making no attempt to cover all aspects of social life.

The concept of mazeway and cognitive map as used by Wallace seems appropriate to both my own models but more especially to my cognitive map in that it stresses the goals sought by the individual and the routes by which these goals might be attained.

The individual is central in my ego-centred cognitive map. Extending outwards from himself is his network of personal relationships with others. In recent descriptions of networks by social anthropologists we are usually presented with complex data on an individual's interaction during a limited period; to collect these data is tedious; yet in constructing the map we need to include all those others with whom ego does not regularly interact but with whom he may have a potential positive relationship and, too, those whom he may avoid. (On a map we note not only the routes to be followed but also the by-ways and culs-de-sac to be avoided.) In interacting with individuals more distantly related to him, ego's expectations of their behaviour are probably couched in normative terms; he expects certain types of response from a wealthy farmer, a priest, a town official. But in interacting with those closer to him he has much more knowledge about the others' behaviour; he may calculate how far their responses might deviate from the norm; he assesses his own resources

—his debits or credits with others. Thus, whilst interaction with those more distantly related to one tends to be in normative terms, with those more closely related one may draw up a detailed balance sheet of resources, debts and credits, sanctions anticipated and thus evaluate the relative costs and benefits of one's proposed actions. On the fringes of the map one has a more generalised image of the structure of relationships; nearer the centre, the picture is much more detailed and indicates to ego the opportunities available to him in pursuing his goals.

Ego has his own cognitive map; the observer may compare the maps of the individuals in society, and thence of different social groups in society in terms of both the concepts used in constructing them and the type of reticulation. The idea of the world-view or cognitive map has usually been applied to the 'common man' in a society, most frequently the peasant. But it is equally applicable at all levels—from the virtual outcast at the bottom of the hierarchy to the member of the social élite at the top. (And even the external observer, if he is a participant observer, has his cognitive map describing his relationships with informants, etc.)

Cognitive maps may be compared on two dimensions—scale and reticulation. In the centre is ego; around him are 'people like me', or 'us' as compared with 'them'; this category appears much larger to him than those at the margins. The 'us/them' dichotomy has frequently been described; some refer to the former as the moral community—it is the group with shared values. Often, in rural settings, it is expressed in territorial terms—our community/village as against others, or ethnic terms—our tribe is different from others. Neither is applicable in urban settings and I would suggest that the limits of the 'us' group are determined largely by social mobility. Within the 'us' group there is relatively free movement of individuals from one status to another and those who move out of the group are lost to it —the relationships with them are severed. Just how rigidly the 'us' group is thus bounded is a matter for empirical investigation. Peasant societies are frequently quite rigidly bounded, but as I hope to show later, in many modern African societies networks are very loosely bounded and the relationships of quite humble people extend into élite groups and thus render the 'us/them' distinction (at least in terms of inequality) less easy to define.

The 'us' are circumscribed by groups of 'them'. Laterally these may consist of like communities, the neighbouring villages, and so on.

On the inferior margins are those who are the drop-outs from 'us', the not-socially accepted. 'Them' usually refers more specifically to those placed in superior rank; they inhabit a world different from one's own; one's own network does not directly penetrate it. But on the margins members of both 'us' and 'them' are a few individuals who link the two groups: in an English village community, for example, the squire, vicar, professionals (doctor, etc.), retired members of the 'them' group.

In comparing the reticulation one may examine a number of criteria—the openness or closure of individual networks, the degree of connectedness between individuals, the types of persons who occupy key positions in networks, the importance to the individual of different zones within his network (intimate, effective, extended).

Power is obviously an important element in the cognitive map because power exists in every relationship—one is using others to gain one's own ends. Each relationship in one's network is seen in terms of debts and obligations. One does not thus see the powerful as a category—at least, if one works within the model of the cognitive map; but if one views the local community in terms of an analytic structure then a dichotomous relationship is possible.

Mutual interdependence within the community together with a possible high degree of social mobility (both intra- and inter-generational) may contribute in fostering a strong sense of equality within the community. Differences in power and reward are accepted but they may be transitory. To achieve this equality of men in the face of obvious inequality of power and reward emphasis may be placed on moral qualities—the poor are honest, the rich are wicked; one may be rewarded in heaven, the other on earth. With equality goes a feeling of community solidarity—the person who seeks to leave the 'us' community, especially to join the 'them', is despised. Such sentiments, of course, strengthen such 'us/them' dichotomy as exists.

Though members of a community may stress equality and solidarity one may nevertheless find intense competition for power and reward. For the equality and solidarity may be stressed primarily in relation to the 'them' group; conversely it may seriously inhibit the development of local leadership within the community.

The degree to which power and equality are stressed within the community, the scale and reticulation in the cognitive map, are all matters for empirical investigation. But it is very likely that, in using one model in appraising social inequality, the individual stresses certain qualities in relationships which are ignored in the other model. In particular the dichotomous relationship seen in the analytic structure gives way to a stress on functional interdependence in the cognitive map. The analytic structure is used by the individual to assess his position in society, to formulate long-term goals; the cognitive map is used in pursuing his limited short-term objectives —perhaps the goals which he feels that he is able to achieve rather than those which exist in his fantasies or in an idealised future.

I stressed at the outset that the distinction between the two models was a heuristic device and that I do not suggest that the individual consciously operates one or the other model in alternate situations. On the other hand we cannot talk of amalgamating the models. In any situation the individual will both appraise his situation as an external observer, using the analytic structure, and determine a course of action with reference to his cognitive map. Inasmuch as both models exist in the same mind and both refer to the same external world (albeit concentrating on the larger society in one case, the local community the other) they must be seen as related. Thus it seems likely (though in need of verification) that a strong 'us/them' dichotomy in the cognitive map of the less privileged members of a society will accompany a dichotomous relationship between 'haves' and 'have-nots' in the analytic structure. Conversely a cognitive map with networks extending throughout the society will be associated with an image of society as open.

From structure to action to structure

The cognitive map of the individual delineates the goals which are available to him and the means whereby these are to be attained; it shows in varying degrees of detail the resources available to himself and to others who might assist or constrain him; it shows the nature of his relationship with others. The map defines not only the oft-chosen goals and the well-trodden paths to them but also indicates to the individual the peculiar opportunities open to him perhaps because he possesses a unique set of resources or can manipulate a particular constellation of relationships. His actions and his values— both those which he enunciates in support of his actions and those which are upheld by his actions—can thus either conform to the existing statistical and jural norms of the society or depart in some degree from them. Thus actions maintain or change the structure of the society and lead all involved individuals to modify their own cognitive maps. However, resistance may be met as new experiences appear to contradict well-established precepts, the modification of which would call for a radical restructuring of the map.

The eventual outcome of the actions of the individual and the subsequent responses of others may be in accord with his predictions, leading him successfully towards his goals. Alternatively the individual may be frustrated. A positive response to such a situation would be to formulate alternative goals or alternative means of achieving the original goals. But persistent and repeated frustration, or the acknowledgment that whilst one's map is accurate one does not possess the necessary resources to attain the goals sought, can lead to a variety of responses. These might be summarised under three heads: fantasy—one hopes that something will miraculously happen to change one's situation, like the arrival of the cargo, a pools win; a denial of the validity of the social ranking hierarchy—an emphasis on upholding moral values as being superior to rank (once again the 'poor but honest' syndrome); the withdrawal from society —either by joining an exclusive sect within the territorial limits of the society or by emigration.

In discussing cognitive maps I suggested that the networks of relationships of which they are constructed could be compared in terms of their manner of reticulation. I wish now to turn to my final theme—the type of relationship which the individual exploits in pursuit of his goals. Basically two types of relationship are possible. He may articulate a relationship which is asymmetrical in terms of power with the purpose of bringing some (though not necessarily equal) gain to both parties. In so doing he is probably competing— in principle or practice—with others seeking similar ends. This is the patron-client relationship. Alternatively he may combine with others of like status in order to pool resources and thus to obtain collective benefits from an unwilling grantor. One can thus define the articulated relationships of each individual in terms of the predominance of one or other type of relationship; or more specifically one might ascertain the degree to which one type predominates in certain situations.

Patterns of patron-client relationships vary widely. One may have gradations in power so that clients are in turn patrons to others below them; alternatively society may be rigidly stratified into patrons and clients. The client may have many patrons, exploiting his relationship with each according to the specific benefits sought; alternatively he may seek everything from his sole patron. Thus patronage relationships may be at one extreme highly diffuse; at the other they may constitute factional groups in the society—these groups constituting major social divisions. (Factions are to be clearly distinguished from the social groups described earlier; the latter are defined in terms of minimal social distance, the former in terms of asymmetrical power relationships.)

In a like manner individuals may combine variously to serve a multitude of specific interests. But these interests may be amalgamated to constitute a broad generalised category of interests; and to the extent that we are concerned still with the distribution of power and rewards in society, the social formations resulting are social classes. Thus I use the term 'social class' to connote not the mere existence of common interests (Marx's class in itself) but the articulation of certain types of relationship.

Class consciousness therefore consists of the recognition of common interests and the articulation of basically symmetrical relationships in pursuit of these; this type of relationship thus dominates the cognitive map of the class-conscious individual. The obverse of class consciousness is not no class consciousness, a kind of blank, but the dominance of asymmetrical patron-client relationships and the possible structuring of society into factions. The class-conscious individual will see the classes in society as opposed to each other; i.e. a dichotomic scheme in terms of our analytic structure. But conversely an individual operating such a model need not be class-conscious. He may see the 'haves' and 'have-nots' as logically opposed to each other, but if he is of the latter category he may well feel that the costs of opposing the 'haves' do not match the likely rewards; he therefore seeks his own personal betterment through exploiting patronage relationships.

The degree to which factions and social classes coincide with social groups is a matter for empirical study. Furthermore I have written above as if the appeal made by the individual to the patron or to the collaborator was simply in terms of a specific interest. In fact an appeal on ethnic grounds is often far more compelling and effective for it cites values which transcend those of specific interests. Thus if individuals continually appeal to others in ethnic terms—'We Yoruba/Italians/any minority must stick together and help one another'—ethnic groups will appear to be the major structural units in the society. However, ethnic groups are not to be seen as alternatives to factions or social classes, for the ethnic relationships articulated can be defined as symmetrical or asymmetrical and an appeal to ethnicity can be seen as variously supporting patron-client or class relationships. Finally social classes and factions can become symbols as compelling as ethnic groups—in fact they appear as primordial categories; a man might appeal in terms of class in a patently asymmetrical relationship, or in terms of faction membership to attain collaboration in a specific economic interest.

Synopsis

It is not difficult to set out a series of headings under which the pattern of social inequality in a society might be studied. The practical problems of implementing such a paradigm are much greater. No individual member of society orders his ideas as simply as this; nor is the image of a single individual being presented, but the generalised image of many—in some respects of different categories within Yoruba society, in others of all Yoruba people in contrast to those of other societies. Furthermore I am aiming not to present a synchronic picture but to demonstrate how the Yoruba image of the structure of social inequality is changing as the society moves from the colonial to the post-colonial era. Finally I wish to interpose my own commentary whilst making it clear to what degree I am interpreting the actions and beliefs of the Yoruba.

I open with a discussion of traditional Yoruba society, using the term 'traditional' in its three customary senses, and hoping that it will be clear from the context which is intended: what Yoruba society was actually like before 1900; those aspects of present-day society that seem to be little changed from the past; the idealised past of present-day Yoruba. I shall outline the basic patterns of relationships in the society, noting some of the concepts used by the Yoruba themselves. This is admittedly *my* reconstruction of Yoruba society but it is a construction which derives substantially from descriptions given by Yoruba informants and would thus be both intelligible and acceptable to them; it is in no sense (save in one or two places clearly noted) a 'deep' structure. Since it is only in recent years that most Yoruba now working in the urban areas have come to the town, entered into wage employment or otherwise become involved in the modern sector of the economy, the description of traditional society serves to present the image of society to which they were socialised in their youth.

The recent experience of these men and women forms the substance of the next two chapters. First, I shall briefly outline the changes in the structure of society that have occurred within the past seventy years indicating the new positions created in society and the changing patterns of the distribution of power and rewards. In chapter 5 I shall delineate the social groups which are to be seen in Yoruba society.

These four chapters provide a description of the conceptual framework and the experiences which the individual Yoruba has as the basic elements of his structural models. They form the background to the discussion of contemporary attitudes which I present in terms of the goals sought, the routes by which these are seen to be achieved, the perception of one's own opportunities, the legitimacy of the existing patterns of social inequality and finally the action which might be taken to alter this.

In conclusion I shall synthesise this material to indicate the models which I see the Yoruba as using in terms of my earlier discussion of analytic structures and cognitive maps.

2 Social rank in traditional Yoruba society

Between the coastal lagoons of the Gulf of Guinea and the rolling savanna 200 miles to the north, between the modern state of Dahomey and the mighty river Niger, live today over ten million Yoruba-speaking people (P. C. Lloyd, 1965a); the vast majority of these are in the Western State—the largest of the constituent units of the Federal Republic of Nigeria—and furthermore live within the forest zone. Culturally the Yoruba people form an ethnic unit quite distinct from the major neighbouring groups—the Fon of Dahomey, the Nupe and the Edo or Benin people. Within Yoruba country dialect differences are quite pronounced; even today some people claim to recognise inter-village variations, whilst a century or more ago men from the savanna towns found the dialect of the Lagos area very strange to them. Yet the differences between the language of the Yoruba and those of the neighbouring peoples are, very crudely, of the same order as between English and Russian. Within Yoruba country cultural unity is displayed for instance in the pantheon of deities, in the symbolism of kingship and chieftaincy. Yet this uniformity masks very considerable differences in social and political structure.

The people

In the east the Kabba Yoruba were organised in small village groups, the village leadership residing in a triumvirate of three chiefs. Kingship, as understood elsewhere in Yoruba, was absent. In contrast the kingdom of Oyo, most powerful between the sixteenth and eighteenth centuries when its dominion embraced perhaps almost half of the Yoruba people, was a highly centralised state. The origins of kingship are obscure. The long king-lists of such kingdoms as Ife or Oyo suggest that the present dynasties date from invasion by an alien ruling group in the thirteenth century; but it is possible and indeed probable that

some form of kingship antedated this apparent conquest. In the
northern Yoruba kingdoms the basic social unit is the agnatic descent
group; in nineteenth-century Ibadan and in neighbouring kingdoms
in the forest zone these groups became very strongly corporate, as I
shall outline. In Ijebu and Ondo cognatic descent groups are found;
in the former area a core of members constitutes a residential unit,
whilst in the latter members are more dispersed. The importance of
this difference is that, with cognatic descent, the individual has greater
opportunity of manipulating to his own advantage his relationships
with the various groups of which he is a member. These differences
in social structure are correlated with differences in political structure. The Yoruba king, or *ọba*, is advised by a council of chiefs
which can be recruited in one of two ways—either each chieftaincy
title is hereditary within a descent group or a man rises through the
grades of a title association to the highest offices. The former mode
is associated with agnatic descent (and indeed helps to maintain it);
the latter is found, though not exclusively so, in societies with cognatic descent groups. These structural differences, readily observable
to the social anthropologist, are not so apparent to the Yoruba
themselves who, blinded by cultural uniformities, suppose the existence of structural uniformities too, save in such obvious matters as
the size of kingdoms. But the Yoruba do clearly recognise distinct
personality stereotypes. The Oyo are smooth-tongued and devious
—the attributes perhaps of the courtiers in the royal palace; the
Ekiti—living in small independent kingdoms and raided for slaves
by their more powerful neighbours until the late nineteenth century
—are more blunt, but are steady, hard-working people. The Ijebu
are the entrepreneurs, the 'Jews of Nigeria', for in the present century
they have emigrated to all parts of the state as traders and craftsmen
—an emigration which might be ascribed variously to a propensity
to exploit new opportunities (deriving from their social structure) and
to the higher density of population in their rather infertile homeland
(P. C. Lloyd, 1966a).

The Yoruba have, for long, lived in towns, the capitals of kingdoms which in recent centuries have had populations of tens of
thousands (Mabogunje, 1962). A rampart and ditch enclosed a
densely built-up area in the centre of which was the *ọba*'s palace—an
assemblage of courtyards with specific ritual and secular uses, facing
a large, open concourse, the whole covering several acres. In front
of the palace was the main market of the town, with roads radiating

to the town gates and beyond to the subordinate towns of the king-dom. Though towns were often evacuated and destroyed in times of war, the siting of most has remained unchanged over the centuries; though individual mud and thatch buildings crumble and decay, others are built upon their ruins, providing continuity of settlement.

By typical African standards the Yoruba were in the pre-colonial era a wealthy people. The indigenous staples—yam, cocoyam, guinea corn and beans—were augmented by the introduction from Asia of the banana and from the Americas of maize and cassava, to give a rich and varied diet. Crafts reached a high standard—both in the quality and variety of articles in everyday use; in pottery utensils and clothing, for instance; and in wood carving, metal work and other artistic forms which constituted the paraphernalia of royalty and chieftaincy, and which furnished the shrines. Trade was highly developed. The majority of town dwellers were farmers who travelled daily or for longer periods to farms; though each man provided basically the foodstuff needed by his own family, it was often advan-tageous for a wife living in the town to buy food in the market rather than walk to the farm. An intricate pattern of trade between the rural area and the town thus developed. Long-distance caravans travelled to the coast to exchange local products—notably slaves and later palm-oil—for European imports, and northwards to participate in trans-Saharan trade.

In the traditional economy all the agricultural work was done by men, save for some harvesting and the collection of wild leaves and fruits used as relish in cooking. Some crafts—smithing, carving, weaving on the horizontal loom—were exclusive to men, others—pottery, weaving on the vertical loom and the preparation of cooked food for sale—to women. Local trade was dominated by women, long-distance trade by men.

This thumbnail sketch of traditional Yoruba society is that of the external observer using historical evidence not available to the Yoruba themselves and employing concepts developed within his own profession. How do the Yoruba see their own society?

In the beginning the high god let down a chain from heaven; Oduduwa, the first man, descended carrying a cock, a handful of soil and a palm-nut; the cock scattered the soil to make the earth and the nut grew into a palm tree with sixteen branches symbolising the sixteen original kingdoms. Thus man, or at least the Yoruba, was created at Ile Ife. (The politico-cultural association founded by the Yoruba educated élite in the late 1940s was termed the Egbe Omo Oduduwa—the society of the children of Oduduwa.) Ile Ife grew into so large a town that one day its king, the Oni, despatched his children to found their own kingdoms. A Yoruba ruler may only wear a beaded crown if he can trace his origin to this exodus or to descent from the Oni or another crowned ruler by a later migration.

The myths of individual towns take up the same threads in the story. The founder, usually a royal prince, either left Ile Ife in this original exodus or perhaps some other town where he had contested the throne and lost. With his followers he wandered until reaching the present site, inhabited only by hunters (for whom it was not a permanent residence) or by a pre-established group which readily acknowledged the royal birth of the new immigrant, conferring upon him the kingship of the settlement. The towns, once established, quickly attracted other migrants—unsuccessful princes with their own retinues, men seeking to overcome their infertility in a new environment, craftsmen or ritual specialists seeking new opportunities, and latterly, in the nineteenth century, refugees in war. The leaders of the larger groups of migrants were, on their arrival, given town and farm land by the *ọba*, and perhaps a chieftaincy title to replace the one lost in their former home; others were directed to existing chiefs for a grant of land. In spite of this complex pattern of migration a pan-Yoruba clanship has not developed. Recognition of a common origin may form the basis of more favoured hospitality to travellers or constitute a barrier to marriage. But within each town it is the relationship with the founder *ọba* which is stressed and prestige in the town derives from membership of an early immigrant group; a later group, though perhaps tracing direct descent from the Oni of Ife, or the Alafin of Oyo, has no special privileges by virtue of its prestigious origin. Whilst the king-list is carefully preserved in each town (though not without discrepant versions) as a means of signifying the antiquity of the towns and to date the arrival of late immigrant groups, the complete list of chiefs within the immigrant groups is not preserved; instead key names are retained in the much foreshortened genealogies. Descent group elders will often cite the name of a female member who became the mother of one of the past *ọba* of the town, thus affirming the relationship between the group and the kingship.

The Yoruba are proud to be town dwellers; it is a mark of civilisation. Neighbouring peoples who live in dispersed settlements are derided and the term *ara oko* (literally 'farm people', now rendered 'bush man' by English-speaking Yoruba) applies to them. A distinction of the same order is made among the Yoruba, between those who are obliged to stay mostly on their farms and those who reside in the town and can spend much of their time frequenting the palace and the compounds of chiefs.

Social categories

Descent

Notwithstanding my earlier comment on the variations in Yoruba social structure, descent is a dominant principle of social organisation in all areas (P. C. Lloyd, 1955b, 1962, 1966a). The following generalisations will however be more apposite to the northern agnatic Yoruba—by far the more numerous category. I write in the ethnographic present except where this is clearly inappropriate.

Members of the descent group trace their descent from a named ancestor who emigrated to the present residence at some time in the past and who is placed in the foreshortened genealogies constructed to establish rights to land or chieftaincy, three or four generations above living elders. The founder is said to have had from two to five sons who accordingly head the constituent segments of the group; this segmentation is, as will be outlined below, a basis for the allocation of chieftaincy titles; it is not usually important in the allocation of land.

Members of a descent group and their wives (who by rules of exogamy must be members of other groups) live in a large compound (*agbo ile*)—a series of linked rectangular courtyards. The compound, including a small proportion of affines, strangers, etc., often numbers several hundred persons, or in very large towns may exceed a thousand inhabitants. Members of the descent groups may be distinguished in the town variously by their facial or body marks, by the possession of certain food taboos associated with the major deity served by all members, by a set of appellations by which members are hailed, by customs practised within the compound, relating for instance to the feeding of small children. All of these serve (together with the myths of origins of the group) to establish its separate identity within the town.

The descent group is not only a residential unit but also a property-holding group. The land of the compound and a large block of farm

land is held corporately by members—all participate in its management and each has a right to use as much as he can, with his various
dependants, cultivate. The descent group is a political unit; the views
of members are articulated through the head of the group (the *bale*,
or chief) and he in turn is the administrative head, collecting tribute
and perhaps organising collective labour. The head of the group is
expected to settle disputes within the group, and to represent the
individual member of the group who is in dispute with a member of
another group. Marriages are seen as the affair of the entire group
which in its regular meetings not only pronounces upon the eligibility
of the match in terms of maintaining the rules of exogamy but also
upon the political desirability of a link with the other descent group
concerned. Members of a descent group are collectively responsible
for one another's debts, to the extent that a creditor was allowed in
the past to distrain any property in the compound. There was however no blood feud, for all cases of homicide had to be referred to
the *ọba* and chiefs.

The Yoruba town is composed of these strongly corporate groups
—strongly corporate in the sense that so much of the activity of the
individual takes place within the group. As an external observer I
stress ʾthe competition between these groups—for power (itself a
function of the rank of chieftaincy title and of the numerical size of
the group), for land (its needs depending upon its size) and for
wives (by which the size of the group is increased). This competitive
relationship is seen by the Yoruba themselves who assert that, but
for the arbitration of the *ọba*, the groups would be unable to co-
exist in the town. An aspect of this competitive relationship is the
equality of the descent groups in the sense that each has an identical
relationship with the *ọba*. But descent groups differ in power and
size; some have high-ranking chieftaincy titles, others lesser titles or
none at all; some groups of later origin are dependent on others,
having received land from them and perhaps being administratively
subordinate; smaller groups are weaker and less able to enforce their
claims on others. The groups with major titles tend to receive more
wives than they give and so grow larger; but a point is reached when
fission occurs. Correspondingly small groups lose their separate
identity and it is debated within the town whether a name refers to a
social group or to a mere geographic locality (but presumably the
erstwhile residence of that group). Prestige attaches to the larger
groups with high-ranking titles—usually deference to the power

associated with the group; for while the external observer may postulate a process of uneven growth and altered ranking, the resident of
the Yoruba town has a more static image of the relationship between
the constituent descent groups.

This ranking of descent groups refers to non-royal groups, for the
royals are in an ambiguous position. The association of the group
with the kingship makes it highly revered, but especially that segment
from which reigning ǫba are chosen. The members of the royal
descent group are not usually eligible for positions on the council
of chiefs nor do they hold large areas of land which have been allocated to migrants. They are denied privileged access to the ǫba. They
are thus relatively powerless and may be said to rank socially below
the commoner descent groups.

Thus on one hand the social rank of an individual in the Yoruba
town is the rank of his descent group. We must now turn to the
principles of ranking within the descent group—principles which do
in fact transcend the group.

Within the descent group each person is ranked in seniority according to the time of entry into the group—by birth for full members, by marriage for wives. The Yoruba distinguish siblings as older
(*ǫgbǫn*) or younger (*aburo*) irrespective of sex, and these words are
used in addressing not only other members of the group of similar
generation level but persons outside the group. Members of ascendant
generations are distinguished in the same way—father's elder sibling
from father's junior sibling; these would be addressed as *baba* (father)
or *iya* (mother) according to sex. A junior brother of one's father
younger than oneself could be addressed as *aburo* though in certain
contexts the term *baba* would be more appropriate. Within a compound a wife must use a nickname for a child born before her marriage.

This ranking is exemplified by the deference accorded to senior
persons—one prostrates to them, one carries their loads and does not
permit them to do any demeaning manual task. A man should never
surpass his father in titled rank—he ought to be helping his father to
gain a title; the success of a junior brother in attaining a title is often
cited as the reason for the emigration of the senior brother—he
could not prostrate before his younger brother. Succession to property, including wives, passes from senior to junior brother—never
the reverse. (Thus a man can sleep with his father's or elder brother's
wife if the senior man is negligent; it is a heinous offence to sleep
with the wife of a junior relative.)

The oldest man in the descent group is its leader, the *bale* (from *baba*, father, *ile*, house or lineage). He succeeds to office without ceremony upon the death of his predecessor. He acts as chairman of the descent group rather than its trustee, for he is not expected to act independently in respect of the property of the group. The power of the *bale* derives from his supposed age, this being associated with his proximity to the ancestors. In fact his age is often exaggerated. Obituary notices of aged Yoruba often cite the age of the deceased as 140 years (though other evidence would suggest 90 or so years). Assistants collecting genealogies for me provided plausible ages for almost all persons (for individuals can calculate their present age by seniority within the compound and by their age at outstanding dates in their childhood—a coronation, epidemic, great fire); but the *bale* was usually described as being over 120 years, the man second in succession to him about 100 years and the third about 70 or 80 years old. When questioned, the assistants asserted that the *bale* was 'so much older than everyone else'.

Ranking within the descent group is important to the individual because so many of his interests are articulated within these groups. In a system of cognatic descent groups the individual has the choice between the groups to which he owes primary allegiance. But the member of an agnatic group has the choice solely between membership of the group and acceptance of its obligations or opting out completely—either in joining his mother's agnatic group or becoming a virtual slave. Women retain, on marriage, full membership of their own groups and they continue to maintain the taboos and to participate in group activities. They frequently visit their natal compounds, taking their children with them. A child may beg for land and be regarded as a stranger of a most privileged status; if he took up residence in his mother's compound his descendants would probably, after an interval of three or four generations, be described in the genealogies as full agnatic members. Exceptionally a chieftaincy title might be bestowed on the son of a female descent group member with the explanation that the group really wished to honour the woman, but she could not hold a title; so instead they asked her son to assume it—thus preserving in part the agnatic principle.

Age

In most Yoruba communities groups based upon age seem to have existed in the past. These were of two types—age sets (*egbe*) constituted at three-year intervals and age grades of perhaps seven-year intervals up to forty-five years of age organised to provide warriors or for public work in the town.

The age set interval ensures, with the operation of a two-year post-partum sex taboo, that two full siblings cannot belong to the same set. Sets were usually constituted when the young people reached adolescence. Those of the men flourished until the death of most members; those of the women were never so important. The activities of the age sets were primarily social—weekly meetings at which members would drink and talk about their problems; an annual dance might be staged. Strong bonds of solidarity existed—a member of the set should not seduce another's wife—and discipline was maintained—fines were levied on latecomers to meetings. One of the primary functions of the age set was to enable the individual to display qualities of leadership among his peers, which he could not so easily do within the compound with its rigid age ranking. Not only might young members of an age set feel that certain of their problems, especially relating to young women, were more appropriately discussed with their peers but they would also assert that attendance at age set meetings had priority over those of their descent groups. Leadership in the age set was achieved, that in the descent group largely ascribed.

Women

I have carefully referred above to 'members' of the descent group without distinction as to sex, though many of the points made refer implicitly to men. The status of women in society may be summarised briefly, recapitulating themes already raised (P. C. Lloyd, 1963, 1968a).

In traditional Yoruba society there is a fairly rigid division between the tasks which are appropriate to each sex; this, together with the almost complete exclusion of women from agricultural work, means that women work independently of their husbands and not jointly or co-operatively with them. Whilst the wife expects her husband to give her a loan to start trading or to establish her craft, all income derived from her labour is her own—to spend on herself and her children. On marriage a woman retains full membership in her own descent group—expressed for example in her attendance at its meetings and ceremonies, her rights to land (to farm with the aid of slaves, to build her own house on). On her death her property passes to her children, albeit not of her agnatic descent group, or in the absence of children to her own junior siblings; it can never pass to her husband (nor can she inherit from him).

Wives of an *oba* have had a privileged status—to abduct one was treasonable and punishable by death. But the status of wives of other men, even of chiefs, derives as much from their age, descent group and occupation as from their husbands. A wealthy man may be generous to his wives, though he usually has many; conversely the husband of a wealthy woman trader is often a nonentity in the town.

The relative significance of age and sex in Yoruba society is perhaps illustrated by the 'magic man' test. Asked 'Which would you rather be—an older sibling of the opposite sex or a younger sibling of the same sex as yourself?' both boys and girls preferred the older siblings, thus demonstrating the dominance of age over sex as a criterion for evaluation (B. B. Lloyd, 1968).

Slaves

In pre-colonial times domestic slavery was widespread. The slaves were initially captured in wars between kingdoms and perhaps later traded in local markets. Nominally a soldier who seized three slaves might keep one for himself, give one to his chief and one to his *oba*. The slaves worked at most domestic tasks, helping their masters on the farm or in trading. The status was hereditary though the children of a female slave by a free-born male would be free. It seems likely that in the space of several generations slaves might become absorbed into the descent group; no formal ceremony existed, but absorption depended upon all recollection of the original slave status being forgotten—it is impossible in a non-literate society to prove that it ever happened. But, at the present time, one may observe situations where an individual who has been regarded as a full member of the descent group in a number of previous situations is suddenly discriminated against—for instance in a chieftaincy contest where slave descent is a most damaging charge that rival candidates can make against each other.

Palace slaves were in a different category. Many performed menial tasks but a hierarchy of titled offices often existed, the holders enjoying close proximity to the *ọba*. Such men were extremely powerful and enjoyed a degree of deference shared only by the high-ranking commoner chiefs.

Wealth

Status in terms of descent, age, sex, slave/free is ascribed—there is nothing that one can do to change it, though one may exploit the opportunities which it provides. But in Yoruba society there has always existed considerable differentiation in terms of wealth—an achieved status largely independent of the ascribed criteria cited. Wealth may be derived from one's occupation—farming, craft or trade—or from political office, the possession of a chieftaincy title.

Farming

Farm land is held corporately by the descent group (Galletti *et al.*, 1956; P. C. Lloyd, 1962). The individual member has a right to use as much land as he and his dependants—his sons, slaves and others —can cultivate. This land is allocated to him at a descent group meeting. If he ceases to be able to cultivate the allocated area, that is if it reverts to bush for considerably longer than the usual rotational fallow, the meeting may allocate the land to others. A man has a preferential right to the land cultivated by his father, but he cannot hold land in excess of his own needs and, in particular, he cannot alienate such land to a non-member of the descent group; only the group acting corporately can so dispose of its land. Wealth from farming thus derives from the control not of land but of skills and labour.

Farming is a skilled operation. The Yoruba recognise, for instance, more than twenty varieties of yam and match these against soil differences and climate. Some farmers are more apt than others even though most might ascribe their success to the correct propitiation of the tutelary deities.

Farmers vary too in the amount of their own effort invested. Young men would combine to form an *aro* group, working on the land of each member in turn and so overcoming a (supposedly) natural inclination to leisure. Some men are sickly and not only is their total effort reduced but ill health at strategic times such as planting can affect considerably the ultimate harvest. All men must divide their time between their work and kinship obligations—ceremonies of birth, marriage and death, descent group meetings.

The lucky man has a wife who bears him many sons. These work for the father until their marriage, when they establish their own independent farms. From adolescence they may have a small plot in which to work in the late afternoons, the produce of which they sell to gain pocket money (the provision of bridewealth on the first wife being the responsibility of the father). Thus, for a period, a a father can amass capital through the surplus produced by his sons.

This capital could be used to acquire slaves or debt-pawns (the debtor, his son or junior brother working for the creditor until the loan is repaid) to augment the labour force and thus increase the surplus. A wealthy man can hold an ọwẹ, calling to work on his land not only his own dependants but others obligated to him—his future sons-in-law for example, and providing food and entertainment for the workers; the advantages of the ọwẹ lie not so much in the cost of the labour, which might be considerable, but in the command of labour at a vital time in the crop cycle, such as making heaps or planting, when members of the ọwẹ ought to be working on their own farms.

In theory a farmer might increase his wealth continually, perhaps to the point at which his descent group could no longer provide land; in practice this did not happen for, as will be detailed below with reference to traders, farmers grow old, their sons marry, they seek chieftaincy titles. A man *could* become wealthy through farming but his affluence rarely rivalled that of the chief or the bigger traders.

Crafts

Most traditional male crafts—smithing, carving, weaving,—were hereditary within descent groups, and generally within groups low in social rank (Callaway, 1967b; P. C. Lloyd, 1953). The organisation of the craft was thus subsumed within the descent group. Differences in skill were recognised but these brought little reward. The good craftsman would be fully employed; the indifferent one would be obliged to farm in addition; the good craftsman would attract apprentices for training but the tasks which could be delegated to such youths were limited and the craftsman could not command labour on the scale of the farmer. Farmers often paid for craftwork largely in foodstuffs; *ǫba* provided free board and lodging whilst the craftsmen worked in the palace. But the mode and amount of their remuneration tended not to produce a surplus which could be invested in wives or a chieftaincy title. Craftsmen generally enjoyed the same style of life as the poor-to-average farmer.

Trade

The big fortunes came from trade—though the term 'trader' embraces a wide range of activities. At one extreme is the petty trader, a woman usually, who buys in one market and sells in another, her profit being absolutely proportional to the capital value of her stock —the goods which she can carry as a head load (with the possible assistance of one or two young girls as well). For some commodities, for example calabashes, this capital can be very little and the success-ful trader transfers to other commodities with a higher value relative to weight—cloth being one of the most remunerative. At the other end of the scale were the long-distance traders in slaves, farm produce such as palm oil, or luxury goods. It is with such men that the follow-ing paragraphs are concerned, though many of the comments upon the nature of trading operations are equally applicable to those engaged on a much smaller scale.

In every Yoruba town one will hear stories of traders who were, at some period within the last century, fabulously wealthy by local standards. Usually such men seem to have had very humble begin-nings—they were born into poor homes and started with little capital; but the legends certainly seem to emphasise their consider-able achievement. Frequently the rich traders seem to have come from those descent groups which migrated most recently to the town and thus either are without major chieftaincy titles or have less land; trade is thus seen as an alternative to political office or farming as a source of power and reward.

The success of the trader lies in his own skills. He must evaluate the market, knowing where to buy and sell, though he is constrained here by the market guilds of each town which substantially fix prices within their own areas. In the absence of written records he had, in the past (as many still do), to carry a record of all transactions in his head. Most of these transactions are of a face-to-face nature and not only in his own popularity a considerable asset but he must correctly evaluate the creditworthiness of his customers and not be blinded by their guile and charm. He must achieve the proper balance between self-indulgence—in acquiring wives and luxury goods perhaps to create an image of affluence and success—and reinvestment of capital in his business. At all times the trader faces the possibility that sudden failure, due to inadequate information as to the state of the market or injudicious transactions, is as likely as sudden success. The traders whose names become legendary are the few who maintain their prosperity for a considerable period.

Trading is an individualistic enterprise, for although a successful man may employ agents and carriers, the management of his business rests with him alone. His skills are attributed to his destiny. He might associate junior siblings with his enterprise but it is feared that the demands of near kin on the profits might prohibit expansion; his obligations to such juniors are to see them set up in business on their own and thus in competition with him. The same fears inhibit partnership with non-related men; here there is an added element of distrust for whilst the junior relative seeks the good of the descent group of which the trader is also a member, the unrelated partner is suspected of working for himself and his group.

The nature of the trading operations and the inability to form partnerships set a limit to the expansion of the enterprise and also inhibit its perpetuation after the death of the wealthy trader. Other factors too contribute to the same end. The successful trader usually reaches the height of his career at between forty and fifty; after this senility inhibits his activity. But at this age his oldest children are still young (for he probably did not marry until he was thirty) and thus not closely associated with him. The children are seen as revelling in the father's wealth rather than appreciating the hard work and self-denial necessary to create it. Even if the trader has sons old enough to take over the business he will be reluctant to treat one of them as his heir and thus arouse the jealousy of the half-brothers and their respective mothers, his wives. If he is eligible for a chieftaincy title the successful trader will probably attempt to attain it, valuing political power above wealth, and in the contest will exhaust much of his capital. Once in office his interest in his business will lapse for the Yoruba hold that the duties of political office are incompatible with private business. Thus if a trader lives to a ripe old age it is likely that in his latter years he has been living off his capital and that little will remain to pass on to his heirs. The laws of inheritance finally ensure the fragmentation of the estate.

A wealthy man acquires many wives, for not only can he afford the bridewealth but many men will gladly give him their daughters in marriage in order to create or strengthen a relationship. Yoruba society is highly polygamous and rich men frequently have ten or twenty wives—and, in consequence, a large progeny (Galletti *et al.*, 1956, pp. 69–74, P. C. Lloyd, 1968a). Children are valued; not only do they provide labour but they increase the size of the descent group; in particular the fame which a man has after his death will depend on the number of children he leaves to sing his praises and arrange lavish funeral ceremonies. Again, the greater the number of children, the higher the chance that one will have a brilliant destiny whose success will reflect upon the father. Yoruba inheritance laws provide that a man's estate should be divided among his *ọmọ iya*, i.e. into as many equal parts as he had wives (or even women not legally married to him) who bore him children (P. C. Lloyd, 1962, ch. 9). In death as in life a man should not favour the children of one woman against another. Movables—money, gowns, slaves, wives— are shared in this manner; indivisible items—a hereditary chieftaincy title acquired by the deceased—are held in turn by one son in each *ọmọ iya*; his house, built by his own efforts, is held corporately by his issue, with individuals having a prior claim to the rooms occupied by their own mothers, and the eldest surviving son in succession taking the deceased's own room and parlour. The children of a wealthy man thus gain little benefit from his affluence; his business dies with him, and his children, as farmers or traders, range from poor to rich according to their individual abilities.

The wealthy farmer or trader continues to live in his own compound, enhancing the admiration with which it is held in the town but not sharing his income with his relatives living in such close proximity. He manifests his affluence in his clothing and in the style of his own dwelling—in the traditional compound by providing a large parlour where he could receive guests, with carved verandah posts to replace the plain ones, or by building a substantial house of modern design. He might keep a horse to ride on ceremonial occasions. He can take more wives. A farmer with labour at his command can stay in the town compound enjoying not only leisure but the opportunity to engage in the affairs of the descent group and in town politics. Just as a chief spends much time sitting in the palace in council with other chiefs, so the trader attends meetings of the guild which regulates the conduct of trade, in the past being concerned with tolls exacted at town gates and markets, the formation of cara- vans and the security of the routes. But this interaction is of a formal nature and when the rich Yoruba man relaxes to enjoy the com- panionship of those close to him it is in his own compound and among the members of his family and descent group that he is usually found—not in some rich man's club. Today however these patterns are changing.

Government

The government of the Yoruba town rests with the *ǫba* (or in the case of a subordinate town, with its uncrowned ruler, the *balę*) and his council of titled chiefs (the *ojoye*) (P. C. Lloyd, 1960). In the past the *ǫba* remained secluded in the inner courtyards of his palace and was seen by his people only at the town's major festivals when he appeared in state, heavily veiled. He did not leave his palace and was attended by his wives and slaves; his close kin were denied privileged access to him. The chiefs met daily in one of the outer courtyards and one of their number conveyed their decisions to the *ǫba* who ordained them with his royal ban. All matters concerning the peace and prosperity of the town fell within the purview of the chief.

   The *ǫba* is still selected from among the sons born to a reigning monarch, the throne passing in rotation between the segments of the royal descent group. Candidates, who were expected to have been born to free, not slave, women and to be free from physical deformi- ties, were presented to the chiefs, who made the final choice, basing their selection upon the pronouncements of the *ifa* oracle as to the characteristics of the reign of each candidate should he be chosen. The new *ǫba* is installed in a series of complex rituals. These usually include: his seizure in a farm village, demonstrating his reluctance to assume office and, notionally, his ignorance of his selection (this in spite of an often bitter contest); his retracing of the route taken to the town by the first *ǫba* of the dynasty; his seclusion for three months in the compound of a minor chief whence the chiefs visit him daily to instruct him in the art of government; finally his coronation during which he assumes a new name, is symbolically re-born, takes a soup prepared from the heart of his predecessor (thus assuming his supernatural powers) and at last enters his palace. The ọba holds office for life. Formerly his reign might be terminated by the present-ation by his chiefs of a symbolic gift telling him that he had lost the confidence of his people and was expected to take his own life; but depositions seem to have been very rare—they have to my knowledge been frequent only in the kingdom of Oyo where the Alafin and his palace organisation contested power with the chiefs and in two towns where the present dynasty is descended from a conqueror who, say the legends, assumed the secular powers of government, leaving the ritual aspects to the previous incumbent, whose descendants are now regarded as priests.

Most chiefs in the Yoruba towns are appointed in one of two ways. Either they are selected by and from among the members of a descent group, the title being hereditary within the group and rotat-ing between its segments; or they are appointed by the ọba and the existing chiefs to fill a vacancy in a grade. In the latter case the support of a large following is a prerequisite for selection; it was not expected that a descent group should provide more than one chief. In a large town the chiefs are ranked in several grades—the senior usually comprising five or six chiefs. The chiefs represent the non-royal descent groups of the town; after his appointment a chief continues to live in his own compound (Ondo is the exception here). Where the title is hereditary in a descent group the compound will usually have a large open verandah and parlour facing the main entrance which is used by the chief. Unlike the ọba the chief is free to move about the town at all times. All untitled persons prostrate fully before a chief, irrespective of their ages; chiefs themselves defer to those of higher rank.

The ọba and chiefs can, but rarely would, withdraw land from a descent group but they might direct its elders to allocate vacant land to a newly immigrant group. They allocate land seized in conquest from a neighbouring town; they determine the use of 'communal' land vested in them—for instance the belt of uncleared land sur-rounding the town. They adjudicate disputes between descent groups. They fix the times for bush firing to begin and for the harvest of new yams.

The Yoruba town had no standing army and a most rudimentary police force. The army was levied by the chiefs—or certain among them—from all adult men of the town; the soldiers provided their own weapons save that in the wars of the nineteenth century chiefs often controlled the supply of gunpowder. Police activities were undertaken by a select corps of men drawn from various descent groups or by palace slaves.

The ọba and chiefs were in the past the richest men in the town, with the possible exception of one or two very successful traders. Their income derived from a number of sources: from annual tribute paid to the ọba through the descent groups and chiefs; from gifts from men seeking benefactions and favours; from entry fees paid by newly elected chiefs; from war booty; from free labour performed on their farms; from fines levied. Prestations to the ọba passed through the supplicant's chief who retained part as his own perquisite. In very general terms this system ensured that the income of the ọba equalled that of all his chiefs.

Much of this wealth was redistributed as gifts, especially to the poor and needy. Since all men had access to land, the recipients were usually those whom sickness and like tragedy prevented from maintaining themselves and their families. This bounty constituted a mode of social security and undoubtedly did contribute towards the equalising of wealth. But the style of life of ọba and chief—expressed in clothing and symbols of office, in diet, in leisure, in house space and in the number of wives—was vastly superior to that of other men. Furthermore the bestowal of gifts created ties of dependence for the recipient. Thus whilst redistribution slightly reduced the inequalities of reward, it increased the inequalities of power.

Upon the death of the ọba his estate passes in its entirety to his successor in office; nothing may pass to his kin. The wealth of the palace is thus cumulative. A chief's estate is distributed according to the general inheritance laws already described and so becomes greatly fragmented; the new chief has to establish his own wealth—first, perhaps, clearing the debts which he incurred in contesting the title.

I have elsewhere described the process of government in the Yoruba town as a struggle for power between the ọba and his chiefs, each using the resources at his command to enhance his own position and to seize for himself new sources of wealth and power (P. C. Lloyd, 1965b, 1968b, 1971a). The Yoruba do not portray the situation in quite these terms; but they take the viewpoint of the chiefs and hold that the ọba should not become an autocrat or tyrant. (Depositions of ọba are justified by their tyranny.) Two aspects of the ọba's role are stressed. First, he symbolises the status of his town *vis-à-vis* its neighbours. Its wealth is reflected in his style of life, the extent of his palace; this in turn is seen to rest upon his good government, the maintenance of peace in the town rather than its perpetual division into factions, whether these be chief versus chief, or chief versus *ọba*. Second, he is seen as an arbitrator, his success in this role deriving from his assumption through the initiation rituals of the powers and wisdom of his predecessors in office. The Yoruba see their *ọba* as a father figure and address him as *baba* as well as by the honorific *kabiyesi*. In selecting the new *ọba* from among the many candidates, the chiefs seek a man who is wise enough to arbitrate successfully but yet is compliant to their wishes; they will avoid a man who seems likely to dominate them. (The selection by the chiefs often takes place none the less in an atmosphere of internal competition between rival candidates each spending lavishly and rallying his supporters—including of course, individual chiefs related to him.) Youth is not a bar to election, and many *ọba* have had very long reigns.

Unlike the kingship, restricted to a few persons only, chieftaincy is open to all, save slaves. (For even in a town where most titles are hereditary within descent groups, some may be openly competed for.) Personal popularity is a prerequisite, either for election by members of one's descent group or to convince the *ọba* and chiefs of one's worthiness for office. The successful candidate usually needs to be wealthy, in order to display his generosity; though in many a contest the early candidates spend lavishly, run out of funds and lose favour, perhaps by their over-eagerness to assume office; victory may then go to a later entrant to the fray. Candidates tend to be elderly men; too great an age is a handicap for it is probable that the incumbent will soon become senile and die; youth too is a barrier for not only will the man lack the wisdom of age, but he will be preventing older men in his own segment from ever attaining the title: they will be dead when the turn of their segment next comes around. The descent group chief is expected to maintain the privileged position of his group in the town; the group must therefore choose its most able man, one who will not let others override him. It frequently happens that such a man is found in a segment not next in turn; his selection upsets the rotation—a frequent occurrence—and leads to considerable wrangling at the next succession contest. In fact the claims of the rival candidates both for the chieftaincy and for the throne tend to be expressed in terms not of qualities of personality but of genealogical fitness: is the candidate of strict agnatic descent, born of a free woman, of the correct segment, and so on? The rotation of a title between segments should never be upset to allow a man to be succeeded by his own son; such a flagrant restriction of the opportunities of others is extremely rare. However, a son who has been closely associated with his father during his chieftaincy is often a strong candidate at a later date. Here it must be remembered that a relatively high proportion of descent group members will be sons of chiefs and that the favours bestowed by chiefs on one or two of their offspring will be seen as reflecting the ability and personality of the latter—not the capricious whim of the father.

Like the *ọba*, the chief holds office for life. In extreme circumstances he may be deposed by the *ọba*, but a more usual sanction is to ban him from the palace. Members of the descent group are anxious that this should not happen; they might formally depose their chief but they would be unwise to weaken him by overt withdrawal of support. A senile chief is an embarrassment, but if this is merely the corollary of great age, the power and reputation of the group is maintained.

Concepts

In the previous paragraphs I have outlined the distribution of power and rewards in traditional Yoruba society, using largely my own terminology yet describing a structure which is as readily apparent to the Yoruba themselves as it is to me. At this point I introduce a few of the concepts which the Yoruba use.

The Yoruba word *agbara* corresponds to the English term 'power' in several of its connotations. It connotes both physical strength (though *ipa*, which one might translate as 'force', is a cognate term) and the command over persons. In its latter sense power derives from a number of factors: from age; from titled office; from wealth which enables one to create relationships of obligation and indebtedness; and from leadership. Thus descent group elders, chiefs, rich men, contemporary leaders of popular movements are all described as *alagbara*. Furthermore, among the Yoruba this power over persons is overtly displayed on a number of occasions. Thus at the Muslim *sallah* festivals, chiefs and rich men ride on horseback from the prayer ground surrounded by their followers; when such men attend a wedding or funeral they are accompanied by a large following; the installation of a chief is an occasion which all his dependants—descent group members, and other relatives, affines, slaves and others owing any obligation—are expected to attend; in fact the chief might 'fine' a man absent without good reason, making him buy drinks to be consumed by all present in order that the breach shall be healed.

The Yoruba distinguish between *owo* (money or riches) and *ọlà* or *ọrọ* (wealth). The *olowo* is the trader, rich today but perhaps penniless tomorrow, the man who has ready cash, but whose fortunes may fluctuate and whose affluence may be based on credit; his net assets are small. The *ọlọlà* or *ọlọrọ* has extensive farm land, house property, a large family, which imply not only permanence but also power. In fact members of a descent group may collectively describe themselves as *ọlọrọ* with respect to other groups dependent on their own, by virtue of a grant of land or because their chief is the administrative head of the quarter which embraces the other groups.

The term associated with the higher social rank is *ọlá* (honour). Title holders and very wealthy men are described as *ọlọlá* and the term implies the possession of power. The reciprocal attitude is deference. (It is intriguing to speculate on the relationship between *ọlà* [wealth] and *ọlá* [honour]; in many Yoruba phonemes a tonal change creates a completely new word; in others the tonal change denotes but a slight change of emphasis.) *Ọlá* is distinguished from *ọwọ* [respect]; the verbal form *bọwọfun* is used for prostration before someone; one respects the *olowo* [elders, creditors and the like], one does not term them *ọlọlá* (unless they are also title holders, etc.).

In showing how the Yoruba distinguish between riches and power we may see why a rich trader is anxious to assume titled office if so eligible. Not only is it a more permanent status, ensuring continual wealth, but it is associated with power and personal following and this is valued more highly than riches and lavish consumption.

Social mobility

When a Yoruba is asked, 'Are all men equal?' the most probable answer is: 'No—for just as the fingers of the hand are of different length so are some men older, healthier, richer, wiser than others.' The term 'equality' is used in the English sense of equal quantity or measure but not of social rank. A tonal change gives us ọgbà (one's age mate); thus when a Yoruba describes someone as being of the same rank as himself, or his equal, he is almost certainly referring to age rather than wealth or power. Two forms of social mobility are thus recognised—an ascribed rise in power associated with age and an achieved promotion associated with economic success and the attainment of political office. On either scale Yoruba society is open.

Our own concepts of mobility are constructed with reference to a monogamous society. Fertility differences between rich and poor may be recognised but they are rarely a factor in the rate of social mobility. In a society which values polygyny as highly as do the Yoruba a very different attitude to mobility must prevail. It is clearly quite impossible that the high rank of a chief or wealthy man is perpetuated in all his children; the more numerous they are the more they must be evenly distributed along the social hierarchy. The equality with which a man is expected to treat his wives and their respective children prohibits direct transference of his own high status to even a single heir. Yoruba technology permitted few durable memorials —large compounds crumbled, stone monuments to honour the dead were not made. The perpetuation of a man's fame rested with his children—hence the desire to have many of them and to stress that they should be of good character so as not to tarnish the name of their father. With a large progeny a man might hope that some would excel, but this would be the result of their destinies and only indirectly of his own efforts. Inversely, in a polygynous society a relatively high proportion of the population can claim close kinship with the powerful and wealthy—both present and past. So when a poor man goes through the streets to a friend's wedding or funeral, the drummers will usually be able to find a few distinguished ancestors in either male or female line, to cite in their praises of him.

The sons of a chief or wealthy man do share in the privileged status of their father—they are usually better clothed and fed; but their very number ensures that the benefits of each of them are relatively small. They grow up in the compound playing with their collaterals, children of less affluent men; they display few subcultural traits of, for instance, language or leisure activities. In fact they are sometimes said by the Yoruba to be disadvantaged—growing up in a household in affluence and security, they do not appreciate the necessity of hard work to get ahead.

The Yoruba belief in destiny is not rigidly deterministic. As a man enters the world he is given his 'fate', though its details are hence-forth unknown to him. Like the puritan ascetic he strives to live up to the standards set for him. A 'poor fate' can be modified if a man is of good character, assiduous in serving his deities; a 'good fate' can be spoiled by recklessness, or by the machinations of others through witchcraft or sorcery. The emphasis on character (*iwa*) im-plies the good opinion of one's fellows—a prerequisite as we have already seen for trading success and even more so for election to chieftaincy (Idowu, 1962, chs. 12, 13). Within the descent group privileges are granted to those whose efforts are directed towards the collective good of the group, withheld from those who display uninterest or selfishness. The social skills in manipulating one's personal network of relationships is seen in terms of assuring oneself of popular support rather than of dividing one's enemies and rivals.

A man does not reach the top by his own unaided efforts; the popular support required has just been cited. But in addition he needs specific helpers—men who will lend him money to start in trade, men who are his main backers in the title contest. The Yoruba speak of the *oluranlọwọ*, one who lends a helping hand, and the *alfẹhinti*, the one on whom one rests one's back. Without such men one's efforts are of little avail; and again one's good character is seen as important in attracting their help. In turn the benefactor is highly regarded. To the Yoruba the ideal man is the *gbajumọ*, a man of out-going personality, always ready to help others with advice or money, unstinting in giving his time and possessing a wide circle of valuable acquaintances through whom he can obtain the favours sought. He enjoys a lavish style of life. But his position is a precarious one. His clients may be able to ensure his further success—in business or towards chieftaincy; equally they may exhaust his capital so that the basis of his status, his initial wealth, is lost. Once he has nothing to give, the followers who had so recently been singing his praises quickly transfer their allegiance to another who has resources to offer. Unlike chieftaincy and great riches, which are available to only a few though all may compete to attain, the role of *gbajumọ* is one that is attainable by a great number, though again, few will be so successful as to achieve widespread fame.

Conversely, the qualities which are most despised are those of miserliness—the exact opposite of those of the *gbajumọ*. The miser is not free with his time, money or services; his efforts are directed exclusively to his own advancement.

The Yoruba can well understand how a man rises in the social hierarchy through the judicious use of his resources, maintaining a careful balance between beneficence and reinvestment, maintaining his network of personal relationships. It is quite conceivable that a man should rise from the most humble origins—the *alapata dide* is 'one who gets up from stony ground'. Sudden wealth demands other explanations, and here the supernatural is involved. A man is believed to be able to use medicines which ensure his success yet at great personal cost—his wives are barren, his children die. In fact the occurrence of such misfortunes is tantamount to proof of the use of the medicine. Naturally the rich man ascribes his success to his skills. And correspondingly, at the other end of the scale, the poor man attributes his poverty to witchcraft, whereas others will describe him as lazy or inept, distinguishing, among the poor (*akuşe*), those who have never had an opportunity to do better (*otoşi*) from those, like the rich man's son, who threw away their chances (*oloşi*). Nevertheless beliefs in witchcraft are strongly held in Yoruba society; the witch increased in power at the expense of others (Prince, 1961). Similarly sorcery enables one to thwart the designs of others. Murder and suicide were very rare among the Yoruba for these other means existed to overcome one's rivals—whether co-wives or chieftaincy contestants—in this highly competitive society.

The very openness of the society creates the possibility that a man might progress from success to success so that he completely outdistances his fellows—a rich man outshines the chief in his style of living, one chief overtops his peers. The location of so much power and wealth in one man threatens the social structure. Thus charges are laid against the man so that he is obliged to spend lavishly to retain popular support and in doing so he is reduced to a more acceptable level. The story of Chief Salami Agbaje illustrates both this ploy and the charges which are assumed to carry most weight (Butcher Report, 1951).

Chief Agbaje was a very prosperous Ibadan merchant who, starting at the foot of the chieftaincy ladder, had risen to within striking distance of the senior office—that of Olubadan. The other chiefs so feared his success that in the late 1940s they instigated a campaign against him, and at one point sent a long petition to the district officer. The following allegations were made: that bribery increased in Chief Agbaje's customary court (a point directed more towards the D.O. than towards other Yoruba), that he maintained a private road to his farm, open to others only on payment of tolls, that he gave his own sons a good overseas (university) education but neglected those of his deceased elder brother, that he reinvested his money rather than showing generosity to others, that he exploited his employees rather than helping them to become independent men; that he was not forgiving of his opponents; that he fomented intrigues rather than sought peace; that he was disrespectful towards a more senior chief; that he was tyrannical. Petitioners cited in the Butcher Report (p. 20) alleged:

> injustice, selfishness, avarice, exploitation, deceit, vindictiveness, machination, ruthlessness, insatiable ambition and soul-less tyranny, these are not bad equipment for an adventurer in the jungle of modern finance. They have never been the characteristics of the Ibadan nobility . . . our chiefs are not meant to be rich, cunning or extraordinary. We prefer them mild, humane, noble, cultured, compromising, dignified and honourable.

The agitation led to a commission of enquiry by a senior colonial administrative officer who found the charges either without foundation or else irrelevant to Chief Agbaje's chiefly office and aspirations. This finding echoed that of a peace mission by the Oni of Ife and Awujale of Ijebu who noted (pp. 23–4) that

> owing to his progressive outlook [Agbaje] has therefore become unpopular with the majority of Ibadan chiefs who are averse to rapid changes. His outstanding success in business and great wealth also contribute to his unpopularity . . the agitation could have been nipped in the bud if Chief Agbaje had distributed largesse according to custom immediately it started.

In the event Chief Agbaje retained his title but he died before he attained supreme office.

Cognitive map and analytic structures

The cognitive map of the individual Yoruba denotes the goals which are open to him—statuses of *ọlọlá, ojoye, olọrọ* or *gbajumọ* and the means by which these are achieved—skill and hard work, the successful manipulation of personal relationships within the overall constraints of one's own destiny and of the supernatural and the machinations of others. The individual's network comprises three categories of persons—members of his own descent group and those related maternally and affinally; members of his age set; and patrons —to whom an appeal may have been made solely in terms of one's own need and character but could have been supplemented by claims of kinship or age. Of these categories the descent group members form a highly integrated central core.

The analytic structure perceived by the Yoruba is of an open society with two hierarchies—those of age and power/wealth. The two are congruent in that a young person is expected to promote the power of his father or elder brother and that power is rarely associated with youth. The power hierarchy is thus a narrow one within the wider age hierarchy. Those who reach the top are deemed to have achieved their position substantially through upholding the values of Yoruba society; the successful are not seen as rising by unfair means whilst the honest remain poor.

The difference between the rewards of those respectively at the top and the bottom of the social hierarchy are, relative to other societies at this technological level, very great. The chiefs and wealthy traders live in luxury at the expense of the poor. How does this exploitation appear to the Yoruba? The rich trader sells his goods at the same price as his poor competitor (the guild enforces this); thus his superior profits derive from buying more cheaply in another area and from the scale of his operations—both attributed to his superior skill. The flow of goods from a son to his father, from subjects to chiefs, is seen as enhancing the power and honour not only of the individual recipient but of the group of which he is head—and which includes the donor. Furthermore the elective nature of chieftaincy and kinship, the checks which constrain personal aggrandisement, the redistribution of wealth to the poor, all emphasise the mutual interdependence of superiors and inferiors. A high degree of polygyny, together with the inheritance laws, renders it impossible for a man to perpetuate his status in most of his children and even, in some situations, in any one of them. If he employs assistants (usually very poorly paid) in his business he is expected to help them become established on their own account, and not to perpetuate a relationship of great inequality.

Some permanent inequalities are however appreciated. Within a small town every descent group will have a major chieftaincy title and though these titles are ranked in seniority the difference in the prestige attaching to the group is minimal—presuming them to be of equivalent size and equally endowed with land. In larger towns titles are ranked in grades and some groups (and in very large towns many groups) have no title. These distinctions are usually reflected in the size and land holding of the group and result in a more marked ranking in prestige. Members of descent groups without hereditary chieftaincy titles may be eligible for other titles and may strive to excel in trade, but they are debarred from the selection of the major council of chiefs, and thus indirectly of the *ǫba*. The same dichotomy appears between the metropolitan and subordinate towns of the kingdom. The latter are structured in the same manner as the former; but the *ǫba* is the supreme ruler and the senior chiefs of the capital individually act as overlords of the subordinate towns, receiving tribute from them on behalf of the *ǫba*, and settling their unresolved disputes. The members of the subordinate towns have no control over the appointment of their overlord or of their *ǫba*.

Finally, within Yoruba country existed a division into powerful states and small, weak kingdoms. The latter were raided by the former for slaves and the stigma of slavery attached to the whole population. Such attitudes tend to persist long after colonial rule has destroyed the relationship.

In such discriminations between rich and poor, powerful and weak, the units are defined in terms of descent, and at the macro level, of ethnicity. Such ranking is closed, inasmuch as chiefless descent groups do not often obtain titles, subordinate towns do not become capitals, nor do the weak enslaved kingdoms suddenly become powerful. This contrasts with the open society which has formed the basis of this chapter. One must therefore modify one's statement that Yoruba society is open by adding these constraints of descent and ethnicity. These, however, do not operate equally throughout Yoruba country. Among the northern agnatic Yoruba one may distinguish between the large Oyo towns (now of Oyo, Ibadan and Oshun Divisions) in which many descent groups lack a chieftaincy title and are seen as dependent upon those which do possess them, and the smaller towns, of Ekiti for instance, in which most men are eligible for a title. In both these cases a further distinction exists between capital and subordinate town. Among the southern Yoruba, the Ijebu and Ondo, with cognatic descent groups, chiefs are selected through title associations and titled office is thus open to all. Descent nevertheless remains here an important criterion in the recruitment of a following.

3   The developing social structure

This book is not the place for a full-scale analysis of colonialism and its impact upon an African people; but to understand the perceptions which the Yoruba have of the structure of their own society, one must at least chronicle and outline, albeit in a simplistic manner, some of the changes which have taken place during the lifetimes and the memories of living individuals. The stress here is placed upon the changing loci of power during the last hundred years and the new economic opportunities which have been exploited. I shall be concerned with new positions of authority and new occupations indicating the routes—in terms of education, financial resources and the like—by which these might be attained; in other words I shall be describing the rules governing the allocation of power and rewards in Yoruba society. In this chapter I merely present the framework or structure of society; in the next I shall describe the characteristics of the individuals who successfully or unsuccessfully manipulate the structure in the quest for positions of great power or wealth.

The pre-colonial period

The nineteenth century is the base line for our study, but 'traditional' society cannot, and indeed must not, be presented as static. Some indications of the processes of competition for power have already been suggested in the previous chapter. Here I present a brief historical sketch (P. C. Lloyd, 1971a).

Yoruba country was dominated in the late eighteenth century by Oyo, whose empire embraced in its widest terms half of the Yoruba people; much of the remainder was dominated in a like manner by the Edo kingdom of Benin. But Oyo collapsed at the end of that century in civil wars which were abetted and exploited by invading Fulani. A massive southward displacement of population resulted as the savanna towns were destroyed and their inhabitants fled to establish settlements along the margins of the forest zone. Ibadan developed from a war camp sited at a small Egba settlement of that name, growing into the strongest state of the nineteenth century. As its population increased, so it had to seize adjacent territory to provide farm land. Eventually its war leaders raided far eastwards into Ijesha and Ekiti for slaves which not only increased Ibadan's population even further but helped to provide these warriors with private armies itching for further campaigns. Many slaves and free-born dependants worked on the land but a plantation economy in the strict sense was not developed. Ibadan was also engaged in wars with the kingdoms of Ijebu and Egba which controlled the trade routes to Lagos, the port through which were imported the arms upon which further military prowess depended (Awe, 1967).

I have described elsewhere in detail, and briefly in the previous chapter, the competition for power between the Yoruba *oba* or king and his subordinate chiefs (P. C. Lloyd, 1968b, 1971a). The civil war in Oyo stemmed, I believe, directly from this conflict. In the nineteenth century the new resources which became available for allocation—the profits of war and European trade—were appropri-ated by the chiefs rather than by the *oba*. Thus this period of quite substantial social and economic change did not result in a greater centralisation of power but rather in its opposite—the strengthening of the chiefs and through them of the descent groups; in fact it was I believe during this century that the lineages of the northern Yoruba became so strongly corporate.

European penetration of Yoruba country came comparatively late. In the 1820s Clapperton and the Lander brothers traversed the trade route from Badagri to Oyo Ile. In the 1840s missionaries ar-rived, also at Badagri, and set up stations at Ibadan, Ijaye and of course Lagos. Simultaneously many Yoruba who had been taken from the slave ships and settled at Freetown and its surrounding villages also returned to their homeland; but most settled in Lagos, though a minority went to Abeokuta, some abetting the work of the missionaries, others becoming quickly re-absorbed into Yoruba life, even to the extent of trading in slaves (Ajayi, 1965). Lagos became a British colony in 1861 and from this bridgehead consular officials often accompanied by Yoruba Christians visited the states of the Yoruba interior in efforts to stop the wars. Ultimately they were successful in dispersing the war camp at Kiriji at which for six years the Ibadan armies had faced their combined adversaries, the Ijesha and Ekiti. In the early 1890s treaties were made, with much publicity, with the *ọba* and chiefs of the several Yoruba states to promote peaceful trading relationships with Britain. With a marked lack of publicity a protectorate was declared in 1901, and the Yoruba, together with many of their British administrators too, entered the twentieth century a little uncertain of the nature of colonial dependence (P. C. Lloyd, 1974).

Lagos developed in the second half of the nineteenth century as an administrative and trading centre. Prominent were the creole families from Freetown, for in their exile they had been vigorously evangelised by the Church Missionary Society and many were well-educated converts. That Africa should eventually be governed by Africans was scarcely in doubt at this period when malaria and other fevers made the west coast so lethal for European settlement; and although many Europeans sought to give primacy to economic development at a low technological level, the missions did establish secondary grammar schools so that Africans could aspire to high positions in their society. Thus Samuel Crowther, himself taken in slavery in the 1820s, became an Anglican bishop, and Henry Carr became director of education in Lagos. This creole élite became substantially Westernised, seeking and being granted near social equality with the European residents of Lagos; the furnishing of their houses, the family portraits with father in starched collar, mother in bustle and children in sailor suits, all bear witness to this process. At the same time many of these men sought to reinterpret Yoruba culture for an educated or Westernised audience. Some creoles became prominent businessmen and although collectively they did not surpass in scale the several small European firms, many did have independent relationships with English commission houses through which they exported their palm oil and kernels and imported manufactured goods (Kopytoff, 1965).

This process of Africanisation came to a sudden halt at the end of the century. With the discovery of quinine Europeans had good chances of surviving several terms of duty, although the hot, damp climate of southern Nigeria made permanent settlement undesired— and colonial policy furthermore discouraged it. The European merchants sought direct access to the interior markets, holding that the coastal African traders were either inefficiently exploiting the available markets, or by their monopolistic position, as in the cases of Nana and Jaja in the Niger River delta, were actually preventing the growth of commerce. In Britain an evangelical revival increased the number of missionaries seeking to work in Africa and the new-comers were often highly intolerant of the laxities in faith and morals —as they saw them—of the African clergy who were with some suc-cess accommodating the Christian message to Yoruba values. These newcomers were reluctant to take positions subordinate to Africans (Webster, 1964). These and other similar pressures culminated in the imposition of colonial rule on Yoruba society.

Colonial rule had two principal consequences for the development of the social structure. First, in the bureaucratic hierarchies of state, church and commerce a rigid division into 'senior' and 'junior' service was created—explicitly in the civil service, implicitly else-where. Senior service posts were, by and large, reserved for English-men and remunerated on a scale equivalent to that obtaining in the home country with added inducements and perquisites to compensate for life in the tropics and separation from the family for long periods. Nigerians filled the junior service posts, their remuneration being determined by the need to attract men from farming or crafts. In general both salary and rank of an African clerk after twenty years of service were below that of the newest English recruit. These distinc-tions followed educational qualifications, for whilst the administra-tive officer was a university graduate or held similar professional qualifications, the Nigerian clerk usually had but primary education; there was little scope for the scholar with post-secondary education and those few Nigerians who did receive a university or similar education became private professionals—mostly lawyers or doctors. Second, the Nigerian role in overseas trade declined. Most Lagos businesses which were flourishing at the end of the century did not outlive their creators, for the reasons outlined in the previous chapter. Furthermore these businessmen invested their savings in house property and education, both of which promised not only a sub-stantial return but also considerable security. Other traders entered the field but against European competition they could not take full advantage of the increase in overseas trade. The European merchants not only prospered individually but amalgamated their businesses, the culmination being the creation of the United Africa Company— itself a subsidiary of the Unilever empire. Thus the UAC exported one-third of Nigeria's cocoa in 1950 and five other firms exported between them nearly one-half of the crop; similarly one-third of Nigeria's imports were handled by the UAC, three other firms accounting for a further one-fifth. However, acting as agents of these big international firms, many Africans gained both the experience and savings which enabled them later to establish modestly on their own account. But the development of a Nigerian bourgeoisie was substantially impeded (Hopkins, 1973).

The colonial period

Colonial policy is summed up in the concept of the 'dual mandate'— the economic development of the colony provides raw material for British industry and a market for its products, and in so doing progress and enlightenment are brought to the African population. Yoruba country has no mineral wealth of export value and its prosperity has rested upon palm products, cocoa and timber— especially cocoa. Palm oil and kernels have been exported since the early nineteenth century, though the Yoruba now use most of the oil in cooking and export only the kernels. The introduction of cocoa dates from the very end of the nineteenth century when members of the Lagos creole élite established plantations at Agege on the out-skirts of Lagos. Since then its cultivation has spread throughout the forest zone almost exclusively through the initiative of the Yoruba themselves—though not, of course, without government encourage-ment. Exported timber comes from the almost uninhabited forests of Ijebu and Ondo, where it has been exploited both by the expatriate trading companies and by Yoruba businessmen. To foster this economic development a minimal infrastructure of roads, railways and essential services was created; some such services, for instance the railways, required a permanent force of skilled and semi-skilled wage labour; others, such as road building, used *corvée* or migrant labour. The emphasis in the early colonial period was on the migrant labourer who worked for a few weeks or months, probably when farm work was minimal, to gain cash to pay tax or bridewealth or to buy new luxuries—a bicycle or sewing machine. The creation of manufacturing industry was scarcely contemplated before 1945.

The colonial administrative service was small. Three or four British officials might be in charge of a division of nearly a million people, assisted by a handful of Nigerian clerks and police; their task was to maintain order and to foster development only to the extent that order was not disturbed. Government was comparatively decentralised with relatively few officials, either administrative or professional, being located in the regional capitals. Primary and secondary education was seen by the government as a means of providing an adequate number of clerks and facilities were limited to this end; missionaries however saw education as the prime mode of conversion and so increased their efforts as funds would allow.

The British government insisted that its colonies should be self-supporting. In the earliest days of colonial rule the only available source of revenue was from import and export duties and this pattern of financing has continued to the present. Taxes raised directly from the mass of the population were largely retained, as outlined below, at the local government level. Thus in substantial ignorance of the world prices of the commodities which he produced or of the duties levied on the imports which he consumed, the Yoruba farmer did not clearly see the exploitative aspects of government.

Local government

British colonial policy certainly envisaged that ultimately—though for most people this meant a very long time in the future—government would be handed over to the Nigerians themselves. But most administrators saw the traditional political structures as forming the basic units in some federal system; the colonial structure of power would somehow wither away—and hence it was useless and misguided for educated Africans to seek positions in this structure. Indirect rule, an administrative policy formulated largely by Lugard with reference to Northern Nigeria, began as an expedient—there were too few English officials to do anything but rule through the traditional rulers and chiefs—and later became dogma. To maintain the authority of the traditional office holders customary modes of appointment had to be overtly maintained, however much officials might engineer the installation of favoured candidates. The integrity of the traditional structure was to be maintained. Political boundaries existing at the beginning of colonialism, often in a rather fluid state, became ossified as modern administrative units were made to coincide with supposed traditional realities. The British did not create ethnic differences, as some Nigerians now argue, but they certainly sanctified them.

An autocratic ruler, as the Hausa-Fulani emir substantially is, fits quite neatly into the administrative hierarchy from colonial governor to Nigerian villager. The Yoruba *oba* does not. With the introduction of the native authority system in 1917 the *ọba* became more dependent upon his British district officer than upon his chiefs; and in fact he could exploit this relationship to enhance his power at the expense of his chiefs. Whilst the *ọba* were illiterate the conflict between them and their equally aged and illiterate chiefs was muted. It became aggravated with the appointment especially in the 1930s and 1940s of educated *ọba* and outbreaks of violence and the temporary exile of *ọba* became common. But the chiefs inevitably lost and, in consequence, forfeited the loyalty of their own people. The educated *ọba* gained in popularity, for though an increasingly autocratic ruler he symbolised the progress of his town. His relationship with the British administration was seen more often as a means of attracting benefits to his town than as a divisive force within the town (P. C. Lloyd, 1964).

With the Native Authority system local taxation was introduced, and there were anti-tax riots in Egba division and elsewhere; but these should be interpreted as protests not solely against tax as such but against the creation of chieftaincy hierarchies which were not in accord with traditional principles. The taxes were modest, rising from about six shillings per adult male in the 1920s to ten shillings in 1950; in the earlier period 70 per cent of this revenue was retained by the Native Authority and in 1950 all but sixpence. Taxation was seen by the British and Yoruba alike as relieving the latter of all customary forms of political tribute. From this revenue were paid the salaries of *ọba* and chiefs. The former were well remunerated, the five *ọba* most highly ranked by the British receiving £2,500 in the late 1940s. *Ọba* of lower rank received considerably less; for instance the Ewi of Ado Ekiti with a kingdom of 60,000 people (1952 census) received £600. Such salaries enabled these men to maintain a style of life, whether traditional or modern, well above other citizens of their towns. The subordinate chiefs in a town tended to receive collectively as much as their *ọba*; their individual salaries were thus very small and this contributed to their loss of prestige, especially in the case of literate chiefs whose status demanded an affluence which they were quite incapable of affording. For, in the traditional manner, chiefs were expected to have no source of income other than their farms.

The Native Authority system, embodying such a substantial overlap with the continuing traditional modes of government, provided a satisfactory mode of administration but it was not capable of self-government, nor with its minuscule administrative service was it capable of promoting economic or social development. From the 1920s advisory boards of local literates and traders had been incorporated into some councils of chiefs and together with the appointment of literate ǫba this was seen as a means to foster development; but the financial poverty of the councils limited their efforts. In a complete reversal of policy the British (Labour) government advocated in the late 1940s the establishment of local government with elected councillors both as a means of creating development and of providing a training in elementary democracy. This policy was being implemented in an *ad hoc* manner when it was statutorily formalised in the first major legislation of the new Action Group government in 1953.

Economic development

The prosperity of Yoruba country rests on cocoa (Galletti *et al.*, 1956). In recent years the income received by the farmers has usually considerably exceeded the total revenues of the Western Regional State government; in fact these revenues are largely dependent upon the proportion of the world market price withheld from the farmers.

From its beginnings at Agege the planting of cocoa spread rapidly to the Abeokuta and Ibadan areas in the 1920s and to Ekiti and Ondo in the 1930s (Berry, 1967). Cocoa needs fertile, forested land, hence it does not grow well in the savanna or on the poor soils of the Ijebu escarpment. Costs of establishing a cocoa farm are relatively low since food crops can be planted between the trees as they grow to maturity. The crop is thus grown by a large number of farmers on small plots of their family land, this land often being allocated at descent group meetings to ensure a fair distribution to all members. Some men obtained land from maternally related groups on favourable terms. In recent decades there has been an immigration of farmers into the less densely populated areas of Ife and Ondo; these men pay an *iṣakǫlẹ* which is larger than a nominal recognition of land title but much less than an exploitative rent. A category of wealthy landowners living entirely from such rents has not arisen. In the early 1950s it was estimated (Galletti *et al*, 1956, p. 280) that there were 175,000 cocoa farmers though later estimates favour a figure of a third of a million; thus a high proportion of farmers within the forest zone—probably one-half—have some cocoa. The distribution of cocoa farms varies somewhat from one area to another but approximately half of all cocoa farmers had less than 2½ acres of cocoa, these accounting for about one-sixth of all land under cocoa whilst only 7 per cent of the farmers had above 10 acres of cocoa, accounting for one-third of all cocoa land. These wealthy cocoa farmers often obtained their land not from the descent group but from the ọba and chiefs, being allocated hitherto unused land at the town's frontiers; but they were able to develop their land because they had capital to hire labour. Most of the cocoa farmers have relied on family labour and there is no supply of local landless labour; men might work spasmodically on the farms of others to get cash quickly; much of the work on the farms was done by seasonal migrants from Yoruba savanna areas. The income of families within the cocoa belt shows a similar distribution. Half of all families received less than £100—accounting for one-sixth of total income—whilst 3 per cent received over £500—accounting for nearly one-quarter of total income (Galletti *et al.*, 1956, p. 458).

In recent years the number of owners of cocoa farms must have increased. There has been relatively little new planting as most of the suitable land is now used. But farms have passed corporately to the original planters' children; in many cases these farms are cared for by one son, acting as a steward, and the income used to maintain the family house or finance the education of junior family members. The doubling of the output of cocoa between the 1950s and 1960s has been due mainly to the control of diseases by spraying with pesticides; but the cost of this has considerably added to the farmer's annual expenditure on his crop. In the Ibadan and Abeokuta areas yields are declining as the trees become old; but the costs of rehabilitation (involving an absence of yield for five years as well as the labour involved in cutting out old trees, planting new ones) amount to £100 an acre—a sum beyond the capacity of most farmers.

The export of the cocoa crop is controlled by the Cocoa Marketing Board. In advance of each cocoa season the Board determines the price which, less a small sum for handling, the farmer shall be paid for his crop. The farmer is thus ostensibly protected against the seasonal vagaries of the world price which often fluctuates considerably with the guesstimates of world production, itself unstable as cocoa yields are highly subject to seasonable climatic variations. From the mid-1950s to 1970 the margin between the average world price and producer price varied between £150 a ton and almost nothing; but as Helleiner (1966, p. 90) estimates, between 1948 and 1961 almost one-third of the price received for the cocoa on the world market was withheld from the farmers.

In the latter part of the colonial period the buying of cocoa was, as indicated above, largely in the hands of the expatriate trading companies. These have now withdrawn in favour of Nigerian licensed buyers, but the organisation of buying remains substantially the same. Below the expatriate farms was, in the early 1950s, a tier of about 1,500 produce buyers, each purchasing an average of sixty tons of cocoa a year (Galletti *et al.*, 1956, p. 40). These men had sub-buyers or 'scalers' working in the rural markets, collecting perhaps twelve to fifteen tons, whilst they in turn employed 'pan buyers' who visited farmers in their villages to collect the cocoa. The success of these men, at all levels of the hierarchy, depended on their turn-over and thus largely upon their personal relationships with their customers, and the skill with which they advanced credit to the farmers; it depended too on their relationship with their firm and success in getting greater cash advances. A produce buyer's credit rested not only upon his own financial investment in his business but also in the security offered; he might mortgage a house though if a descent group held land this was hardly a viable security; often he relied on the personal bond of a more wealthy man.

In the savanna areas there are fewer opportunities for cash incomes from agriculture. In Oyo province tobacco growing has increased in recent years under the tutelage and close control of the tobacco companies, but this crop is not as lucrative as cocoa. Although almost all cocoa farmers produce a large part of the food which they consume, the cocoa belt has a food deficit met in part with imports from the Yoruba savanna areas. Emigration is frequent and the Yoruba traders found in the north of Nigeria, in Ghana and the neighbouring French-speaking states come largely from such towns as Ogbomosho, Ejigbo and Shaki.

The flow of money directly into the rural area stimulated the demand for manufactured goods. These were imported by the expatriate firms and distributed through a hierarchy of commission agents, often ultimately reaching a petty trader hawking a small tray of wares from compound to compound. As in traditional Yoruba society the big traders were the wealthiest citizens and they depended upon the same skills. A further category of prosperous businessmen were the lorry owners carrying both cocoa and imported goods, and passengers. For those who could accumulate the initial capital a lorry was a profitable investment for it *could* pay for itself in less than a year if its owner were both careful and lucky. In practice these three enterprises—produce buying, trading in imported goods and lorry owning—were often combined in a single business, controlled by its creator and employing relatively poorly remunerated scalers and pan buyers, drivers and touts. As in the pre-colonial period the amalgamation of these individually managed businesses was very rare and their ultimate size depended largely on the owner's capacity to control his staff and cope with the financial complexity of his enterprise.

Imported goods have killed some traditional crafts—blacksmithing for instance. Others have survived and some have prospered. The highest prestige still attaches to gowns made of locally woven cloth and the output of the weavers has probably increased over the past century. An interesting development in Iseyin, a town noted for its weaving, is the rise of entrepreneurs who buy cotton thread in Lagos or Ibadan, supply it to the weavers who are paid for the cloth produced, and then sell this cloth in the city markets. The new crafts and professions—tailoring, carpentry, goldsmithing, shoe-making, barbering, bicycle hiring—are still invariably individual enterprises. Since there is no traditional skill here to be transmitted through the descent group, entry to the craft is by apprenticeship; the youth often lives with his master and the fee paid reflects the cost of his board, the amount of work done by him and the speed of the tuition. After completing his apprenticeship the craftsman gains his 'freedom' and, if he can buy the necessary tools, sets up as a master; if he has no tools he works for other masters as a journeyman using their equipment and receiving a daily wage. The crafts are organised into guilds (save where the number of craftsmen makes control difficult) very similar to those of medieval Europe, though clearly deriving not from these precedents but from traditional Yoruba modes of organisation. A successful craftsman has several apprentices and the necessary equipment for them but his scale of operations at this technological level is limited by his inability to control a greater number of apprentices or to do the skilled work which they cannot perform. He is usually ill educated and lacks the technical skills to move to a higher technological level. (And there is a dearth of viable small-scale industries into which the craftsman might move.) The range of incomes of these craftsmen and professionals is commensurate with those of cocoa farmers, save that few can equal the wealth of the largest farmers. (Callaway, 1967b, 1973; P. C. Lloyd, 1953).

During the latter years of the colonial period a new local élite came to dominate the provincial Yoruba town. At its head still stood the popular autocratic *ọba*, often wealthier and better educated than other citizens; but the chiefs were poor and rather discredited. Literates who obtained jobs as clerks and teachers were rarely employed in their home towns, though with their frequent transfer they developed few ties with the towns of their temporary sojourn. Wealthy businessmen were usually ill educated and continued to live in their own compounds, though in the sudden affluence of the early 1950s they built flamboyant houses therein. They were often politically powerful and usually sought to achieve traditional chieftaincy titles; they constituted an independent local bourgeoisie, often in opposition to the traditional rulers. They were universally admired both for their own success and for the prestige which they bestowed on their entire community—both descent group and town. They were in almost all cases a local élite, looking inwards to their own communities, rather than a cosmopolitan élite looking towards the national capitals and the new opportunities there emerging (P. C. Lloyd, 1974).

Independence

Colonial rule was not so rigid as to deny a higher education to any Nigerian who could gain admission to a university and pay its fees; it merely did little subsequently to employ such persons. They therefore became private professionals—and leaders of the nationalist movement. In the mid-1920s Nigeria had but fifteen African lawyers and twelve doctors, almost all members of the Lagos creole élite (Coleman, 1960, p. 142). Their political demands—and we must here add to these professionals a larger number of less well-educated men, businessmen and others—were largely conceived in terms of greater participation in colonial government. The nationalist movement was largely confined to Lagos and though it claimed to speak for all Nigerians, the government could argue that the paternalist district officer trekking from one bush rest house to the next was far better placed to represent the views of the rural mass of Nigerians. The nationalist movement exploited local political issues (as in Lagos chieftaincy disputes) as well as industrial unrest though they never allied themselves closely with the growing trade union movement. After the war the nationalist demands turned to control of government but the movement, though much stronger, still represented the same interests. The founder members of the Egbe Omo Oduduwa Action Group were predominantly lawyers and Lagos-based businessmen. With the establishment of democratically elected parliaments in the regional and federal capitals the dominance of the Lagos creole élite vanished, for members could be elected only in constituencies of which they were 'native'. The political parties thus attracted a number of elected parliamentarians who had hitherto been apolitical (P. C. Lloyd, 1955a). Yet during the decade leading to independence in 1960 the overwhelming majority of those elected were either lawyers, headmasters or businessmen. In Lagos in the early 1950s the Action Group was seen as the party of the bourgeoisie, the National Council of Nigeria and the Cameroons (NCNC) as representing the proletariat; but these 'class' labels were quickly dropped as each party sought universal support. Similar divisions were threatened during the 1950s with the founding of Muslim parties which appealed to the illiterate farmers and craftsmen, but these parties were short-lived. In some specific situations divisions based on wealth coincided with ethnic divisions; thus the Action Group was associated in Ibadan with the Ijebu—traditional rivals of the Ibadan who were now amongst other activities making fortunes from houses built upon Ibadan land; the NCNC was associated with the indigenous Ibadan people—predominantly farmers and craftsmen and not sharing in the new affluence of their city. Politicians were well remunerated. Ministers argued that they could not receive less than their permanent secretaries and so were paid £3,000 a year; ordinary members of parliament were paid £800 a year. Both received very generous allowances for their cars.

The first parliamentary elections were held in 1951 and within a few years the regions had obtained internal self-government with a ministerial system. Nigeria became fully independent in 1960. The policies of the political leaders have been rapid social and economic development of their country and concomitant with this an increasing control over its activities.

Foremost in the Western Region was the scheme for free and universal, though not compulsory, primary education, together with the rapid expansion of secondary education and increased support of university education. Nearly half the region's recurrent expenditure is devoted to education. This policy, together with the improvement of health facilities, derived from a belief that for economic progress a literate and healthy population was a prerequisite. In addition the politicians felt compelled to reward their electorates with the services so vociferously demanded by them; the re-election of a parliamentarian often depended upon his gaining these benefits for his home area (Abernethy, 1969).

The civil service

The provisions of these and other services and the excursions of government into economic activities have contributed to the rapid and continuing growth of the civil service at all levels. The senior administrative and professional grades have doubled in size in the last fifteen years, the executive and higher technical grades quadrupled. The salary structure of the service has however remained substantially unaltered. At the bottom are the sub-clerical grades earning in the mid-1960s between £130 and £350 a year; these grades account for almost half the total Western State service of 15,000 people. The executive and higher technical grades (now numbering nearly 4,000) commenced at £340 a year and rose to £1,500—lengthening of this scale occluding the marked distinction between the former 'senior' and 'junior' services. This grade is commensurate with the attainment of a full secondary grammar education and further training or experience. The administrative and professional scale, including the superscale, ranged from £720 to almost £3,000 for a permanent secretary; this category now numbers over one thousand. To salaries above £600 a year is attached the right to a loan to buy a car together with an allowance to run it. The car is thus the status symbol of the 'senior service man' as now popularly labelled. Only very gradually have other perquisites held by expatriate officials been eroded as the service has become Nigerianised. Apart from the civil service proper there has been a great expansion of posts in the educational and health services. A substantial proportion of Yoruba university graduates are in fact teachers. Here the same discrepant salary scales prevail, for while the graduate teacher starts with a salary above £600, the grade II teacher receives between £200 and £400, starting only a few increments up the scale if he has A Level qualifications.

Recruitment of British administrative officers to permanent civil service posts ceased in 1953 but the first large intake of Nigerians occurred only in 1954. These were newly graduated men whose university training was financed by government scholarships and who were hence 'bonded' to the government. Today with a much greater number completing university education, the entry to the civil service is by competitive examination. Promotion rates were rapid in the 1950s consequent not only upon the expansion of the civil service but also upon the compensated retirement of British officials. On the eve of national independence expatriates constituted a little over a third of the senior grade, and three-fifths of these were on contract. Those Nigerians who were first on the lowest rungs shot to the top; of those who attained permanent secretaryships when these offices were Nigerianised in 1960, several had been in the civil service for less than ten years. (Similarly in the university the first Nigerian professors spent, on average, seven years in reaching their post from their first appointment as lecturers; in the army it took those commissioned in the 1950s eight years to reach the rank of lieutenant-colonel.) Moreover, promotion was more rapid in the administrative cadres than in the professional, thus creating ill-feeling in the latter. Subsequent promotion rates have of course been far less rapid, for those first reaching the top were relatively young and have several years of service before their retirement. Frequently it has been suggested that civil service salaries are too high, related to other incomes, and should be cut by a token 10 per cent; this has been successfully resisted by the civil servants—perhaps the most powerful pressure group in the state.

Local government

Nationalist politicians have usually viewed the traditional rulers as rival heirs-presumptive to colonial rule; on attaining power the Action Group leaders however professed reverence for the kingship and overtly supported it as an instrument of their rule. Nevertheless their policies have contributed to a decline in the prestige of the ọba (Awolowo, 1947; P. C. Lloyd, 1964).

The Local Government law of 1953 provided for councils with three-quarters of their membership elected by ballot, ọba and chiefs filling the remaining places *ex officio*. The ọba and chiefs, acting through the House of Chiefs, successfully forestalled several moves to reduce their power but the new government held the same power

over their appointment and deposition as did the colonial rulers—
and used it in the same way to assert its superiority. As the elected
councillors attempted to wrest from the *oba* many of the more lucrative duties, so did the *oba* lean on the government for support. But
whilst in the early 1950s the Action Group leaders relied on the *oba*
and chiefs to ensure their electoral victories, in the later years of the
decade the elected councillors were, *de facto*, the local party branch.
Party political divisions in the Yoruba towns often followed traditional factional units, but instead of appearing to stand aloof, the
oba was now usually strongly identified with one or other party.
With the Action Group split in 1962 and the increasing political
violence, their position deteriorated.

To maintain the increased scale of local social services made
possible by government grants-in-aid, the local government service
has expanded greatly and increased in professional competence.
Under the military government elected councils have been disbanded
and a colonial-type administration reimposed—but today the
Nigerian district officer deals with the local government officials,
and *oba* and chiefs, as well as ex-councillors, merely contribute to a
generalised public opinion (Adedeji, n.d.).

The chiefs have, in addition, lost many of their judicial duties as
their places on the higher customary courts have been taken by
lawyers or by well-educated (and often politically appointed) laymen.

The revenue of local government councils still comes largely from
direct taxes and fees for the services which it provides. In 1953 the
Action Group government imposed a ten-shilling increase, infelici-
tously termed Capitation Tax, to boost its own revenues, and this
engendered considerable opposition, causing riots and political
defeat at the next federal election. However, though local and state
income taxation are now merged, the local authorities retain all
revenue collected in respect of incomes below £300—i.e. from the
vast majority of the population.

Economic control

In the past twenty years the Nigerian political leaders have gained
a very substantial measure of control over their country's life and
activity (Ekundare, 1972). Parliamentary government was established
and the civil service almost completely Nigerianised, most of the
remaining expatriates being on contract rather than in pensionable

posts. The direction of economic growth was determined on one hand by the investments made in the infrastructure—new roads, social services and the like, and on the other hand by the fostering of private companies. A few state-owned industries were set up by the Western Nigeria government but these have not been very successful. Between 1957 and 1966 the government also invested nearly £20 million in twelve companies to which expatriate investors contributed a slightly larger sum—such companies included Dunlop (Nigeria) Ltd, the Premier Tobacco Company, Guinness Nigeria Ltd, Nigeria Textile Mills Ltd, West African Portland Cement Co. Ltd (Iwajomo, n.d., p. 25). The financial returns from such investments have been most favourable. Finally the government has given a large number of loans to small Nigerian businessmen and farmers for the improvement of their enterprises. Though several thousand people have benefited from these loans, the total sum advanced is not comparable with the investment in the expatriate-dominated firms; furthermore the repayment of these loans was most unsatisfactory—in March 1966, of £2 million loaned by the Finance Corporation, repayments on £1·8 million were overdue and outstanding.

Finally the Nigerian governments are changing the development of the social structure through their educational policy; but this will be considered in more detail in the next chapter. In 1955 Western Nigeria instituted a system of free primary education—though parents must still pay for books and uniforms; but secondary and university education is still extremely costly for most Nigerians, and a relatively small number of scholarships are awarded by public bodies. This of course enables the children of the rich to obtain higher education, whilst depriving the children of the poor.

One marked feature of the economic control exercised by the government is the increasing degree to which the individual must seek benefits and favours from the government. Contracts for building roads, schools, dispensaries have been awarded by regional or local governments; contractors must be licensed to undertake contracts of a certain value; produce buyers are similarly licensed; development loans to small businessmen are given by the public corporations rather than by the banks; scholarships are awarded by committees of public bodies. Customary court presidents are appointed by the government. Such a situation is a fertile field for nepotism and corruption. Men are apt to be rewarded not for their ability or financial probity but for their allegiance to the dominant political party, or even a faction within it; and part of the loan received or a perquisite for an appointment made is returned either to the individual responsible for its allocation or to party funds.

Thus, whatever its other images, the political party comes to be viewed as a vast patronage machine with its members waxing rich as a result of the services provided for their clients. The picture of the successful politician portrayed by the Ibo writer Chinua Achebe in *A Man of the People* (1966) was only too true throughout southern Nigeria; Aluko's novels vividly portray the Yoruba scene. But such politicians are highly vulnerable. When, as happened in the 1950s, the favours to be allocated were increasing, the politicians were popular; with the erosion of national savings, with falling prices for export crops, with the high cost of the growing administration and the relative lack of capital for new economic developments, the politicians were forced to turn for support to their party rather than to the electorate, and the parties turned to coercion and violence to maintain their positions of power. Such was the situation in Western Nigeria, which, exacerbated by the split in the Action Group, finally resulted in the military coup of January 1966 and the politically dominant role of the army ever since that date (Panter-Brick, 1970; Post and Vickers, 1973; Schwarz, 1968).

The military

Nigeria reached independence with a very small army—a mere 8,000 men; it symbolised the coercive power of colonial rule. As Luckham (1971) describes it, it was the last public institution to be Nigerianised; in 1960 only 18 per cent of the officer corps were Nigerians and none of these occupied any of the top fifteen positions (p. 163). By 1966 the army had grown to 10,000 and had been fully Nigerianised. The youth of the officer corps follows from this extremely rapid process of Nigerianisation; 85 per cent were under thirty and the majority in their lower twenties (p. 98). The army has tended to frown upon highly educated men and yet, unlike the police force, has not appointed its officers from the ranks; thus only one-sixth of the officers—mainly the recent entrants—have university degrees while two-thirds were recruited from secondary schools. (The combat officer corps has an even lower university component— 2 per cent—and a correspondingly high secondary school element— 84 per cent.) Army officers have tended to come from the same wide range of social backgrounds as other educated men; the fathers of four of the highest Yoruba officers were respectively a railwayman, a tailor/farmer, a tax clerk, and a carpenter/farmer. The salary scale of army officers is commensurate with those in other spheres of public life—a second lieutenant starts at £768 a year (1967), a major at £1,392 and a brigadier at £2,700; privates start at £200, sergeants at £300 and RSMs at £492.

In the early years of independence the image held by the Nigerian army officer of his position in society was strongly influenced by British tradition; as Luckham (1971) describes it, 'Officers are gentlemen'. They were substantially divorced from life in their own society and tended to remain within their barracks. Subsequently they have become highly visible. In acceding to supreme power they have been brought into close contact with civil servants and erstwhile politicians; but the latter have higher educational and technical qualifications for the training given to the officer recruit was usually short and limited to military matters. Luckham thus reports a strong sense of inferiority among the Nigerian officers.

Following the coup of January 1966, the counter-coup in July and the two-and-a-half-year civil War which opened in July 1967 as a result of the attempted secession by the Ibo-dominated Eastern Region, the Nigerian army grew to about 200,000 men. Whereas the colonial army recruited its lower ranks largely from northern Nigeria, as the Yoruba appeared to disdain military life, the new army drew large numbers of unemployed school leavers into its ranks, the private's salary of nearly £20 a month seeming a fortune when compared with other opportunities. Similarly more Yoruba were recruited into the officer corps, reversing a trend seen in the early years of independence when Yoruba dominance in the senior posts was countered by a substantial recruitment of men from Northern Nigeria in order to redress the ethnic imbalance.

This large army was recruited for combat purposes. Administration has remained largely in civilian hands. Initially the permanent secretaries were directly responsible to the supreme military councils at regional and federal levels, but subsequently, in an effort to appear more susceptible to public opinion, 'leaders of thought' were selected and later these men became commissioners with a role very similar to that of minister. In fact most of the appointees have been erstwhile political leaders, though today they owe their posts to the military leaders, not to the popular electorate.

Industrial and commercial expansion

The foregoing sections have described the development of the rural economy during the colonial period and the political changes consequent upon Nigeria's attainment of independence. Here I wish to outline developments in what is usually termed 'the modern sector' of the economy (Aboyade, 1969; Iwajomo, n.d.).

Whilst the production of foodstuffs has scarcely increased in recent years, and whilst cocoa incomes, though fluctuating, have rarely risen (most of all in real terms) above the levels of the 1950s, the rate of growth in the manufacturing sector has been phenomenal. Its contribution of 4 per cent to the gross domestic product in 1958 had risen to 8·4 per cent in 1967—an annual rate of growth of 16 per cent. Yet this contribution is still only one-sixth that of agriculture. The products of newly established industries are largely consumer goods, substitutions for imports—food preparations, beverages, tobacco, textiles and shoes, furniture, transport assembly plants and the like. They fall into three categories: first, firms established by Western expatriate companies, perhaps with local participation—the government providing a substantial part of the capital and one of the expatriate trading companies providing capital and/or local experience; second, firms managed by Asians; and third, firms established by Nigerians. The expatriate firms tend to be large, the Nigerian firms small; thus of the 135 firms surveyed in Western Nigeria in 1965, 66 had less than 50 employees whilst 30 had between 100 and 500 and 8 had over 500 employees (at this period Ikeja fell within the Western Region). The eight big factories accounted for over two-fifths of the total employment, the sixty-six small firms for less than 10 per cent of it.

The expatriate companies tend to be capital-intensive; in textile mills one worker is employed for each £1,000 investment; in other industries the investment figure is often ten or more times greater. The British- and American-owned firms tend to be organised on Western lines; working conditions are generally good and as a consequence the turnover of labour is small. Wages tend to be above those paid by governments—in the mid-1960s £10 a month for unskilled labour rising to £150 to £300 for trained artisans. In some of these industries, tobacco and beer for instance, wages form but a very low proportion of the cost of the total product; such firms can readily pay higher wages and at the same time pass the cost on to the consumer. (In contrast a very high proportion of government expenditure is on wages and salaries and any increase in these must immediately be reflected in increased taxes.) These firms also employ a substantial number of expatriates—an average of over twenty in each of the eight biggest firms cited above. In manufacturing industries over half the senior, or managerial and highly trained technical, personnel were expatriates. The firms are anxious to preserve the public image and widely report their appointment of Nigerians to senior positions—usually to posts in personnel management, or sales promotion, and least often to positions of active economic control over the business.

The industries of the type described above are for the most part located close to Lagos port or in the Ikeja industrial estate—areas of modern, well-laid-out factories. The Nigerian businesses are more likely to be found in cramped situations in the hearts of the major towns. They are small; in a survey made in the mid-1960s Harris (1971) estimated that there were in Nigeria nearly 200 Nigerian firms employing more than twenty persons and about 500 employing between ten and twenty persons. Of the larger firms only 15 per cent employed more than 100 persons, and a further 25 per cent employed between 50 and 100 persons. Most of these firms were located in Lagos and the Western Region; dominant activities were sawmilling, printing, baking bread, garment making, furniture. The men who controlled these firms—predominantly owner-managers—usually started with little capital; over half with less than £1,000 and a further fifth with between £1,000 and £5,000. They tended to have relatively little education—for as will have been seen already, there is little inducement for a university graduate to go into a risky independent business when a secure salary of £700 and more awaits him in a bureaucratic post. Thus one-quarter of Harris's sample had less than a full primary education and a third a complete primary schooling; only 15 per cent had a full secondary education and of these nearly half had had subsequent academic or professional training. Education was, according to Harris, only weakly correlated with the size of the firm. These businessmen tended to come from families with fairly high status in traditional or rural society; those with the bigger businesses were initially traders or in clerical, teaching or government posts; a greater proportion of the small businessmen had previously been self-employed. Thus Harris distinguishes between the craftsman-entrepreneur who 'has emerged earlier in the process of industrialisation but has remained primarily a traditional artisan' (p. 344) and the trader-entrepreneur with greater commercial experience and familiarity with markets.

In these predominantly small businesses the relationship between owner and employee more closely resembles the patriarchal ties between master and apprentice. Harris states that the average monthly wages paid were only £7—that is considerably less than the government minimum; and only thirty-one firms paid over £40 to any of their employees. The owners' rewards were equally modest— in only one-half of the sample did the entrepreneur receive more than £50 per month (i.e. less than a university graduate's starting salary) though two-thirds earned more than this sum from their combined businesses.

These generalisations are amplified by the detailed studies by Harris of printing (1968) and sawmilling establishments (Harris and Rowe, 1966), by Kilby (1965) of bakers, by Callaway (1973) of business in Ibadan and by Akeredolu-Ale (1972). (See too Kilby, 1969, ch. 10.)

A survey by Olakanpo (1968) of Lagos shopkeepers paints a similar picture; of these, one-half started with a capital of less than £100, only one-sixth with more than £500. Less than half had a complete or post-primary education, and nearly one-half were illiterate in English; most had previously been traders or craftsmen. Studies such as those of Harris and Olakanpo emphasise that the constraints upon the growth of these Nigerian businesses are not primarily lack of capital as the respondents usually claim but rather the lack of technical skills and managerial experience, and the small size and highly competitive nature of the market within which they operate. These Nigerian entrepreneurs, both traders and craftsmen, have specific interests to maintain but they are poorly organised as a political pressure group. In fact in the early 1960s Harris found Yoruba businessmen divided along ethnic lines in support of the Awolowo and Akintola factions.

The Nigerian entrepreneur—the owner of a shop or a small manu-facturing business—has thus risen from the ranks of traders and craftsmen; the bureaucrat is the product of the educational system. In the 1950s the teacher or civil servant usually had no income other than his salary; but in recent years an increasing number have gained second sources of income. House property is the most popular form of investment of savings; and those in secure posts can obtain mortgages from the housing corporations. Buildings for rent to urban immigrants yield a return of up to 15 per cent while the 'plums' are the houses rented to expatriate businessmen whose firms do not wish to invest such capital within Nigeria and are anxious to have as their landlords men who are influential patrons in Nigerian politics. With rents often paid for several years in advance, such houses cost their owners relatively little. Other savings are invested in businesses, often in the names of a wife or brother to preserve some propriety; those also in positions of political power can then influence the awards of contracts and the like. One of the first tasks of the military regime was to establish commissions of enquiry into assets and their findings demonstrated that it was not only the politicians but also many civil servants who had rapidly become wealthy men.

The upsurge of commercial and industrial activity has led to an increase in the number of professionals. The number of lawyers has rapidly increased, partly because the length of training and the initial qualifications required make it an easier field to enter than those professions requiring university training. Most lawyers are self-employed—and such a level of saturation has now been reached that some find little more than the simplest legal tasks. Of other professionals—doctors, engineers, architects, accountants and the like—almost three-quarters are still employed in the public sector and an infinitesimal minority are self-employed.

One corollary of this pattern of industrial and commercial development is the rapid growth of the major cities—in our case of Lagos and its suburbs and, to a lesser extent of Ibadan. It seems likely that one-quarter of the population of Yoruba country is living away from home—in neighbouring provincial towns, in other areas of Nigeria or in the cities. The rural area becomes unattractive. In many areas increasing population has created a shortage of land such that an individual cannot obtain enough to maintain a family. For the young man who does have land, the methods of farming suggested are little different from those of his forebears—for some crops high-yielding and disease-resistant strains are now available and fertilisers are advocated, but the traditional hoe culture has not been superseded. The failure of real incomes from cocoa to rise has limited the growth of rural-based crafts. Governments have tried with little success to persuade firms to locate industry in the rural areas—notable exceptions were the siting of a tobacco factory in the town of Chief Akintola during his office as premier, and of a textile factory at

Ado Ekiti, near the home of Brigadier Adebayo, during his term as military governor. Local government administration has expanded in the provincial towns but it, and the services which it controls, are quite unable to provide jobs for all school leavers. It is still not long ago that a holder of a primary school leaving certificate was assured of bureaucratic employment; today's school leaver does realise that conditions have changed but he sees in the town the sole opportunities for advancement even though an indefinite waiting period of unemployment may be a prerequisite for ultimate success.

Government and industry are quite unable to absorb this flow of urban migrants. For instance the number of boys who leave Western Nigerian schools each year, with or without completing their primary

TABLE 1 *Occupational status of school leavers (percentages)*

	Attending school	Apprentice	Working on own account	Employee	Unemployed
Primary school	56	8	1	4	31
Sec. modern	26	4	—	15	55
Sec. grammar	23	—	—	36	40

Percentages rounded to nearest whole number.
Source: Report of a sample survey of unemployment among 1969 school
    leavers (Western State of Nigeria, 1966).

schooling or obtaining further qualifications, is approximately equal to the persons currently in wage employment in the state (Callaway, 1963, 1967a). Against this, national plans aim to increase wage employment by a very small percentage each year. An unknown number of school leavers find intermittent work in the service sector. But the officially given picture is one of severe unemployment. The results of the Western Nigerian survey for 1969 school leavers are given in Table 1. The survey, taken a year after the youths left school and with a rather poor response rate, perhaps presents too gloomy a picture, for many of the unemployed will eventually find work. But there are as yet no reliable figures of adult unemployment.

Nigeria is now producing about 3,000 university graduates a year and, given the slow expansion of the administration and the paucity of opportunities in industry, overproduction seems imminent. But to date there seems to be little real unemployment, for graduates have been appointed to executive posts or to teaching posts normally held by grade II teachers, though at the salary appropriate to their education (and thus contributing directly to the rising costs of these services). Their discontent lies in their appointment to posts ranked in prestige below the level of their aspirations.

The structure of employment and income

In the previous sections we have looked piecemeal at the different sectors of employment. One tends to emphasise these sectors which are modern and expanding, creating new relationships. But these sectors still employ a relatively small proportion of the population. At the present time about 600,000 Nigerians are in wage employment in enterprises of more than ten persons; almost as many are perhaps in smaller establishments. In the former category almost 100,000 are in Western Nigeria where they account for almost 3·5 per cent of the

TABLE 2   *Income distribution in the mid-1960s*

Income (£)	% of persons	% of gross income
1– 50	62·8	39·7
51– 100	26·2	20·4
101– 500	9·9	24·6
501–1,100	0·7	7·3
1,101–2,000	0·3	4·4
over 2,001	0·1	3·6

Source: Western State of Nigeria, *Digest of Income Tax Statistics.*

total labour force. In the 1963 census 53 per cent of the region's gainfully occupied men were farmers, 21 per cent were craftsmen and labourers and 10 per cent were traders. Of those in wage employment (enterprises with over ten employees), 6 per cent were in senior posts (i.e. managerial, administrative or professional), 22 per cent in intermediate (the executive and higher technical scales), 19 per cent in skilled, 13 per cent in clerical and 29 per cent in unskilled posts. In the senior category one-quarter of the employees were expatriates. Of the Nigerian men in this category about one-quarter were civil servants, one-sixth teachers.

The result is a population with very low incomes. The average *per capita* income in Western Nigeria is only about £30. And although tax returns are not the most reliable of statistics, Table 2 gives emphasis to this poverty.

In ·distinguishing between the 'modern' and 'traditional' sectors of the economy we must direct attention towards the public services and large expatriate-dominated businesses of the former and the peasant farmer in the latter. But as we have seen, only a very small proportion of Nigerian men are wage-earning employees, even in the urban areas. Yet it is only recently that economists have come to recognise the significance of the 'informal' sector of the urban economy—the small entrepreneurs just described, the numerous self-employed craftsmen and professionals with their apprentices and journeymen, working in a manner similar to those in provincial towns, though trades concerned with mechanical and electrical equipment are far more prevalent—for instance, the motor mechanic and battery charger, the radio repairer. The scale of the enterprise together with a high seasonality of work results in the development of strongly dependent relationships between the master and his more permanent workers whilst a large number of men are engaged as occasion demands as casual labour. The secondary or secondary-modern school leaver is apt to roam the streets describing himself as an 'applicant'; the less ambitious gain a few shillings as daily paid labourers, taking whatever transient jobs are available. Even in localities adjacent to the industrial estates or administrative centres those employed in the 'informal' tend to outnumber those in the 'formal' sector of employment, and the patterns of life determined by the former dominate urban social relationships (Gutkind, 1967, 1973).

In this study I focus upon the perceptions by the urban workers of their social structure; I shall emphasise their own traditional and rural backgrounds; but one must not forget that a largely tradition-ally oriented rural population still forms the major part of Yoruba society.

Trends in inequality

The growth of the Nigerian economy was slower in the 1960s than in the previous years, ranging from nearly 7 per cent in good years to only 3·8 per cent in poor ones; against these figures must be set an assumed population growth of 2·5 per cent. Only at the very end of the decade did the reopening of the Niger delta oil wells give a great boost to the economy. The fortunes of the cocoa farmers and of the Western Region have been mixed, varying with the producer price, the world price and the yield. But the *real* incomes of the farmers were probably no greater in 1970 than in 1952; the costs of producing cocoa have in fact increased due to the measures of disease control, so the farmers are in fact less well off. Salaries in the senior civil service grades and comparable remained unchanged during the decade, though individuals benefited from promotion and annual increments. Wage earners received modest increases consequent upon the report of the Morgan Commission in 1964, and in many of the big expatriate firms regrading of jobs improved wage rates. During the 1960s it is estimated the wage differentials between skilled and unskilled labour widened, though over a longer period the trend has been in the opposite direction. Against this relative stagnation of wages and salaries must be set an increasingly rapid rate of inflation. Price rises were modest in the 1950s. The Ibadan consumer price index (1953 = 100) rose to 117 in 1960 and 128 in 1963. During the Civil War it stood at 140 but then rose to 180 in 1971. The sharpest rises were in basic foodstuffs—a rise of about 40 per cent in the year 1970–1—and thus indicate an even greater hardship among the poorer wage earners than the overall consumer index would suggest. It was in this atmosphere that the Adebo Commission sat. The Nigerian trade unions urged that a minimum monthly wage of £48. 10s. 0d. be established whilst the salary peak should be £4,092 a year (UCCLO, 1970). In the event the Commission awarded increases ranging from 30 per cent above existing rates to some of the lowest paid workers to 10 per cent for those at the senior level (Adebo Final Report, 1971).

Area inequalities

Development never benefits all areas to an equal degree. In Western Nigeria cocoa growing was confined to the forest zone in which some two-thirds of the region's population live; and, as already described, the production is now declining in the west of this area, in the farms established in the 1920s or earlier, whilst the more easterly and late-planted areas of Ekiti and Ondo are still highly productive. Differences in the rate of acceptance of education have given strong ethnic biases in the leadership of the country, and though it is generally assumed that leaders will act to further the interests of their home areas, the civil servant or teacher has relatively little scope here. Political parties on the other hand distributed ministerial offices and such benefices, with a marked degree of ethnic equality.

The major distinction today is however not between one rural area and another, but between the rural area and the city. Administration, as we have said, is centralised in the state and federal capitals; thus half of the Western State's civil servants are stationed in Ibadan. Greater Lagos probably has one-third of Nigeria's wage earners and over half the industrial enterprises. There is thus a flow of wealth, in the form of taxes, marketing board surpluses and the like, from the rural area to the cities which is not balanced by the remittances by the urban workers to their home areas. Almost all the signs of affluence are in the cities, and these increase daily whilst the rural scene remains largely unchanged.

The rural-urban dichotomy, paralleling the traditional-modern dichotomy, is often stressed in the current literature. A theme which must be emphasised, however, at least in respect of the Western State, is the growing interpenetration of the rural area by the modern state. The local élite described earlier in this chapter is today much less in evidence. The ọba and chiefs have for different reasons and at varying periods lost much of their prestige. The produce buyers and traders are less conspicuously affluent; they may perhaps be poorer but certainly they are not now building flamboyant houses as they did in the early 1950s. They are probably investing more heavily in education or in house property—often in the cities rather than in their home towns. In such activities, and in their attempts to obtain loans and licences, they look not to their local communities but to the state. Much of the commercial activity in the provincial towns is furthermore now directed by men who live in the bigger towns and cities. Finally the big houses which are now being built in the rural towns and villages tend to belong to these city-based businessmen and to civil servants and professionals; they are their country seats from which they aspire to influence the affairs in their natal areas.

Inequality of wealth

Although the Nigerian governments have abolished the rigid distinction between senior/expatriate and junior/indigenous services, the income range subsumed within it has been maintained. Even the recent Adebo award has made relatively little difference to the basic salary structures though it did slightly reduce the differential between the minimum wage level and the top salaries in government. In the 1950s these top government salaries represented the peak incomes for Nigerians but in subsequent years opportunities have increased for high salaries in industry and for secondary incomes from property or private business; one should now distinguish between the poor university graduate living off his salary and the wealthy one with an additional private income (Teriba and Philips, 1971).

Although the public services have been almost completely Nigerianised, there are in fact nearly five times as many expatriates in Nigeria now as in 1952. The dominance in the colonial period of the administrative officials and missionaries, deeply committed in their different ways to the country and its people, has given way to that of the technician and adviser who stay for a few years or even months and expect to be generously rewarded for the discomfort and disruption in their lives occasioned by their tours in the tropics. However, the Nigerian who is similarly qualified not unnaturally aspires to the same degree of affluence in his own living style.

Income disparities such as experienced in Nigeria are, furthermore, not ameliorated by taxation policies (Orewa, 1962). In the Western Region rates of direct tax have been, for the most part, regressive. Thus a married man with three children with an assumed income of £50 paid 11 per cent of this in tax; on an income of £100 8·75 per cent was payable; on £300, 7·75 per cent, and only when the income reached £2,000 was 10 per cent again payable in tax. In this respect the burden of the low-income man in the Western Region was much heavier than on his counterpart in Lagos or the Eastern Region. The Ayoola Commission enquiring into the Agbekoya movement attributed (Ayoola Report, 1969) the disturbances to protests against the high taxes and new modes of tax at a time of economic depression among the poor and mounting affluence among the rich. In the words of the Adebo Commission (Interim Report, 1970 p. 11):

It is clear not only that there is intolerable suffering at the bottom of the income scale, because of the rise in the cost of living, but also that *the suffering is made even more intolerable by manifestations of affluence and wasteful expenditure which cannot be explained on the basis of visible and legitimate means of income.* [their italics.]

Though this point of view is widely proclaimed, successive governments have, through wages and salary awards and through the failure of assets tribunals to punish more than a few isolated scapegoats, done little to change such a state of affairs.

Political control

The ringmasters in the Nigerian political arena are no longer the nationalist politicians but the senior army officers. The latter, like those whom they supplanted, seem to find the temptations of power severe, and rumours now abound of officers with expensive property in Lagos, with wives given generous contracts. After the Civil War there were suggestions of demobilisation of part of the vast army, though many feared the consequences of sending back to unemployment youths who were now trained in weaponry. The army itself has an interest in maintaining its size and power; and it has suffered no reduction.

Three groups compete for economic power. On one hand are the civil servants anxious to enhance state control partly for avowed ideological reasons (though as individuals they exploit the opportunities open to private enterprise), partly to strengthen their own sector of the administration and to increase their own opportunities for patronage. On the other hand are those who support the development of private enterprise—those who are employed by or closely associated with the expatriate companies and the indigenous entrepreneurs, two groups which are at one in resisting state control yet are in many cases competitors for the same limited markets.

Among the have-nots who suffer relative deprivation are: those senior civil servants, teachers and the like who have had no income but their salaries in the period of rapid inflation; the executives who aspire to higher posts and the much larger salaries attached thereto but who through family poverty or misfortune dropped out of the educational system before reaching its summit; the really poor— the cocoa and food farmers, the independent craftsmen and petty traders, the wage-earning factory workers and labourers.

Between 1951 and 1966 periodic federal, regional and local government elections gave the Yoruba an opportunity to voice their general approval or disapproval of the party in power even though in the latter years violence, coercion and ballot rigging distorted this voice. The political parties functioned as webs of patronage through which the demands and opinions of the ordinary man might be represented to those in ultimate power. Today these channels no longer exist, for although many of the politicians are back in office as commissioners, political parties as such are banned. The army officers seem to seek popular support to legitimise their rule but permit its articulation only in the most diffuse form. Nevertheless organised protests were not met with military repression for the army was used neither to quell the wave of illegal strikes in January 1971 following the announcement of the interim Adebo award nor in any great show of force to stamp out the Agbekoya movement. But short of violence and organised action no way now exists for the Yoruba to express his political views save through voicing them to someone in a more powerful position in the hope that ultimately they will reach those at the top.

Ideologies

A dominant theme of this monograph is the manner in which new social situations are interpreted by the Yoruba in terms of their traditional concepts; but we must allow for the modification of these concepts through the introduction of alien ideas. Here I shall be briefly concerned with the ideologies disseminated by national leaders. In neighbouring Ghana, President Nkrumah enunciated his principles of African socialism; and it was one of the major tasks of the Convention Peoples' Party to ensure the popular acceptance of these. But there is generally a reluctance to receive an ideology couched in alien terms. As Strickon (1967, p. 114) writes of Perónism in Argentina, it was

> an ideology . . . which did not reorient every-day operations of the locality. It was an ideology and model of the social system which could not order or predict the events which were significant within [the local community]. One might talk of class warfare but there was no way to activate it. One had to act in terms of basically traditional expectations.

Nigeria's political leaders have in fact made little attempt to formulate a national ideology; for obvious reasons consensus between Yoruba, Ibo and Hausa-Fulani leaders would have been hard to achieve. The leaders have instead overtly adopted a pragmatic approach to the development of their society.

Broadly the improvement of the lot of the poor may be achieved by either of two means—by a rate of economic development which brings benefits to all sections of the community or by a redistribution of the national wealth in favour of the poor. The national leadership has obviously preferred the former. National and regional five-year plans have been concerned exclusively with rapid economic development. The Action Group of the 1950s not only united local business interests and the liberal intellectuals but was also supported by men of a much more radical political orientation; it therefore eschewed any detailed ideological programme, and both the 'principled' welfare statism of its centre and 'pragmatic' welfare statism of its right wing were subsumed within the party's slogan 'Life More Abundant'. During this decade this party, more so than others, emphasised planning and welfare. However at the end of the decade the party was split, with Chief Awolowo leading a faction which emphasised an egalitarian socialism and as a corollary, anti-regionalism. Following a visit by Awolowo to Ghana the annual congress of the party adopted a manifesto of 'democratic socialism' which envisaged a mixed economy combining public and private enterprise (Sklar, 1963).

Awolowo (1968, 1970) developed his ideology during his imprisonment and wrote two books outlining its principles. But whilst he is now perhaps Western Nigeria's foremost and certainly its best known ideologist, the masses almost certainly know much more about Awolowo the man than about democratic socialism. The first half of his autobiography (1960) dealing with his rise to power has been locally published in a cheap paperback edition; his recent manifesto circulated only among the highly educated. Thus we have the image of Awolowo the self-made man—the youth who struggled to get an early education (see p. 105) and then moved through a succession of jobs, clerical and trading, until he managed to go to England to study law. His reputation as a barrister of great ability and probity won him not only the admiration of the mass of the people but also of commercial interests and the like who retained his services. His wife, moreover, is an astute and now very wealthy trader; she facilitated her husband's study abroad; but her position as a leading wholesaler of locally manufactured cigarettes and textiles is seen substantially as evidence of political patronage. But in his blueprint for Nigerian development Awolowo calls for full employment and a national minimum wage, free education at all levels, free health

services, a comprehensive social insurance scheme and schemes for
the care of the aged and sick. Socialism is defined as social justice for
all (1970, p. 36):

> ... the just and equitable distribution of the nation's wealth
> among those factors which have made positive necessary and
> effective contribution to its production. And such factors are
> labour and entrepreneurship—which are two species, degrees or
> gradations of the same phenomena—the application to the land
> of the efforts of man, assisted by capital which is wealth accumu-
> late from an antecedent union of labour and entrepreneurship
> with land.

He emphasises most strongly the modernisation of the economy but
sees two antecedent stages to full socialisation—nationalisation and
Nigerianisation. In discussing various modes of production he ad-
vocates co-operative farming but envisages the continuance of the
independent peasant, though 'no one working alone or with his
family should be allowed to cultivate more than a given acreage of
land, or to employ more than a given number of workers on his
farm land' (p. 40). All forms of manufacturing would ultimately be
nationalised save those of individual artisans and co-operative enterprises. Again, 'taxis would be socialised; but ... owner drivers ...
would be assisted by government with finance and expertise to run
their own taxis' (p. 42). All levels of trade would be left in private
hands though subject to government direction and control; professionals would be free to practise privately. A farmer, driver or
retailer should be able to earn as much as the highest-paid civil
servant. A stringent control of landlordism is however advocated;
the incomes of existing landlords should not exceed the higher
salaries of employees, their houses should pass to the state upon
their death and the emergence of new landlords be discouraged. A
man might however build as many houses as he wished for occupation by his family. Awolowo prefaces this book (1970) with a poem
by Mrs Southey, 'Never Say Fail':

> Keep pushing—'tis wiser than setting aside,
> And dreaming and sighing and waiting the tide.
> In life's earnest battle they only prevail
> Who daily march forward and never say fail! ...
> Ahead then keep pushing and elbow your way

Unheeding the envious and asses that bray;
All obstacles vanish, all enemies quail,
In the might of this wisdom who never say fail!

In marked contrast are the ideologies of the radical left. But these, too, are little known to the mass of the population. Some avowed Marxists joined the Action Group in the early 1950s and these later identified with the more liberal policies of the left wing of the party. Dr Tunji Otegbeye, now a wealthy private doctor, founded his own party—the Socialist Workers' and Farmers' Party; he has visited Moscow on a number of occasions and has been continuously under police surveillance and in detention for periods. His pamphlets and manifestos contain all the clichés of vulgar Marxism, interspersed liberally with quotations from Marx, Lenin and Stalin; but they seem to contain little specific analysis of the Nigerian scene.

The trade union leadership has given little ideological leadership, split as it is in its allegiance to Western and Eastern trade union blocs. A newspaper, *Advance*, has had a small circulation in recent years. It has given considerable publicity to strikes and its columns have contained open letters to managements. One of its major demands has been the freeing of the Nigerian economy from its ties with foreign capital—though giving little specific indication of any alternative mode of economic development. Its feature articles repeat the most orthodox Marxist analyses with little attempt to apply them to Nigeria; many are devoted to the adulation of the Soviet Union. Both Otegbeye and *Advance* saw the Nigerian Civil War as a fight between rival ethnic 'bourgeoisies' and advocated the unity of the workers.

At a different intellectual level is the analysis of Eskor Toyo, a trade unionist who has recently spent much time in eastern Europe. In his booklet *The Working Class and the Nigeria Crisis* (n.d.) he provides a basically Marxist account of Nigerian society without recourse to the worn clichés and quotations. He identifies three classes —the bourgeoisie, the petty bourgeoisie (including independent professionals, petty traders, artisans, the peasants and managerial groups among the workers) and the working class (wage earners) (p. 5). He postulates conflict in Nigeria at two levels—between the feudal aristocracy of Northern Nigeria and the commercial bourge-oisie of the South; and between the ruling bourgeoisie and the mass of the people, here including the poorest of his petty bourgeoisie.

Socialism is defined in terms of workers' power in government, nationalisation of large enterprises and workers' control of factories, the abolition of poverty and unemployment, scholarships to ensure equal educational opportunity for all. 'Socialism means freedom for all and life more abundant for everyone equally, not for the few on top' (p. 38). Rather than give a detailed blueprint for the future society Toyo directs his attention to the need for the workers to gain control of the government. He castigates the petty bourgeoisie and opportunist mentality of most of the trade union leadership but argues that it is the workers—the wage employees—who by virtue of their better organisation should give the lead to the peasants and poor petty bourgeoisie.

This is not the place in which to evaluate the probable historical significance of either of these two ideological statements—the 'democratic socialism' of Awolowo or the Marxism of Toyo. Nor is it easy to assess their impact on popular thought. What one must stress, however, is the positive role which Awolowo envisages for the self-employed man in the future Nigerian economy, a role which will enable him to use his skills and abilities to amass wealth so long as he is not too blatantly exploiting others and as his income does not exceed that of salaried persons. Toyo's manifesto is significant in that it says so little about the self-employed farmers, artisans and traders, in spite of their numerical dominance in Nigerian society; he postulates a commitment to wage earning which, as we shall see later, is shared by relatively few of the workers whom he is addressing.

4 Social mobility

In the previous chapter I set out the new occupational categories which emerged during the colonial period in both the rural and the urban sectors. I sketched briefly the resources necessary to achieve these occupations and the range of rewards and the nature of power which they commanded. In this chapter I shall be concerned with the individuals who move through this social structure. Who possesses the necessary resources and moves to the top of the social hierarchy? Who is constrained, and by what factors, so that he remains near the bottom? A major difficulty in describing the pattern of social mobility is that it is forever changing and the circumstances of one decade often differ from those of the next. In particular the experiences of the man in his fifties, which have moulded so much of his own thinking, are radically different from those of his children at present being educated. In this chapter I shall first outline the educational system as it has developed in Western Nigeria, briefly describing the types of institutions; next I shall survey attitudes towards education; in a third section I shall present data illustrating the statistical chances of individuals of varied categories for obtaining specific types of education; finally I shall look at routes of advancement open to those who drop out of the educational system.

The educational system

The placement of individuals in occupations in the modern sector of the economy is largely determined by their educational attainment—more so perhaps than in a Western industrial state where we talk so often about meritocracy. The language of the modern sector is English and fluency is demanded of those active in it; furthermore a fairly high level of technological competence is required in both clerical and manual occupations. Again, such a high proportion of the employment is in vast bureaucratic structures, the civil service in particular, but also in the major expatriate firms, where appointment and promotion depend quite rigorously on examinations passed.

In Western Nigeria the introduction of schools rested largely with the missionary societies though government has subsidised them and now embraces them in a state-controlled system (Abernethy, 1969). The missionaries saw in education the best opportunities for proselytisation, the main source of converts. But primary education was slow to develop. The 1921 census recorded only 14,000 Yoruba with a complete primary education. In the 1920s there were but 140,000 children in school in the whole of Southern Nigeria and this figure rose only to 220,000 before the Second World War. Many of the schools were in the villages, with a single teacher in charge of several classes, though others were much better staffed. Fees amounted to about £1 a year, though many children were excused this by working as house servants for the teachers. Enrolment varied widely from one province to another, being highest in Lagos, and, in the 1920s, seven times higher in Ijebu than in Oyo. Ijebu maintained this lead and in the early 1950s it would seem that 70 per cent of the boys of primary school age were in school—a figure almost equalled by Ekiti Division but far ahead of the 20 per cent of Oyo and Ibadan provinces.

One of the first major acts of the Action Group government elected in 1951 was to institute universal free primary education. On the one hand it was believed that a literate population was a necessary prerequisite for economic growth and development; on the other hand the electorate clamoured for a reward for their political support of the party and major party leaders vied with each other to launch schemes which would establish their own popularity. At first compulsory education was mooted but in the early years of the decade the party was somewhat insecure and unwilling to jeopardise its position.

When the scheme was launched in January 1955 the intake into the lowest class far exceeded expectations, due to census deficiencies. Many of the schools were of inferior construction. The increase in teacher-training facilities proceeded simultaneously and thus, for several years, the schools were often poorly staffed. Although tuition is free, parents are expected to pay for books and uniforms and the annual cost of these should now amount to £5 though it is estimated that most parents pay only half of this amount. The scheme attracted to the schools a higher proportion of girls than had hitherto attended, but in the past decade the numbers of girls entering each year has been only 80 per cent that of the boys. One can presume however that, since 1955, almost all boys have at least started primary education (Banjo Report, 1961).

One distressing feature of the free education scheme during the decade and a half since its inception has been the high drop-out rate— barely half the boys entering class I reaching class VI. The major loss occurs between the first and second years but there is a steady attrition thereafter. The drop-out rate is highest in village schools, perhaps amounting to 80 per cent, and relatively low, say 20 per cent, in schools in the urban areas. Furthermore, of those children who complete the year in class VI, many fail the terminating exam, the necessary qualification for many types of employment. In the early 1960s 70 per cent were passing, but by the middle of the decade this figure had fallen to below 50 per cent. Here too the rural schools showed a lower pass rate—rarely exceeding 40 per cent whilst greater successes, 75 per cent and above, were obtained in the towns.

In consequence it is widely believed by the Yoruba that the primary school leaving certificate of today is a far inferior qualification to that of earlier decades. Two outcomes might be noted. In 1956 a three-year secondary modern education was instituted, substantially following the British example. It was intended that these schools should give training in commercial and technical subjects which would qualify leavers for jobs in the modern sector and compensate for the literary bias in primary education. However, by a cynical interpretation they merely tried to bring students to those minimal levels of literacy and numeracy hitherto reached in primary class VI. These schools are not grant aided and tuition fees have been charged ranging from £12 to £15 in the 1950s to £25 today. They were initially popular and total enrolments of boys rose from 6,500 in 1956 to 46,000 in 1962; subsequently numbers have fallen off dramatically, to about 15,000 at the end of the decade. In these schools too the drop-out and failure rates have been very high. The meagre chances of successfully completing the course and the relatively slight chance of obtaining employment significantly better-paid than with a primary VI certificate have contributed to the declining popularity of these schools (Taiwo Report, 1968).

The affluent have circumvented the poor quality of state primary education by other means. In the 1950s they used their influence to get their children into the better urban schools, notably those run as practising schools attached to teacher training colleges. A school established in the University of Ibadan campus for the children of domestic servants, clerks and labourers had, due to the prestige of the University and the policy of the school's governors, a very highly qualified staff; in consequence, children of the élite arrived from all parts of Ibadan in their parents' cars whilst the servants' children trekked two miles to the nearest ordinary primary school. The 1960s have seen the rise of private primary schools, 7,000 children being enrolled in these (mostly in Ibadan) by the end of the decade. These range from extremely well-organised and equipped schools attended by both expatriate children and Nigerians to smaller establishments run by educated women largely as a profit-making enterprise. Fees may be as high as £50 a term.

Before 1955 a youth who successfully completed primary education was qualified for employment as an untrained teacher. In subsequent years he could attend a two-year training course to gain his elementary teachers' certificate (grade III) and after a few more years teaching, a second two-year course to gain the higher elementary teachers' certificate (Grade II). Though tuition fees were charged, these were remitted in the case of teachers deemed to be undergoing in-service training. Teaching was thus a cheap if slow route to academic success. The free education scheme necessitated the employment of a very large number of untrained teachers, but its deficiencies have spurred the government into improving the quality of the teaching staff by raising its academic standards (and thus of increasing the costs of education). At the end of 1964 the grade III colleges were abolished. Grade II colleges give a two- or three-year course to students who either already have a grade III certificate and have taught for two years or have the West African school certificate. To an increasing degree entrants to these colleges, and thus to the teaching profession, come from the grammar schools.

The major constriction in the educational system of Western Nigeria occurs at the secondary grammar school level. By the end of the nineteenth century five such schools had been established in Lagos by the main missionary societies and by 1930 two more had been added in Lagos and six in Western Nigeria. These early schools served a wide catchment area and were of necessity boarding schools. Even, as in Ijebu Ode where the grammar school served a more local population, it was obligatory to board in the senior classes; by withdrawing children from their home environment, Christian values could more easily be inculcated; by doing homework in school the differential effect of home conditions was obviated. In 1954 there were still only 59 grammar schools in the Region, but in the next decade the expansion was phenomenal—to 216 schools in 1969, with the number of pupils quadrupling in the decade 1955–65. Most of the incentive in establishing the new schools came from local communities with the Ministry in Ibadan trying to apply a brake and enforce adequate standards. Although many of these schools now serve a local population, almost all have boarding facilities and there are in fact twice as many purely boarding as purely day schools. In spite of the rapid expansion the quality of these schools has been substantially maintained, due in part to the employment of expatriate graduate teachers, and to the necessity of achieving a reasonable rate of success in the West African school certificate (WASC) examination. The drop-out rate has been relatively low—for boys in the latter part of the 1960s a little less than one-quarter.

Grammar schooling is, however, expensive, even though heavily subsidised by the government. Fees for tuition and boarding range from £40 a year for day pupils to £80 for boarders. Tuition fees alone were, in the 1960s, usually below £30 but schools made a number of compulsory levies to increase their income and sometimes demanded elaborate school uniforms. The Ajayi Commission (Ajayi Report, 1963) was led to recommend that 'woollen blazers, boater hats, panama hats, scarves of any type should be abolished as unreasonable or outmoded in present-day Nigeria' (p. 27). Such costs are obviously beyond the means of most Yoruba, amounting in fact to their entire annual income. There are very few government scholarships for grammar schools and inasmuch as they are awarded by committees of local élite it is widely felt that they are won by the children of the affluent rather than those from poor homes.

The first established grammar schools were fairly uniform in quality but recent expansion has produced a wide differential. At the top are King's College, Lagos, and Government College, Ibadan (both directly run by government) and the major and older missionary colleges: at the bottom are the newly established, struggling schools in the rural areas. The former attract the best Nigerian teachers, can employ more expatriates and in consequence have a higher success rate in the WASC examinations. Entry to all these schools is by competitive examination in which children from educated and affluent homes have obvious advantages. Parents are anxious that their children should enter the better schools for not only are their chances of academic success greater but they will meet in these schools children of similar social background who will be their companions for life. In the early 1950s the entrants to King's College, Lagos from Western Nigeria were drawn largely from the better primary schools in provincial towns; in the late 1960s the entrants came overwhelmingly from fee-paying primary schools and from one state school sited in the élite area of Ibadan where tuition was officially free but expensive extra-curricular cramming classes were provided.

Whatever the quality or prestige of the schools above, their fees are relatively uniform. But in the early 1960s an international secondary school was established adjacent to the University campus in Ibadan; this received considerable American support since its foundation was stimulated by the growing number of teenage Americans, children of AID experts and the like. Such schools cannot be exclusive to expatriates and so they endeavour to attract a sizeable number of Nigerians. The initial fees at this school (now somewhat reduced) were £200 a year for day pupils, £400 for boarders. But many rich Nigerians still prefer to send their children to England for secondary education, and the admission to Eton of the son of Chief Akintola, then Regional Premier, was hailed in the press both as a personal achievement and as a triumph for all Yoruba —he had breached the bastions of white power!

The colonial government made very little provision for higher education (Ashby Report, 1960). As late as 1937–45 only sixty-nine scholarships were awarded for overseas university study, and in 1945 only 193 Nigerians were studying in Britain (Coleman 1960, p. 124). In 1932 the Yaba Higher College had been established to provide professional education, notably in medicine, of a quality more appropriate to local conditions. But the recipients of these diplomas then discovered, in seeking appointments and promotions, that theirs were judged inferior to the overseas qualifications held by expatriates. When the idea of a university in Nigeria was mooted, nationalists insisted that it should be similar in quality and in content of curricula to the best in Britain. With this aim the University College, Ibadan (later University of Ibadan) opened in 1948, and grew rapidly so that its student population surpassed 2,500 in the mid-1960s (Mellanby, 1958; Saunders, 1960; van den Berghe, 1973). Of the other universities created in the early 1960s, two served the Yoruba West—Ife and Lagos. These three universities together with those in the Northern and Eastern regions were producing over 1,000 graduates annually, nearly one-half of these being Yoruba.

Initially entrants to University College, Ibadan, were admitted on the basis of their WASC examination results and a university entrance test; they took a two-year preliminary course before entering the degree courses. However the university provided the stimulus for large numbers of young people to take their GCE A Levels both by private study and with the help of correspondence courses; in the mid 1950s most of those who obtained the necessary number of A Levels were admitted. Clerks and teachers spent much of their free time (and some of their office hours) preparing for these examinations. When the Western Region government reorganised working hours in the mid-1960s, instituting an afternoon session from 2 to 5 p.m. (in lieu of the closure at 2 p.m.) a cry went up that senior civil servants were maliciously preventing their juniors from furthering their own education and thus perhaps threatening their seniors.

The colleges of arts, science and technology, set up to provide professional and technical training, became instead A Level colleges. The high cost of such education then led to their being merged into the newly created universities, while A Level teaching (or rather the West African higher school certificate) was made the responsibility of the sixth forms which the better grammar schools were encouraged to provide. The number of university applicants with A Levels or HSC increased to exceed the available places. Henceforth applicants were admitted on the quality of their examination results with a strong bias against older applicants and those who had sat their A Level subjects in consecutive years—a process which increasingly favoured the entrant from the grammar school sixth form at the expense of the person who had struggled to get his A Levels by private study. During this period two distinct categories of students could be seen in the university—one from the affluent homes and prestigious grammar schools, the other from poor homes who had risen via teacher-training colleges and private study; the former blasé and 'intellectual', the latter keen only to get a modest degree by whatever hard work was necessary. One of the more intelligent of these once said to me: 'Are we allowed to put our own ideas into examination answers or should we simply recapitulate what we have been told in lectures?'

University education is heavily subsidised by the government, to about seven-eighths of its total cost. Yet the fees payable by the student range from £150 to £200. In the early 1950s most students received a government scholarship or were 'bonded' by grammar schools or teacher-training colleges (the school paid the fees in return for a promise that the student would work there—a means of ensuring a steady flow of graduate teachers at a period when competition for the limited numbers leaving the universities was very high). But the number of scholarships has not increased at a rate commensurate with university expansion; in 1968 nearly 2,000 students from Western Nigeria entered a Nigerian university but only 250 of these received government awards whilst a further 300 were financed by schools. The 'indigent' student has become a problem in all universities. He pays his first year's fees from his savings; when, late in his second year, it transpires that he is unlikely to be able to afford this year's fees, it seems wasteful and unjust to expel him—yet to waive the fees would encourage mass default. The main argument against completely free university education is that its financial benefits to the recipient (and his family) are so great that he ought to contribute something towards it. This rests of course on the, usually unchallenged, premise that the income differential between the graduate and non-graduate is fair and immutable.

Figure 1 presents in a schematic manner the progress through the educational system of boys born *c*. 1950. The figures are approximate only, allowing for distortions caused by regional boundary changes and marked annual variations in some data; the diagram ignores the intervals of work which sometimes separate primary and secondary schooling and usually divide secondary and university education. The dotted line indicates the teacher-training route; the numbers cited are of students in colleges at the stated period; these are not included within the thousand entering primary school in 1957 for they will be much older men, their training being interspersed with periods of teaching. 'Drop-outs' refer to the entire periods of primary or secondary schooling, not to a single given year.

Attitudes and constraints

The foregoing paragraphs, in indicating the cost and number of places available at different periods and at different levels of the educational system, have outlined the opportunities available to the Yoruba. They have said nothing about Yoruba attitudes towards these opportunities—the value which parents have placed upon

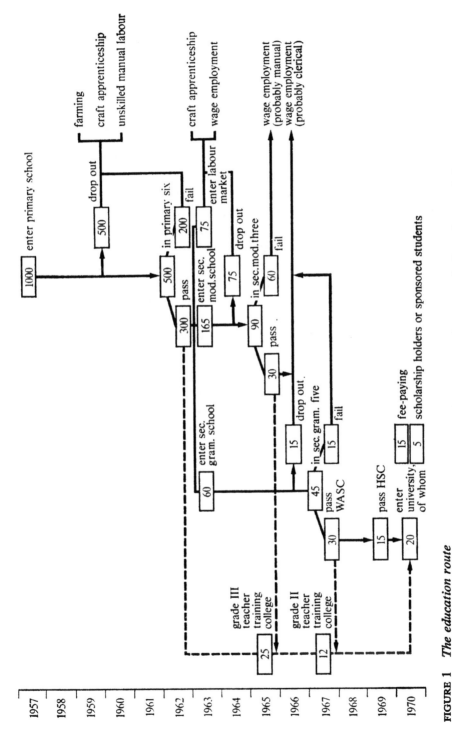

FIGURE 1 *The education route*
Source: Western region or state education reports and digests or abstracts of education statistics.

education and cost-benefit analysis which they continually make in assessing their sons' chances of success against the financial outlay and the loss of his labour. Here one must distinguish between an early period—varying in time in different areas—when education was still viewed with much suspicion and the present time when it is almost universally accepted.

There are today as many Yoruba Christians as Muslims, Islam having spread rapidly in western Yoruba country in the nineteenth century, especially in the towns. The proselytising activities of early evangelists and school teachers threatened both Islam and the indigenous cults, but the former, being a universal religion too with its own formal mode of education in the Koranic schools, was much more resistant. Christianity seems to have spread with economic growth. The relative lack of success of the American Southern Baptists in Oyo would seem to derive more from the poverty of the savanna areas than from the more fundamentalist faith of this mission. Other historical factors too explain the early acceptance or rejection of both Christianity and education. The settlement of the returned Yoruba slaves in Abeokuta made this town an early centre of Christian activity and of education. The kingdom of Ijebu, in contrast, was impervious to foreign influence during the nineteenth century, believing that its power and integrity rested upon its exclusiveness; however, after a dramatic military defeat by British forces in 1894 when they closed the trade routes, the Ijebu began to embrace Christianity at a speed which embarrassed even the missionaries. It seems that they suddenly realised where power and opportunity now resided and were anxious not to be left behind. Ibadan, the great military power of the nineteenth century, was slow to accept education, in spite of the existence of a CMS mission in the town from the 1850s. On the other hand the Ekiti were quick to accept education once their country was opened up by roads. Thus the underprivileged community more rapidly exploits the opportunities which seem to provide it with an alternative route to power. Conversely of course a ruling group can accept such opportunities to maintain its position— the late nineteenth-century Baganda chiefs and people are perhaps the best-known African example. A Yoruba equivalent is perhaps provided by the Ondo, some of whose prominent chiefs both became Christians and promoted their country's development by opening a new trade route via the lagoon into the heart of Yoruba country.

Within individual Yoruba ethnic areas one often finds that villages have educated their children in greater numbers and to higher levels than has their metropolitan town. Thus Awe, with several PhDs, contrasts markedly with neighbouring Oyo; some Ijebu villages too have very outstanding records. One possible explanation is the weak initial development of Islam in the villages. Another, and I believe stronger, argument is that the people in the dependent towns and villages, being denied access to the positions of greatest power—the chieftaincies in the metropolitan town—sought this alternative means of asserting themselves. In like manner these towns often sent to the local government councils men of much higher educational calibre than those elected within the metropolitan town.

The same arguments which have been adduced to account for differences in acceptance of education between Yoruba ethnic areas and between the town and its rural hinterland, apply too within each community. Men of high social status feared any assault on that religion which underpinned this status; in particular they feared the disgrace which would befall them if their sons were encouraged by their teacher to violate the local shrines to prove the ineffectiveness of the traditionally held sanctions. Ultimately they feared the loss of their sons altogether as the teachers urged them to abscond from their families if life at home grew intolerable. In contrast men of low social status, seeing little opportunity to achieve chieftaincies (because of poverty or because their descent group had no title), turned more readily to Christianity and sent their children to school. Nevertheless the wealthy chief or trader often saw the need for an educated son to help him with his correspondence and accounts and so sent one or two sons to school; conversely the farmer needed his sons' labour as a means of ensuring his own social advancement and so was reluctant to send them to school. Lastly there are differences in individual personality; in so many autobiographical statements is to be seen a dominating—or as we might say achievement-oriented—mother or grandmother.

In accounting for their failure to attend school many men describe their fear of school discipline, the caning which was held by most people to be a necessary accompaniment of learning. The scholar was a drain on his family finances. His age mates worked, could indulge themselves in fine clothes and had plenty of free time for recreation; the scholar had virtually to withdraw from the company of his peers. The severity of life at school was perhaps easiest for those who came from Christian homes for not only did parents here support the violence of the teacher but they themselves maintained almost as strict a regime of godliness, cleanliness and punctuality.

Today it is accepted that without education a highly rewarded occupation is almost impossible to achieve. Parents are willing that their children should receive as much education as possible; one does not hear a father say, 'What was good enough for me is good enough for my son.' More schools are now managed by local authorities and Muslim bodies; and in any case, the intolerance of the early Christians has completely disappeared. The difference now lies not between those who accept and those who reject education, but between those who understand the system and can manipulate it and those who do not and so cannot. Thus when asked what they can do to help their children to do well at school most men answer in terms of paying the fees regularly, buying uniform and books as required, seeing that the children are fed before going to school and are punctual. In other words they fulfil the demands made by the school but do little to stimulate their children's intellectual development, as by coaching them at home, providing a quiet place for homework, stressing achievement. Such attitudes are however found more frequently among those parents who have themselves been educated. In addition the better-educated parent is more discriminating in choosing schools for his children while the affluent parent has both the influence and the resources to gain admission for his children into the best and more prestigious schools.

Attitudinal differences today are reflected more by the drop-out rate than by initial enrolment in school. Here the main reasons are of an economic nature. Parents are reluctant both to finance the education and lose the labour of those children who show no aptitude at school. They become disillusioned when the successful completion of primary schooling heralds not, as in the past, immediate entry to a clerical job but indefinite unemployment or a job as an unskilled labourer yielding an income no greater than a self-employed craftsman might achieve, with less prospect of advancement. It is alleged that the teachers abet these attitudes by favouring the withdrawal of the dull children who might otherwise reduce their pass rate in the school leaving examination—a magic figure on which their own chances of promotion are seen to rest (Taiwo Report, 1968, pp. 9–10).

Almost all Yoruba ascribe the termination of their education to a lack of money. In some cases their parents clearly suffered absolute poverty; in most cases some money was available but it was deemed more advantageous to spend it in some other manner, perhaps in fact because the future educational success of the supplicant was dubious. Several factors, which are of little importance in a modern industrial state, constrain the education of the Yoruba youth.

First, the amount of money in circulation varies greatly from year to year. Between 1948 and 1964 the amount of money (in real terms) received by the cocoa farmers in the best year was well over double that in the worst year—a difference reflected strongly in the money available for investment and saving, as education is seen to be. (The income received by the cocoa farmers is, it will be recalled, greater than the annual expenditure of the regional/state government.) In turn the income of cocoa farmers directly affects that of craftsmen and traders.

Second, the polygynous family head is expected to treat equally the issue of each wife. Not only is the rate of polygyny high among the Yoruba—at any one time a third of all married men have two wives, a third more than two—but the divorce rate is also high so that a man may in fact practise serial monogamy and so have two or more wives during a lifetime. A man who educates a son of his first wife will be under strong pressure from each of his other wives that one of their own children should benefit to an equal degree. It is a matter of chance whether these women have children requiring simultaneous education or whether they may be educated consecutively. A wife who has little claim on her husband's income, one or more of her sons already being educated, is expected to finance the schooling of the remainder of her issue from her own earnings as a trader or craftswoman. To decide whether to educate one son well, so that he will earn enough to help the rest of his family, or to spread the benefit more equally, is a difficult problem for any parent. A son for whom a good education is provided feels a moral obligation to repay the debt by financing the schooling of his junior siblings— though those immediately junior to himself have probably passed the age of schooling before he is able to help them. Alternatively if a junior sibling himself, he will educate the children of his elder brothers who were not so fortunate as himself. Such a method of financing education is of course only possible when the age of the siblings covers the full span of the mother's childbearing years. It depends furthermore on the cost of primary education being low—a man will not have to spend much on his own children until several years after his marriage. Although a few men now subscribe to life assurance schemes to cover their children's education or their own sickness or death, the great majority still see in their loyalty to their family the best mode of insurance.

Third, disasters may hit the family. Men have tended to marry late and to continue to father children for several decades. Sickness, senility and death of the father occur frequently in the life of Yoruba children. Although customary law provides that the father's junior brothers or elder sons should maintain the child, family animosities or the preference of the uncle for his own children often result in a raw deal for the orphan. Again, if his mother should divorce his father, the latter may well vent his displeasure on his own child; and if the child follows the mother to her own house, he has even less claim on his father's money. Deaths in the family, necessitating expensive funerals or the maintenance of extra dependants, involvement in a land dispute with costly litigation, are tragedies in which obligation to the descent group transcends that to one's own children and may well result in the premature termination of their education.

Finally, when the number of grammar school places was small, a youth who passed the entrance examination to a good school could tap a wide circle of relatives for a contribution towards his fees—his success brought glory to his entire descent group or village. Today, with the greater availability of places, these wealthy kin will have children of their own who are able to enter, by one means or another, at least a poor quality grammar school. The youth of today are far more dependent upon their own parents and full siblings.

Although the statistical data available are insufficient to substantiate it as fully as one would wish, the picture that emerges from the descriptions above is one of increasingly restricted opportunities for those from the poorer families. A grammar school education is, to an ever-growing degree, a prerequisite for academic success; yet it remains costly and scholarships are few; though the number of places is increased, the chances that a brilliant boy from a poor home can find the fees are in fact reduced.

Today's parents, however, grew up in a very different atmosphere. The childhood of Chief Obafemi Awolowo, as most vividly portrayed in his autobiography (1960), is not atypical and the virtues of perseverance and hard work which he stresses are widely held in his generation. Awolowo's grandfather was the Oluwo, the senior commoner chief in Ikene, his paternal grandmother a dominant figure in his life. His father was a wealthy farmer and timber contractor who embraced Christianity when it first came to Ijebu. Like most adult converts he was rigid in his adherence to his faith. Awolowo started school at five and was initially coached by his father. When he was only eleven, his father with other Christians raided the smallpox shrine during the 1920 epidemic and subsequently died of the disease. His mother refused to be inherited by a junior brother of her husband and returned home but could not finance Awolowo's education. His uncle, though wealthy, would not pay either. For four years he drifted in Abeokuta from one master or relative to another, occasionally attending school. Eventually, with money earned, he stayed in one school long enough to reach standard V, then the senior class, and subsequently became a pupil-teacher and entered Wesley College (teacher training) in 1927 for a four-year free course. After a year he left to become a clerk in Lagos at a higher salary than teachers earned but the job lasted only a few months. After a year and a half of unemployment he went back to Wesley College as the school clerk, then left this to become a journalist on the *Nigerian Daily Times*. Next he took up produce buying and in an initial good season made a considerable sum, which he subsequently lost in the next season, leaving him indebted for several years. Eventually in the mid-1940s he came to London and in two years qualified as a lawyer and returned to Lagos to take a foremost place in Nigerian political life.

Some data

Social mobility is even more difficult to measure in an African context than in western societies. First, has the factory worker, son of a chief, moved upwards or downwards? Second, occupational categories such as chief, farmer, trader embrace both the richest and the poorest in the society; furthermore it is useless to ask such respondents for their income, let alone that of their father. Educational qualifications are however unambiguous and give some indication of the status of an individual in his community.

The data presented in Table 3 were collected not from surveys explicitly designed to explore educational mobility but as a by-product of others. One of the surveys, carried out in 1971, was designed to explore the attitudes of urban workers towards social inequality;

an occupationally stratified sample was selected in Agege, where all respondents were immigrants, and in Ibadan, where they were indigenes. The other survey was carried out in 1962: question-naires were sent to primary schools in Ibadan most likely to include a large number of children from affluent and educated homes, in order to select a sample of such children for further physiological studies. The data used below refer exclusively to Yoruba males.

TABLE 3   *Inter-generational mobility of Yoruba*

Survey 1: 1971	*Respondent's education* (%)			
Father's education	*None*	*Primary*	*Sec. modern*	*Grammar*
None	98	89	79	66
Some	2	14	21	34
n =	124	71	24	38

Survey 2: 1962	*Respondent's education* (%)							
Father's education	*None*	*P1–5*	*P6*	*P6+*	*SG1–5*	*WASC or grade II*	*H.S.C. etc.*	*Univ. degree*
None	100	76	67	62	52	53	46	38
Primary	0	24	26	38	26	31	25	35
More than primary	0	0	7	0	21	16	29	27
n =	113	33	121	13	132	147	119	145

A number of features are readily apparent. First, most respondents have had more education than their fathers; in view of the expansion described earlier in this chapter this is hardly surprising. Second, very few respondents have received less education than their fathers. The educated parent above all recognises the value of education and tries to ensure that his children do better than himself. The level of the respondent's education rises consistently with that of the father. In the parental generation there were of course very few highly educated men and so it is difficult to judge whether men with the past secondary education of that early period have been as successful in maintaining such a standard for their children. And of course the majority of Yoruba university graduates are still young, having received their degrees post-1950, and their children are not yet old enough to go to university. Lastly, the data demonstrate that a high proportion of men who do have high educational qualifications today were born to illiterate parents.

Some further elaborations on these data are possible. From survey 1 it appears that illiterate Christians are more likely to have given their sons a good education than illiterate Muslims. From survey 2 a breakdown of the better-educated respondents into their ethnic groups shows some striking variations. Thus Ekiti university graduates had the least well-educated parents—eleven out of fifteen being illiterate; this is consonant with the recent rapid expansion of education in that area. In contrast five out of ten Egba graduates had fathers with more than a primary education. (Lagos-born graduates had even better-educated parents.) Economically backward areas with little enthusiasm for education produced graduates with relatively highly educated fathers; thus, of the twenty-nine graduates from Ibadan, Oyo and Oshun divisions, only ten had illiterate fathers but seven had fathers with post-primary education.

The mothers of the above respondents had less education than their fathers; but here too a rising level of education correlates with higher respondents' education. Among Ondo and Ijebu university graduates, mothers seem to be rather better educated, reflecting perhaps the degree to which Ijebu mothers take financial responsibility for their children's education. In the generations with which these surveys were concerned far fewer women than men received education at all levels. There is however a similar correlation between the education of parents and daughters. But of women graduates only 6 per cent had illiterate fathers and over one-half had fathers with post-primary education; only one-quarter of these graduates had illiterate mothers.

We have no data which succinctly show the social background of youths at present attending grammar schools in Western Nigeria. Table 4, reproduced from Abernethy (1969, p. 245), refers to a sample taken in 1964 of 480 youths in grammar schools in southern Nigeria. In addition he states that 14 per cent of the youths listed their fathers' incomes as below £50, 26 per cent as over £200; 32 per cent had illiterate fathers, 18 per cent had fathers with some secondary education. These figures are similar to Foster's Ghanaian data, in which the selectivity indices for farmers, traders, and administrative, etc., categories were 0·6, 2·9 and 4·9 respectively (1965, p. 241). The selectivity index of the administrative, etc., category is probably too low, for the majority of men embraced herein in the census are young and relatively few children of secondary school age.

A comprehensive survey of the students of the University of

Ibadan carried out by van den Berghe and Nuttney corroborates the data already cited (see Table 5).

The authors conclude: 'Students are drawn disproportionately from the more educated and well-to-do families, but on the whole no more so today than fifteen or twenty years ago.' However, they note that the average age of students increased in the late 1950s. From 1948 to 1955 29 per cent were under twenty at matriculation, from 1956 to 1966 only 7 per cent. This reflects, in my belief, the increasing proportion who had taken A Levels by private study whilst employed, perhaps for as much as ten years, between leaving school

TABLE 4 *Occupational distribution among the fathers of grammar school students and among Southern Nigerian men*

Occupation	Fathers of sample (%)	Southern Nigerian men over 15 (%)	Selectivity index
farmer, fisherman	35·8	70·0	0·51
craftsman	8·5	6·7	1·27
trader, clerk	25·7	9·6	2·68
administrative, professional, technical	19·2	3·5	5·49
other	10·9	10·2	1·07

Sources: Nigeria, Department of Statistics, *Population Census of Lagos, 1950* (Kaduna, 1951), pp. 73–4; Western Region, *Population Census of the Western Region of Nigeria, 1952* (Lagos, 1953), pp. 2, 8; Eastern Region, *Population Census of the Eastern Region of Nigeria, 1953* (Enugu, 1954), pp. 2, 6. This table is reprinted with permission of the publishers from *The Political Dilemma of Popular Education: An African Case*, by David B. Abernethy (Stanford University Press, 1969),. p 245.

and entering university. The same survey showed that the children of farmers reached the university at a much later age—over half of such students were over 30, whilst only 18 per cent were below 20; the figures for students whose fathers were professionals or semi-professionals were almost the exact reverse—45 per cent under 20, 16 per cent over 30 years of age (van den Berghe and Nuttney, 1969, p. 371).

These striking figures suggest that as university entry increasingly favours those coming straight from grammar schools, so will the proportion of children of wealthy, educated parents increase at the expense of that of farmers' children. The older students tended to be found in the education faculty (being trained teachers undergoing further training) and in the social science and arts faculties; the students in the faculties of agriculture, science and in particular medicine, were younger than average. In the initial years of the university, 1948–52, only 20 per cent of the students were self-supporting (i.e. their fees paid by themselves, family or friends), a figure which rose slowly to 30 per cent in 1958–62 and then very rapidly to 71 per cent in 1963–6. This rise reflects in part the development of the faculties of social science and education in the late

TABLE 5   *Occupations of fathers of University of Ibadan students (percentages)*

Occupation	1948–52	1953–7	1958–62	1962–6
farmers	29·2	26·1	31·1	38·0
traders	12·9	19·7	16·3	14·6
traditional chiefs	1·2	1·1	1·7	4·0
unskilled workers	0·2	0·5	0·8	1·3
artisans	7·7	8·7	8·2	4·0
clerical and sales	8·6	7·7	6·3	2·3
semi-professionals	23·0	22·0	25·4	18·2
professional	13·6	11·3	7·3	15·5
others	3·6	2·9	3·0	2·3
	100	100	100·1	100·2
$n =$	418	804	933	556

Source: van den Berghe and Nuttney, 1969.

periods, for in both of these, over the entire period of the survey, three-fifths of the students were self-supporting.

The data of van den Berghe and Nuttney, based on the entire period of their survey and on the 1952–3 census, shows that Ijebu were over-represented in the student population, there being over six times as many (in proportion to the total population) from this province as from Ibadan province. My own data, based upon 1967 entrants to the University of Ibadan and an estimate of the total population based upon the 1963 census, adjusted to compensate for obvious overcounting in some areas, show that Ekiti and Ilesha divisions then had the highest proportion of students, followed closely by Ijebu, with Oyo and Ife divisions with the lowest proportions—a quarter those of Ekiti and Ilesha.

These figures bear out a popular belief that among the educated
élite the preponderance of Egba and Ijebu men is now challenged by
the Ekiti.

Among the senior administrative class in the Western Region civil
service, Ijebu and Egba men accounted for nearly half of the total,
though Ekiti men were prominent as permanent secretaries; by a
historical accident the first two military governors of the Western
Region/State were Ekiti. Among the Ibadan University teaching
staff the Ijebu still predominated but were closely followed by the
Egba and Ekiti, with men from Oyo, Ibadan and Oshun divisions
far behind.

Alternative routes

This chapter has been concerned thus far with the educational system
and with showing how individuals pass through it to gain appropriate
jobs in the modern sector. But what happens to those whose schooling
is prematurely terminated, the primary and secondary modern drop-
outs, and even many of those with a primary VI certificate, who
cannot obtain clerical employment? The answer given by most
parents is that their sons should learn a trade, or craft (*iṣẹ ọwọ*, hand
work); that is to say, they should undergo an apprenticeship in one
of the small-scale crafts found in every town and village.

The costs of such apprenticeships vary widely, with the amount
of technical knowledge to be imparted and the period involved;
where a boy stays with his master for a short period and thus con-
contributes little of his own labour the fee is higher than if he stays
longer working first as a houseboy then as a helper in the craft.
Again some boys continue to live at home, others stay with the
master. My own data (Iwo, 1949–50) shows the payment of fees
for an apprenticeship in bicycle repairing ranging from £3 for a
six month's training, £2 for one year, £1 for two years and free
training for an apprenticeship lasting for three years (P. C. Lloyd,
1953). Callaway's (1967) later examples from Ibadan describe a
master carpenter who receives £5 a year from his apprentices—
they stay four years and receive free board and lodging, and a
mechanic, a tailor and blacksmith whose apprentices work for four
or five years and pay no fees. Apprenticeships, therefore, are within
the means of virtually all parents—the only necessary cost being
the loss of the boys' labour in their own work.

However, to set up as an independent master upon completion of the training requires a capital outlay on tools amounting usually to a minimum of £50. Those who have been trained as lorry drivers—a glamorous occupation in the eyes of most young men—need £35 for their licence fee. These are sums which parents are often unable to afford; in fact had they possessed such sums their son would in many cases have continued his formal education. As an alternative the qualified craftsman can work as a journeyman, using the tools of his employer and saving slowly to buy his own. However, the general stagnation of the rural economy, consequent upon the failure of the real income from cocoa to show a consistent rise, means that there is little opportunity for the newly trained master to break into the local market where the existing masters already have close ties with their customers; nor can the latter expand their business by hiring journeymen. Thus the trained craftsman is forced into wage labour.

Our own data show that men trained as craftsmen have a low level of education. Of the men sampled in the questionnaire survey who had undergone craft apprenticeship, one-half had no education at all, one-sixth had received some primary education and only one-quarter had successfully completed primary schooling; less than one-tenth had received any post-primary schooling. These figures are very similar to those for traders; they may be contrasted with those for farmers—90 per cent of whom had received no education.

Of those men currently working as wage-earning manual workers in the civil service or in the factories about a half have received training as craftsmen. Those with a rather better education, who initially aspired to bureaucratic clerical work, have also tended to work for small employers perhaps as clerks to traders, as pools agents and the like. The craftsmen allege that they enter wage employment in order to save enough money to buy their tools, pay for their driving licence and the like, when they will revert to self-employment. Not only do very few men enter manual employment as a chosen career directly upon leaving school (even allowing for periods of unemployment) but few, once so engaged, express an intention to remain in such employment.

Unlike the clerks or teachers, many of whom are privately studying for higher educational qualifications, the manual worker—whether labourer or factory hand—does not continue his studies. As a school drop-out he is probably not very bright; but the explanation given by such men is that their work gives them no opportunity to maintain their skills of literacy and furthermore leaves them physically tired and thus unable to study in the evenings. In other words once a man enters manual employment he will not, save in the case of the highly skilled or well-trained artisan, get back into the educational system. Equally the chances of promotion within the factory are slight; he may rise to a supervisory post of foreman but posts involving much superior technical skills will go to men with higher educational qualifications.

The hope for such men is thus to re-enter the sector of self-employment, pursuing the craft learned in their apprenticeship or exploiting some other manual skills learned in factory or workshop. Having saved enough to establish themselves in this way they hope to expand their business to the relatively low limits which seem feasible. From this point they hope to become traders—the bicycle repairer and mechanic will sell spare parts, the carpenter will trade in planks, the tailor will become a cloth trader. For it is only by trade, first in a limited and later a more diverse range of goods, that great wealth is believed to be achieved.

The realism of such hopes is difficult to assess. In the colonial decades seasonally migrant labour and target workers constituted a large part of the wage-employed labour force. We have no data on the subsequent activities of those who leave factory employment— whether they do in fact become traders or craftsmen or merely move into another wage-paid and presumably better job. The affluence of industrial areas such as Agege certainly provides opportunities for the self-employed man which the rural area does not. But the wages of most employees, save the more highly paid factory workers, seem too low, in the present period of rapid inflation and with their increasing family responsibilities as they grow older, to permit savings on a sufficient scale to make self-employment seem a more attractive option.

It is of course possible for a man to start trading without first becoming a craftsman or wage earner. As Olakanpo's (1968) survey of Lagos shopkeepers cited above (see p. 77) shows, one-half started with capital of less than £100. But here too the parents with this sum to bestow upon their son are more likely to spend it on his education (or that of another child). Most men have built up their capital by slow savings, or have received a lump sum payment—a pension or demobilisation gratuity. Interestingly Olakanpo reports a lower rate of success among traders who had no other previous occupation than among former teachers or craftsmen; nevertheless half of his shopkeepers had been traders from the outset of their careers.

The careers of the wealthiest Yoruba businessmen do not provide statistical evidence of the degree of openness or closure of the possible routes to success. But they do provide, for the mass of the population, models of the means by which a man can pass from the wage-earning sector into that of successful self-employment.

5 Social interaction

Two themes have dominated the previous chapters. First, the range of incomes between rich and poor is not only very great but lies furthermore in non-overlapping zones, largely determined by education. Added to this is the traditional Yoruba liking for ostentatious display and the fact that, in the tropics, life is lived out of doors to a greater degree than in temperate countries. Second, the rate of social mobility has been very great. It is not uncommon to find a university professor who has illiterate parents; in fact as we have seen, a substantial proportion of the well-educated men have come from humble homes. Ties of kinship and, usually, previous schooling link these successful men with the rural area even though their occupation demands that most of them live in either Ibadan or Lagos. Equally those remaining in the rural area can usually name a relative or classmate who has done well and reached a high social position.

People *need* not mix as social equals with those of equivalent wealth; nor *need* they maintain ties of kinship and schooling. The purpose of this chapter is to outline, in a very summary manner, the prevailing patterns of social interaction in order to determine the degree to which status groups based upon income—rather than ethnic criteria—are developing in Yoruba society; and to examine the nature of the personal networks which are maintained by individuals.

Living styles

Only to a partial degree have rich and poor become residentially segregated. As we have already noted, the wealthy provincial produce-buyer or lorry owner has usually built his own magnificent house on the land of his descent group. Most Yoruba towns are expanding with the development of estates of modern houses on their fringes along the major roads, but the older and traditionally oriented man prefers to live within the compound where he can exercise such power as his wealth and age defines. Thus in the provincial Yoruba town, as in the indigenous quarters of Ibadan, the traditional 'compound' is maintained even though its outward appearance is vastly altered (Mabogunje, 1962). As the mud-walled, thatched roof structures have crumbled, in recent decades they have been replaced by bungalows and two-storey houses; these are the property of the individual builder but later become the corporate family property of his children. At first these houses faced into the traditional court-yard of the compound but later they were aligned to the new roads and the courtyard itself occupied by new buildings. Today the ob-server beholds but a sea of rusting corrugated iron roofs of houses of widely differing pretentiousness; no visible boundaries separate the compounds but to the descent groups concerned a gutter between two houses, an isolated tree or rock outcrop is highly significant as a jealously guarded limit. The compound, if no longer a physical unit as a single structure, is certainly still a social unit with a strong sense of its unity and cohesion displayed at its regular meeting in the house of its head. In most towns the compound has been a tax collecting unit and one or more compounds have constituted a local government ward. However there is an increasing tendency for new roads to cut through the traditional compounds and for these roads to constitute the modern administrative boundaries. Thus the unity of Oje in Ibadan has been substantially destroyed by such adminis-trative parcellation.

A few immigrants find lodging within these traditional compounds as men rent a spare room in their house. But most live on the periphery of the towns. In the early colonial period the administration built houses for its clerical staff alongside their offices; barracks were provided for the police; the Nigerian Railway housed its staff. In recent years only a few employers have provided such houses. Thus many of the junior employees of the Universities of Ibadan and Ife are housed within the campus (van den Berghe, 1973, ch. 6). But most urban migrants are accommodated in privately owned houses. These are built on the edge of the town on land purchased from a descent group. Most are two-storey houses and have on each floor from three to six rooms of identical size on each side of a wide corridor. Communal rooms for washing and cooking are provided at the back of the house. In such a house the rooms may be let singly or in pairs; alternatively a family may occupy the whole of one side of the corridor; or again, the owner may live upstairs, occupying the whole area, while he lets the ground floor rooms. With such arrangements it is possible to find people of very different incomes occupying the same building. Again housing is scarce and although a man will usually notify a relative or townsman of a vacant room in his building, it is unusual to find a house rented to people of a single community; instead ethnic diversity is the rule. In Ibadan, for instance, Yoruba from different areas are intermixed with non-Yoruba, Edo or Ibo and there are no quarters identified with a single ethnic group. The one exception is the Hausa quarter of Sabo. Residents of a house are in very close daily contact with each other, yet intense personal bonds rarely seem to develop as friendships seem to be determined more by ethnic ties or work place than by co-residence.

The colonial administration provided luxurious houses for all its, mostly expatriate, senior staff in the park-like residential areas (Government Residential Areas) on the periphery of the towns (Mabogunje, 1967). Many of these houses are now occupied by Nigerians, though with the expansion of the civil service only the most senior qualify for such houses—the remainder must find their own accommodation. The universities however do still accommodate all their own staff—save those who opt to take a loan and build their own home. In Ibadan, the Western Regional Housing Corporation developed the Bodija estate with larger houses mortgaged to persons with incomes well above £1,000 a year, and smaller ones to senior executives earning above £600 a year. The various styles of house are not segregated; the larger ones line the main roads while the smaller ones lie behind them in culs-de-sac. In recent years the government has made available plots both in the Bodija estate and on some of the GRAs on which the wealthy have constructed their own houses (often of course securing a mortgage or loan). In such areas the owners are assured that their neighbours will be of similar status—in terms of income. Many of the wealthy have however bought land privately—and in some secrecy as they fear to increase the popularity of an area and so raise the price of the land. Many have built modern, architect-designed houses. But they may well find that nearby plots have been sold to landlords building multiple-roomed houses solely for letting to migrants. Furthermore, though the landowning descent group lays out regular plots and reserves land for roads, the latter are initially developed by the purchasers and usually remain rough tracks for several years while the houses themselves are often irregularly sited. Thus the wealthiest families, usually but not invariably, live in the exclusive government estates. The young graduate will probably start his life in rented rooms and later build his own house in one of the privately developed areas, where he will be in close physical proximity to much less wealthy immigrants.

With wealth and education the style of life within the home becomes overtly more and more Western. But one must clearly distinguish the technology—the car, television or radiogram, refrigerator, common now to all industrial societies—from values of family life; many a recently arrived expatriate has been rudely shocked in finding that the African family which has exactly the same material style of life as himself nevertheless has a very different ideology. To some extent the Yoruba have inherited a material style of life created by the colonial administrators in moving physically into their houses—houses built for men who were expected to keep their children in England and containing therefore spacious reception rooms but few bedrooms. Modern houses are designed for the larger family, but there are no marked differences between the houses of expatriates and of indigenes. On the university campuses houses pass from expatriate to Nigerian and back again; many wealthy Nigerians lease their own house to expatriates for a few years, the high rents quickly paying off the entire mortgage, before themselves occupying it (P. C. Lloyd, 1967b).

Between persons of like income the styles of living are very similar. First, there is a uniformity in house style and hard furnishing in government or university housing. The shops carry a limited range of imported furnishings and the few local furniture manufacturers tend to copy the imported styles. It would be difficult to be very different from one's neighbour. Second, expenditure patterns tend to be uniform. Most people spend relatively little on the education of their own children, though extensively aiding their junior relatives. Few have a choice, as is available in England, between spending nearly £1,000 a year on a public school education or using this sum for a higher standard of everyday living or for holidays. Life assurance is growing in popularity though it is not yet widespread; saving is more usually achieved through house building or assistance to relatives. Except for the very rich, holidays are spent at home or in visits to friends and relatives. As a result, the wealth of a man tends to be readily visible—in the style of his house and its furnishings, the size of his car, his dress. It is thus not difficult to scale one's acquaintances in terms of their wealth. Furthermore the income of the civil servant may easily be established by reference to the staff list—a booklet readily available to all in the public service.

The foregoing paragraphs have referred to the affluent educated man, not to the wealthy but more traditionally oriented traders living perhaps within their own compounds. For these latter too their wealth may be assessed with equal facility, for few will invest so heavily in their children's education or in house property in the cities as to deny to themselves the locally recognised symbols of affluence. One readily notices qualitative differences in styles of house furnishings which can be scaled from the more traditional to the more modern. At the former end of the continuum one may find, for instance, expensive imported settees and armchairs lining the walls of the living room; almanacs decorate the walls rather than prints of well-known artists. Such differences are usually paralleled by variations in marital roles to be noted later.

One of the most important status symbols is the car. Those in public service with an income above approximately £600 are entitled to a government loan and an allowance which substantially facilitates both running the car and repaying the loan. With public transport almost non-existent a car is essential for visiting both within the town and in the rural area. In Ibadan, for example, the affluent residential areas are up to eight miles distant from each other. Only with a car can one maintain the pattern of interaction expected of a person of high status; only with a car can one be freed from the constraints of one's neighbourhood.

Dress remains for the modern Yoruba a most important sign of affluence. Yoruba gowns, whether of locally woven or imported cloth, are worn for almost all formal occasions and ceremonies; the locally woven cloth is more prestigious but imported laces and brocades can now be much more expensive. For a funeral weekend, including wake-keeping, a church burial service and subsequent festivities a wealthy man or woman may appear in several changes of costume, each costing up to £100 exclusive of gold ornaments.

Speech patterns identify the educated. Schooling encourages fluency in a basic standard Yoruba but tends to eradicate much of the richness of phraseology and dialect differences. Whilst educated Yoruba usually converse in the vernacular, their speech is heavily laden with English phrases, the use of which can be increased or decreased according to the impression that one wishes to create. It remains possible to identify the ethnic origin of an educated Yoruba by his pronunciation but these differences are now overlain by those correlated with educational level.

Finally, the Yoruba are still obsessive about rank. Thus to address as 'mister' a man who has a doctorate, or as 'doctor' a man recently elevated to a professorship is felt to be as heinous as failing to address a traditional chief by his proper honorific, and the guilty will apologise most effusively for their error.

To sum up: differences in wealth are overtly displayed to a very high degree, for among the affluent and educated Yoruba to hide one's affluence would, as in traditional society, draw accusations of miserliness. Yet, save for the very rich who live on the government estates, and those on university campuses, the wealthy are not segregated to any marked extent from the poor.

Families and communities of orientation

A vast gulf both in material styles of living and in values separates many parents and their well-educated sons. Many factors necessarily inhibit interaction between the generations. The children probably live in the city, parents in the rural area or provincial town; the children's house is not designed to accommodate dependants; cooking by gas or electricity is frightening to the parents; the diet of the children's family is different from that to which parents are accustomed. Equally, a visit by an educated family to their home compound creates problems—they may have to take with them camp beds and bedding, water and much of their food. Yet it is a rare parent who is not inordinately proud of his successful children. It is he who arranges the motorcade for the graduate returning from overseas, the church service of thanksgiving, and who demands that the son should wear his English winter suit as a public demonstration of his success. Achievements not available to the parents are realised in their children and their status and prestige in their own community are enhanced thereby.

For the children whose schooling has focused so largely on Western learning and values, the parents remain the embodiment of their own culture which they are anxious to retain. An educated man who professes to be ashamed of his 'uncivilised' parents is almost certain to be ridiculed by his peers. Wealthy children therefore send remittances home to enable their parents to live comfortably in the style to which they are accustomed. Since they are likely to be elderly there is no question of setting them up in a new and more lucrative occupation—they should enjoy their retirement and be free to indulge in public affairs. Only when they fall ill are they removed from their surroundings into the modern hospitals for the best treatment that money and influence can provide.

Children thus remain in close touch with their parents; the car owner can visit them several times during the year whilst the poorer man makes, at best, an annual visit and relies otherwise on correspondence, or more probably, on news carried by travellers to the home area.

Many an illiterate and traditionally oriented parent has been willing to support one son who has shown scholastic aptitude whilst others were given no encouragement to go to school and were trained as farmers or craftsmen. Other parents strive to give all or most of their children at least a minimum education. Within the polygamous family one achievement-oriented wife may have struggled to educate her own offspring from her trading profits whilst her co-wives were unable or unwilling to do likewise. As a result the sibling group often displays wide disparities of status. One rarely hears of a successful man assisting his elder brothers. Traditionally a junior brother served a senior brother, helping on his farm, assisting him in house building; at death, property could pass only from senior to junior brothers. The elder brothers of an educated man are invariably too old to be sent for schooling or apprenticeship —their occupational careers are already charted. Nevertheless it seems unusual for a man to give his elder brother a substantial loan, for instance to improve his business. Thus these status disparities are maintained.

All of a man's efforts are however directed towards the assistance of his junior siblings or of the children of his older brothers. Not only do the emotional bonds of kinship demand this, but in addition the successful son realises that a disproportionate share of the family wealth was invested in him and he has an obligation to repay this by financing the education of junior relatives. In some cases his own education actually prevented his siblings from continuing theirs, and he must compensate them for their truncated careers. In recent years a further explanation has been given: with increasing unemployment and poverty among the less well-educated, the successful men profess anxiety that the former may turn to crime and bring disgrace to the family.

Physical separation from siblings does not seem to reduce the feeling of obligation to help them. It enables one to plan one's beneficence, paying the school fees of those who will gain most benefit, rather than exhausting funds in frequent gift giving which often yields no lasting benefit to the recipient. It also makes it easier to confine assistance to the financial sphere, resisting requests to take the junior siblings or nephews into one's own household and thus destroying the unity of the nuclear family and perhaps threatening the advantaged training of one's own children. Nevertheless ties between siblings remain close; it is said by Yoruba that the principal disadvantage of a white wife is that she will be unwilling to provide food on demand on the unexpected arrival of members of one's family. Kinship obligations may grow irksome, but they cannot be denied in totality.

When several siblings have been educated, it is likely that some of them will be living and working in the same city—either in Ibadan or in Lagos. What is the relationship between them? Casual observation suggests that differences in status and in age, the two factors probably being correlated, are significant. A man will interact more frequently with siblings close in age and of similar social status, least with those different in age and status. The frequency of interaction with the latter probably falls well below that with friends, though the intensity—measured in strength of emotive feelings and of obligation—will be greater.

The successful man finds many demands made upon him by his home town or village, especially if he is one of the few of its sons to have prospered. If he is a civil servant and cognisant of the intricacies of bureaucracy his help will be sought in the building of a new school or road; if he is in the relevant ministry he will be expected to steer the community's requests through the appropriate channels. But perhaps the prime task of the successful man is to find employment in the cities for others from his community, either through the power to make appointments, as a clerk who can manipulate the files so that some applications are submitted for scrutiny whilst others are deemed late and ineligible, through being in a position to recommend a 'brother' to an employer or by merely notifying the applicant of a known or potential vacancy. The reputation of the man in his home community will depend upon his success and his willingness in accepting these obligations.

But why should a man be so active on behalf of his community?

Would it not be in his own interest to ignore it especially when these obligations might conflict with those towards colleagues and associates in the capital? First, there is probably pressure from parents who will lose respect if their child defaults in his obligations. Second, one's beneficent actions not only result in the voiced commendations of the recipients of favours but these quickly reach the other members of one's community in the city and so enhance one's reputation in their sight. Indirectly, the respect of most of one's social equals is gained, for it is generally held, by the educated and affluent man, that one *ought* to be active in promoting the interests of one's community. For the man who envisages a political career, mass support in his home area is a prerequisite of success, for it is only in this area, effectively, that he can stand for election. Others recognise that local popularity will enable them to get the desired plot of building land at a reasonable price, to hear of commercial opportunities. The poor man relies much more directly upon his home community for his status and security in his old age. If he cuts himself off from his family he will find that his rights to land have become a legal fiction, for all is being used by his kin; in his compound he will be accorded the respect due to his age but his chances of gaining a chieftaincy title, for instance, will be ruined.

Thus there are strong pressures on the city dweller to identify with his home town or village. If he can afford it he should build a house there—conversely, not to build when one clearly has money is seen as a denial of one's origins. Thus a large proportion of the houses on the outskirts of the Yoruba towns today belong to their successful sons in the cities; many of them outclass in size or design the residences of the local élite of ọba, chiefs and traders. The weddings of educated couples often take place in Ibadan or Lagos, especially when the spouses come from different communities, but funerals are almost invariably in the home community. These and like ceremonies —the enthronement of a bishop, the opening of a school—regularly draw large numbers of the car-owning élite to their home areas every Saturday. (With the increased number of refrigerated hospital mortuaries, bodies need not be interred immediately but may be kept until the weekend; in fact I heard of one instance in which the interment of an important man was delayed for three weeks, for the two Saturdays following the death were already pre-empted by ceremonies which required the participation of a large number of élite and of clergy.) At these ceremonies, as at city cocktail parties, much private business is done between persons of high status; men who are unavailable in their offices are vulnerable in such situations. But the participants at these celebrations are to a large extent ethnically defined, and ethnic cohesion is thus enhanced. Again, weddings, funerals and the like bring men and women into renewed contact with their more distant kin, their erstwhile school and age mates who have remained in the community. By a simple greeting the successful emigrant recognises his origins whilst the home-dweller affirms his relationship with the eminent. Those migrants who have built houses in their home town may furthermore spend the whole weekend there, returning to the city early on Monday morning; their interaction with their home community is thus increased.

In general, interaction with the home community increases with affluence. The wealthy man with a car and a house not occupied by tenants can spend the weekend there; with a car but no house one must return the same day; those without cars may beg lifts if they are sufficiently close to a car owner, or collectively hire a taxi or bus; the poor are unable to travel home, being both unable to afford the fare and unwilling to donate as lavishly to relatives as their infrequent visits demand.

Within the city interaction with co-members of one's home community takes place at formal and informal levels. For most Yoruba, ethnic associations—the town and district improvement unions and the like—are, as will be described below, relatively unimportant. But at the large gatherings—a Christmas party, a naming ceremony—to which the Yoruba invite a wide circle of friends and acquaintances, one may often see a number of persons not usually associated with the host but who come from his home town and would probably be offended were they not invited.

Families of procreation

As we have seen, educated Yoruba men, and to a lesser extent, educated women, come from a wide social base. To what extent are mates selected on the basis of education, of home background or ethnic area? Very few educated men and women have their spouses chosen for them by their parents and a high proportion of marriages result from friendships contracted in school or university. In making their own choices, are they contributing to a closure of the stratum of the educated élite or are they maintaining and increasing the relationships between rich and poor homes?

Educated men prefer to have educated wives. The stated reason is not so often in terms of companionship but of the need to provide a home, to entertain guests according to the standards of one's own social rank. A considerable disparity in education often occurs when an untrained primary school teacher takes as wife a girl who has only a primary education; he subsequently advances through teacher training college and university whilst she remains, perhaps in his parents' home, bearing his children and becoming increasingly set in the manners and habits of a traditional compound. However, a man is reluctant to take a wife with more education than himself, or even in many cases of equal education. In the former situation she will almost certainly be of superior rank in the public service or teaching field; in the latter the shortage of educated women results in their relatively faster promotion. Thus if husband and wife are both graduate teachers, there is a strong likelihood that she will become a headmistress, associating on equal terms with men to whom her husband, still an assistant master, must defer. However the education of Yoruba women has lagged far behind that of men so that it would in fact be impossible for all men to find wives with the same education as themselves.

The better educated women tend to come from literate homes. Thus in the 1962 survey (see above, p. 106) of 110 women with post-secondary education, 83 had fathers with post-primary education and only 41 had illiterate mothers. Table 6 illustrates the relative education of husbands and wives.

Among the early Christian converts—small, closed minority groups viewed with hostility by the remainder of their local communities—intermarriage (provided that it did not contravene customary laws of marriage) was common. And inasmuch as these converts educated their children well, one finds today some close-knit groups of kin, many of whom hold high office in church and state. The Awosika family in Ondo, with its ramifications, is an excellent example (P. C. Lloyd, 1962, pp. 104–5). But such kin groupings are localised and have in the past been feebly interlinked across ethnic boundaries. Apart from such marriage preferences, there seems to be a tendency for men and women from literate homes to intermarry. In the Ibadan sample, of those men with mothers having a complete primary education over half had wives whose fathers had had post-

TABLE 6 *Relative education of husbands and wives (percentages)*

A Wife's education	Husband's education								%	n
	1	2	3	4	5	6	7	8		
1 Nil	44	12	21	1	13	8	1	—	100	237
2 Primary 1–5	9	6	37	3	26	12	6	1	100	68
3 Primary 6	1	—	17	3	27	28	17	7	100	232
4 Primary 6+ ETC, nursing	—	—	4	4	12	30	30	20	100	56
5 Secondary grammar 1–4	—	—	7	—	17	31	26	19	100	72
6 Sec. gram. 5–6 grade II teacher	—	—	3	—	7	25	26	39	100	61
7 Post-secondary	—	—	—	—	1	1	29	69	100	73
8 University graduate	—	—	—	—	3	6	6	86	100	35

B Wife's education	Husband's education							
	1	2	3	4	5	6	7	8
1 Nil	92	88	41	15	23	14	2	—
2 Primary 1–5	5	12	21	15	14	5	3	1
3 Primary 6	3	—	31	54	45	42	32	10
4 Primary 6 + ETC, nursing	—	—	2	15	5	12	14	8
5 Secondary grammar 1–4	—	—	4	—	9	15	16	10
6 Sec. gram. 5–6 grade II teacher	—	—	2	—	3	10	13	16
7 Post-secondary	—	—	—	—	1	1	18	34
8 University graduate	—	—	—	—	1	1	2	21
%	100	100	100	100	100	100	100	100
n=	113	33	120	13	132	147	119	145

Percentages rounded to the nearest whole number.

primary education and whose mothers had had a complete primary education; in a further quarter of the cases either the fathers had had post-primary education or the mothers had complete primary education. Of the women in the sample with fathers with post-primary education, three-quarters had mothers with complete primary education. But of the latter one-half married men from homes in which the father had primary education or less and the mother little or no education at all; only 30 per cent married men with parents as well educated as their own. But the proportion of educated men with literate mothers is well below this figure. Today some of the grandest weddings conspicuously unite two well-known and powerful families, but spectacular as these might be they are of little statistical significance in themselves. Nevertheless, with entry to grammar school and hence to university becoming increasingly the prerogative of the wealthy families, the linking of these by marriage is certain to increase in the coming years.

Traditionally Yoruba men took their wives from descent groups within their own town or closely neighbouring settlements. Today almost all men with less than a full primary education take wives from their own ethnic area—Oyo, Ibadan, Oshun, Egba, Ijesha, Ijebu, Ondo, Ekiti, etc. But this proportion falls with increasing education; of those with post-primary education one-third, and of those with post-secondary education almost a half take their wives from ethnic areas other than their own. These proportions are higher for the wives—over two-thirds of the women graduates marry outside their own ethnic group. The Ijebu men seem to marry out of their own group with less frequency, a feature which may be associated either with the well-known exclusiveness or clannishness of the Ijebu among other Yoruba or with the greater number of their educated women. For it does seem to hold that the greater the number of educated women—i.e. eligible wives—from one's area, the greater the likelihood of marriage with one of them. When husband and wife are both from the same home community, and especially if both come from prominent families, their interaction in the affairs of the community will be substantially greater than if their loyalties were divided.

Marriage among the educated Yoruba is monogamous—at least in the sense that whilst a man may have a sequence or plurality of 'outside wives' whose children he acknowledges and maintains, these latter women do not challenge the superiority of the married wife in her own home. I have described in more detail elsewhere (P. C. Lloyd, 1967b) the diversity of patterns of marital roles obtaining among the more highly educated. These range from a more 'traditional' style in which the women have considerable economic independence and in which roles tend to be highly segregated, to an 'egalitarian' style in which shared roles are more in evidence—the couple may have a joint bank account, decisions concerning the family and home are more obviously taken jointly, the couple go out together in the evenings, rather than seek separate entertainment and recreation. The latter style predominated among men and women who came from literate homes, especially from those of the local Christian élite of teachers and clerks of a generation ago; among such parents (and many of them are still alive today) a 'Victorian' marital relationship prevails, stressing the superiority of the father and the dependence of his wife upon him, together with a strict regard for Christian morality. These marital role patterns affect both the mode of entertainment—egalitarian couples give dinner parties, traditional ones hold mass gatherings—and also the style of house furnishing; in turn these probably affect friendship patterns though I have no data to prove it (save as outlined below). They are also likely to affect attitudes towards their children's upbringing and education.

Conscious of their continuing links with their kin and community, educated Yoruba often allege that they have no 'class' feelings; though the expatriate often notices the frequency with which reference is made, especially by educated women, to the 'natives'. However these same people are bringing up their children in the most circumscribed social environment. In spite of the juxtaposition of families of very different income levels in the newer suburbs of the cities, the children of wealthy and educated parents are discouraged from playing with children from poorer homes—the latter often being described as rude and dirty (B. B. Lloyd, 1966). The children from the affluent homes are sent to the fee-paying private primary schools and in their leisure hours play with their classmates. Distance between homes is little constraint, for the parents may have two cars and almost certainly a driver who ferries the children to and fro. Growing up in the city suburbs these children know little of their wider circle of kin. Often but not always they visit the home area with their parents but for such brief periods that they learn almost nothing about the community. In fact when the parents have a large house in the home town, the children are sometimes encouraged to take their playmates on the weekend visits and to amuse themselves fishing whilst the parents fulfil their obligations at the sequences of ceremonies.

Friendships and associations

The foregoing sections have dealt with ascribed relationships—those of kinship and community. We consider now those entered into by the free choice of the individual—friendships and voluntary associations. To the Yoruba friendship means much the same as it means to us; a symmetrical relationship in which there is a sharing of values and a high degree of mutual obligation.

In traditional Yoruba society bonds of close friendship were often created within the more formal age group associations. Ceremonies of blood brotherhood, though not institutionalised as in some African societies, were sometimes conducted to intensify the link. Membership of the age group itself created obligations which exceed those normally accepted by modern associations. Thus it was held to be a heinous offence for a man to seduce the wife of his age mate. Many of these obligations associated with age sets have, however, been transferred to modern institutions. Thus in Iwo in the early 1950s the postal agent ran away with the wife of the dispenser; although such abductions are not an uncommon feature of Yoruba life this action was construed as a serious wrong for both men were government employees and should have abjured such behaviour; the patron of the postal agent, fully supported by public opinion, thereupon withdrew his bond and the post office was obliged to dismiss its agent. With the vast expansion of the bureaucracy these sentiments have probably ceased to exist in all but the smallest communities. However, the type of relationship engendered by the age set is widely carried over into the school system. The Yoruba had no formal ceremonies of initiation into adulthood but passage through primary school in the same class seems to instil among boys the same feelings of brotherhood as are associated elsewhere with co-initiates. Schooling, with its discipline and flogging, particularly pronounced in earlier decades, was in many senses an initiation into the modern sector of the economy which paralleled traditional African practices. Thus today one finds frequently that a high proportion of friendships which last into adulthood were first created at school. However it is equally apparent that friendships among the literate urban dwellers fall within socio-economic strata and not across them.

The well-educated man or woman who takes up an appointment in the city has already a large number of acquaintances in his new abode—family perhaps and certainly classmates from secondary grammar school and university, for a high proportion of persons with this level of education are employed in Ibadan or Lagos rather than in the provincial centres. His task is to activate old relationships as well as to create new ones. The study of well-educated couples in

Ibadan showed that their friends (ten close friends being cited by each partner) were almost without exception of the same age, education and income as themselves (P. C. Lloyd, 1967b). Most friends lived in Ibadan. About half the friends cited came from Yoruba ethnic groups other than those of the respondent, though the Ijebu seemed to have more friends from their own area; again men who participated strongly in the affairs of their home community had more friends from their own ethnic group. Two-thirds of the friendships were made before marriage and one third of the total were school or college friends; such figures may be thought to reflect the youth of the selected sample, but it was noticeable that the number of school friendships did not decline with increasing age.

Men and women seem to choose their friends in a similar manner and hence the friends cited by the wife were usually quite unrelated to those of the husband. In the more 'egalitarian' marriages a few friendships were shared—the husband naming Mr X as his friend, the wife citing Mrs X as hers. A high degree of shared friendships seems to exist however in the 'Victorian' marriages. Very few friendships seemed to have been established through the medium of the marriage partner.

In this sample only a half, on average, of the ten friends cited by each respondent were known to each other, suggesting a relatively open network; a higher degree of openness seemed to exist among 'egalitarian' couples, a lesser degree among the older men and women.

Among the less well-educated urban migrants the same features are found. Friends are drawn from one's own socio-economic level and, to a greater degree perhaps than among the better-educated, from one's own ethnic group. For these migrants are far more likely to move from one town to another on transfer from one job to another, so that relationships established through co-residence or working together are more likely to be ephemeral.

The voluntary associations found in West African towns have been described at some length by other writers (K. L. Little, 1965), emphasis usually being placed on the manner in which they assist the migrant to adapt to urban life. Here I wish to comment briefly on the degree to which they either transcend or exist within social strata.

Formal age grading has almost ceased to exist in Yoruba towns, for public work is no longer organised on such a basis; again with the growing size of the larger towns the creation of regularly spaced age sets has fallen into desuetude. But the place of the formal age set has been taken by the *egbẹ*, a voluntary association but strongly based on age and locality. Members meet regularly, probably weekly, for recreational purposes. Once a year, at the major Christian or Muslim festivals, they hold a dance and procession through the town with drummers, all members wearing gowns of identical cloth, the costs of which can be quite substantial. Thus, in addition to age and locality, affluence becomes one of the major criteria for membership and *egbẹ* will be formed catering for men of different incomes.

In the churches too the societies formed within the congregation for the purposes of Bible study and fund raising tend, in the same way, to be established on the basis of wealth as well as of age, sex and locality. In the larger Protestant and Catholic churches the wealthy or titled members of the congregation sit in the front pews lavishly dressed whilst the poor occupy the back of the church; status differences are emphasised. The popularity of many of the small sects which have mushroomed in the larger urban centres derives, in part, from their assertion of human equality through the wearing of humble clothes or simple white gowns.

The *esusu* savings clubs do of course stratify their members by income, for the membership of a club is composed of those who agree to pay a fixed sum, weekly or monthly. But although members must share a mutual trust, they meet, if at all, for no other purpose than to collect or distribute the saved moneys.

Other urban associations, such as the guilds of craftsmen or traders, do have more extensive activities. In addition to regulating the craft or trade, guild members will attend each other's marriages, the naming ceremonies of their children and their funerals. But the social security of the individual, his maintenance in sickness and senility, is deemed to be the responsibility of his descent group rather than his guild. The incomes of craftsmen do not vary as widely as do those of traders and the guilds of the latter thus bring together members with assumed similar interests but quite dissimilar incomes.

For the urban migrant the most obvious association to join is his town or village 'improvement union', the ethnic association. But these are not nearly so strongly developed among the Yoruba as among the Ibo. A number of reasons may be adduced. A Yoruba man from one area, say Ekiti, is not such a stranger in Ibadan or Ijebu Ode as, say, an Ibo—a man from a substantially different cultural group. The smaller Yoruba settlements, and some Ijebu villages in particular, have more highly organised associations than the larger towns, from which the majority of migrants must come. A town of 40,000, for example, would find it difficult to mobilise *all* its migrants and those in either Ibadan or Lagos are still too numerous to organise locally on an effective and universal basis. The improvement unions of the larger Yoruba towns and districts direct their activities more towards para-political issues, the provision of services in the home area, than towards the social security of individual members; in so doing they attract as active members those aspiring to political careers. The functions neglected by these unions but which are assiduously carried out by, for example, the Ibo unions, are in the case of the Yoruba performed by informal groups. Thus the migrant who arrives in the city will almost invariably find there some close relatives or school mates and it is upon these that he depends for his initial accommodation and for advice and recommendation in job seeking.

The poorer urban migrant has few close relationships other than those of kinship and community and common employment. Membership of formal associations costs money which he can ill afford. Outside the churches there are in fact few associations open to the urban worker. The government organises youth clubs, ostensibly for teenagers though many members are older, but these cater for relatively few individuals. Tennis clubs are for the more affluent. Most men spend their leisure hours either at home, involved in domestic activities, in studying for examinations or in visiting friends in their homes. Employees of large organisations usually belong to the relevant house trade union but its activities take little of the time of most members. For craftsmen and traders guilds are weakly organised if at all, for the sanctions which are effective in the provincial town, where guild members belong to the same community and are well known to one another, become inoperable in the city suburb where most of them are comparatively recent immigrants.

For the affluent educated Yoruba a much richer choice of associational membership is presented; furthermore most of these associations are exclusive, either *de facto* or *de jure* to those of such high social rank. The Masonic lodges, together with that syncretic association the Reformed Ogboni Fraternity, were more prominent in the past than they are today; the former brought together expatriates, mainly of the commercial community, and wealthy Nigerians;

the latter united within a single town the wealthy traders and senior clerks. Mutual help and patronage were among their most significant functions. Today the Rotary Club has greater prestige and influence. Expatriates also established, in the colonial era, the major charities— the Red Cross, YMCA and YWCA, RSPCC and RSPCA. Positions of leadership are held by those near the summit of the social ladder while executive tasks are performed by those of middle range incomes. Grammar schools and the major teacher training colleges have their Old Boys' clubs which meet annually for a formal dinner but require little other direct participation; however they do help to maintain the bonds between classmates. At the present time most highly educated Yoruba have come from a few old-established schools; the recent proliferation of schools and the possibility of entry to Nigerian universities via the teacher training colleges is broadening the recruitment of the educated élite. But the selective entry into the more prestigious schools and the subsequent social and educational advantages gained thereby will, in future years, continue to be reinforced by the alumni associations of these schools.

The associations cited above demand little of the time of the well-educated, city-dwelling Yoruba; his leisure hours are spent either in semi-formal recreation—tennis or golf at the (ex-European) Club, dancing at a night club, or the innumerable cocktail parties—or in the interminable round of visiting, not just to pass the time of day but to arrange something—a children's party, a forthcoming wedding, a business deal. All these activities are largely restricted to members of similar socio-economic status.

When one visits the house of well-educated Yoruba one will meet the members of his immediate family in the living quarters, the servants in the kitchen and outbuildings. In the parlours of the wealthy but less literate trader or businessman one frequently meets men for whose presence there seems little purpose. They arrive, greet their host profusely, sit down, accept a drink and look through a newspaper or photo album and then with further greetings they leave. Such men hope that in noticing their presence and perhaps in requesting some small favour, the wealthy patron will provide a lucrative opportunity for his client's advancement. But, as with membership of an exclusive club, such activity has its costs as well as its rewards. In identifying with one's patron one must accompany him to ceremonies, purchasing the necessary *aṣọ ẹbi* and spending generously. Whilst such activity is a well-recognised means of getting ahead, for many men the costs in time (and hence lost income) and money spent seem to exceed in either the short or long term the likely benefits. They cease to be so assiduous in visiting their patron, but nevertheless attempt to keep the patron within their personal network.

Networks and status groups

In the opening chapter we distinguished between two dimensions of the perception of social inequality—the ego-centred cognitive map and the analytical structure. By the former the individual defined his own goals and described the routes for achieving them; by the latter he characterised the relationship between the groups or strata which he delineated in his society and asserted its legitimacy. This distinction underlies our present discussion of social networks and status groups.

The individual's social network comprises the totality of his social relationships, described with reference to himself; it is thus ego-oriented or ego-centred. The network may be described in terms of the categories of persons involved—kin, friends, age or work mates, etc., and the type of relationship—simple or multiplex, the frequency of interaction, its intensity (i.e. the degree of obligation), its symmetry or asymmetry in terms of power. The overall pattern can be described in terms of density—the degree of interconnectedness between the individuals, other than ego, who comprise the network; of scale—the number of individuals involved linked to ego both directly and indirectly—and in the latter case, the distance in terms of number of links from ego (Mitchell, 1969). Some writers would use the term 'network' to embrace only those persons with whom ego was in everyday contact and communication and to exclude those relationships with acquaintances which are but potentially or very rarely activated. This is useful if it is one's task, for instance, to assess the effect of daily interaction upon values. But for our purposes it is necessary to use the wider definition. Again writers have distinguished zones within the network—for instance, intimate, effective and extended; whilst the qualities used in defining these zones—usually intensity and frequency—are important, one should not compound them. The Yoruba urban migrant maintains an intensive, or intimate, relationship with his close kin, but may, if they remain in the rural area, interact with them but infrequently.

Zoning or segmentation of the network can be defined in terms of spheres of action, distinguishing perhaps between the kinship sphere and the work sphere. The reality of this definition is seen in the composition of the action sets—those individuals and relationships which are mobilised for specific ends. Thus in the case of the dismissed Ibo worker two action sets were activated—his work mates and the trade union officials in order to fight for his reinstatement, and the members of his ethnic group to find him alternative employment (Peace, 1973).

If one is using the concept of the personal social network one cannot operate in terms of social groups or quasi-groups; at best one can discern factions, especially if ego is the faction leader. But one may superimpose the personal networks of each individual in the society to obtain the total network pattern of that society. A perfectly even reticulation is theoretically possible, but in practice one finds a clustering of individuals and relationships. Such will be produced when a number of individuals constitute a status group—being linked by multiplex, intense and frequent interaction. Such groupings may however be defined by various criteria, for our discussion the ascribed criteria of descent and age and the achieved criteria of income and rank being the most relevant.

In the traditional Yoruba community the individual's personal network is largely confined within his town or village, save for maternal or affinal links with persons in nearby settlements. The individuals in the network can be classified almost entirely in terms of kinship, age and occupation. The dominant social groups are defined by descent and age, the latter being composed of symmetrical relationships, the former of asymmetrical relationships expressed in age ranking.

Personal networks are, today, geographically extensive for they include both men and women who have remained within the home community and those who have emigrated to a variety of urban centres; among those so separated are close kin—parents and children, siblings. Furthermore descent groups and age sets, now defined in terms of primary school attendance, comprise men at all social levels: the farmer or craftsman in the home community, the local wealthy trader, the urban wage employee, the educated teacher or civil servant. The pressures on the poor to seek their ultimate social security in the home community and on the rich to identify with it, cause both to assiduously maintain those areas of their network in which individuals are separated from them by great physical or social (in terms of rank) distance. For while the poor seek to preserve their relationship with the rich, their potential patrons, so the rich need either the direct support of the poor or else the approval of their equally affluent townsmen. Thus, in spite of the social differentiation produced by economic development, ascribed relationships of kinship and community remain very strong.

The poor urban migrant develops relatively few new relationships within the town. Upon his arrival he is heavily dependent upon relatives or classmates already resident and quickly becomes encapsulated within a small circle of kin and friends from his own ethnic area. Other highly specific relationships made through co-tenancy of a house or through work lack the intensity and permanence of ethnic ties. Poverty constrains a more active participation in town life which might perhaps bring new categories into his network.

In contrast the affluent educated Yoruba at the top of the social hierarchy are not only better able to maintain, through possession of a car, their relationships with the home community but are also intensifying the cohesion of the social élite across ethnic boundaries. Links established by marriage and through higher education bind men and women from different ethnic areas; city friendships too are diverse. Whilst those individuals frequently stress the humility of their own social origins and the importance of their social heritage, they are not only ensuring that their children maintain their own high social rank but also providing them with minimal contact with families of lower rank.

Within this élite, social differentiation based upon occupational criteria seems relatively unimportant; civil servants, private professionals and businessmen, teachers, do not move in mutually exclusive circles. Various reasons may be adduced: friendships often antedate the selection of a career; there is, apart from university staff, no residential segregation; in Ibadan a few shops and clubs serve the entire élite. In fact such social differentiation as can be seen, within given limits of wealth, seems largely based upon ethnic criteria.

6 Yoruba attitudes

It is easy to talk glibly about the world-view, mazeways or cognitive map of the individual, discussing the components of such a map and suggesting their origins and interrelationships. To describe the map itself is a task of a very different order. It is as if one were asked to describe a view of a landscape presented either as a painting or a photograph, or perhaps in the symbolic form of an ordnance map. Furthermore the view is not a static one. For just as the individual stresses one set of relationships or one field of activity in specific situations, so it is as if we were asked to describe a view which was repeatedly altered through the use of distorting lenses and colour filters. Wallace, after describing his own cognitive map of the drive from his home to his office concluded (1965, p. 292): 'Whether a homologous frame of reference would be appropriate to behaviour in social organisation remains to be seen.' The cognitive maps described by experimental psychologists cover but minute fields of activity. But in taking social inequality as the theme for our own studies we have selected a field which impinges on almost every behavioural act. Can we be methodical in presenting the patterns of social inequality as perceived by the Yoruba or should we admit to a frankly impressionistic presentation? Too many social anthropologists in eschewing the crudity of the formal questionnaire have in default of an alternative rigorous approach, fallen back upon the latter. Yet I believe that we must try to be methodical albeit admitting the simplistic and often naïve nature of the attempt. Accordingly in this chapter I present responses gained through structured interviews and questionnaires; the interpretation which I give to these rests however upon the impressions which I had already gained in two decades of life among and study of the Yoruba. I think I can truthfully say that the responses substantially confirmed my impressions. The choice of questions asked provides a framework for the description of Yoruba attitudes which, however biased by my own preconceptions, is more methodical than would be the selection from the vast quantum of observed behaviour of items which, without overt rationalisation, I deemed to be significant.

In the opening chapter I argued that it was a useful heuristic device to distinguish between the analytical structure of society as seen by the individual and his cognitive map. The cognitive map is concerned with action in the world of here and now; it delineates the goals perceived by the individual and the routes by which these are attainable, together with the values accorded to such routes and goals. The main component of the map is the individual's perception of his social network—the relationships which he manipulates in order to attain his goals. It is therefore an ego-oriented map. The analytical structure presents a view of society by an individual who, as observer, is external to it (though he can, of course, locate himself within it). It is concerned with the basic social groupings in the society and their relation to each other. In viewing society in this way the observer is concerned not only with the existing structure but also, and according to his intellectual abilities, with possible alternatives. In other words he is concerned with the legitimacy of the perceived structure. As I stated earlier we cannot suggest that the individual separates these two images and consciously uses either the one or the other as occasion demands. The distinction is ours; but in this chapter it seems useful to continue the distinction and to present in sequence those Yoruba attitudes which are pertinent to the cognitive map and the analytic structure—with the obvious corollary that the two sets of attitudes overlap considerably and that their separation is but a heuristic device. In particular many of the concepts and propositions to be described are common to both.

I have further eased my task in presenting much of the material germane to the discussion of Yoruba perception of social inequality in the preceding chapters. For in this monograph I am attempting to present not only a static picture of present-day attitudes but an account and rationalisation of the changes which are taking place. Thus in chapter 2 I outlined traditional Yoruba social structure with the aim both of providing a base line for the process of change and of indicating the attitudes and values to which most urban Yoruba, having grown up in humble rural homes (or in the heart of Ibadan) were socialised in their youth. I tried to distinguish clearly between analyses which were my own—for instance, the presentation of the relationship between ọba and chief in terms of conflict—and those descriptions and explanations of society which were articulated by the Yoruba themselves. Similarly in the two succeeding chapters I outlined the changes in the social, political and economic structure of Yoruba society and described the movement of individual Yoruba from traditional to modern occupations and social positions. The statistical data is not available to most Yoruba; yet it was possible, I hope, for the reader both to follow the available paths traced by individual Yoruba and to see their own view of the goals and routes open to them, of the constraints operating to limit their effective choice. Again in the previous chapter I briefly summarised Yoruba interaction patterns in a similar manner. Thus in each of these chapters I have presented my own analysis of the structure of Yoruba society, comparing this on occasion with a description of Yoruba perceptions of the same structure. This has been possible because my own analysis was, for the most part, based clearly upon observations of Yoruba behaviour and their own explanations of it and to a relatively slight extent upon concepts alien to the Yoruba. (I might for example have presented an account of development in the abstract terminology of economists or Marxists which would be quite unintelligible to the Yoruba subjects of this monograph.)

The nature of inequality

Once again we must return to a question posed in the opening chapter: I am concerned with social inequality—but is this a theme which has any significance to the Yoruba themselves? And, even if the Yoruba do have such a concept which is synonymous to a large extent with our own, is it synonymous in all respects, or are there areas of meaning which are absent in the Yoruba language? In discussing social inequality we are concerned with the distribution of power and rewards—wealth, leisure, prestige—in the society together with the differential access to social positions, that is with social mobility (Rees, 1971). But furthermore we are concerned with the degree to which value is assigned to those positions with greater power or rewards and, in a substantially closed society, the degree to which such value is ascribed to superior social groups. In this latter sense however the concept of social equality (or inequality) has assumed its present significance only within the last two centuries. As Bottomore writes (1965, pp. 11–12):

The division of society into classes or strata, which are ranged in a hierarchy of wealth, prestige and power is a prominent and almost universal feature of social structure which has always attracted the attention of social theorists and philosophers. During the greater part of human history this inequality among men has been generally accepted as an unalterable fact. Ancient and medieval writers, when they touched upon the subject of the social hierarchy, always tended to provide a rationalization and justification of the established order, very often in terms of a religious doctrine concerning the origin of social ranks. This is most apparent, perhaps, in the Hindu religious myths about the formation of the caste system. On the other side, the sporadic rebellions of the poor and oppressed were usually revolts against particularly irksome conditions rather than against the whole system of ranks, and they did not give rise to any clear conceptions of an alternative form of society.

Only in modern times, and particularly since the American and French Revolutions, has social class, as a stark embodiment of the principle of inequality, become an object of scientific study, and at the same time of widespread condemnation in terms of new social doctrines. The revolutionary ideal of equality, however variously it was interpreted by nineteenth-century thinkers, at least implied an opposition to hereditary privileges and to an immutable hierarchy of ranks. The revolutions of the late eighteenth century and the early nineteenth century, directed against the legal and political privileges which survived from the system of feudal estates, brought about an extension of civil and political rights and a greater degree of equality of opportunity. But at the same time they created a new social hierarchy, based directly upon the possession of wealth, and this in turn came to be attacked during the nineteenth century by socialist thinkers who believed that the ideal of equality ultimately implied a 'classless society'.

Thus our own concern with social equality derives largely from our reaction to the structure of the feudal society of medieval Europe. This is not an experience which we can expect to be replicated in much of Africa—examples of the exceptions being the caste-like societies of the interlacustrine Bantu of East Africa where origin myths sanction the division of society into rulers, cattle herders and agriculturalists, or the savanna societies of West Africa with their rigidly ranked occupational castes. And in fact social inequality (within African society) is not a theme which has been raised in the philosophical and political writings of Western-educated West African leaders, their assimilation of so many of the main currents of Western thought notwithstanding. In part this may be because of their desire to proclaim the equality of black peoples with white. Their own stress is upon the communal nature of traditional African society—a feature which they seek to preserve, perhaps because with economic change it is seen to be becoming so anachronistic. Thus while Western philosophers debate the nature of social equality and argue whether its attainment is either desirable or practicable, West Africa's philosophers largely take such equality for granted.

The Yoruba term *dogba* is used, as is its English equivalent 'equal', in the context of measurement. If one asks, 'Are these two bowls of gari equal?', one gets a response in terms of the quantity of gari, not of its quality of texture or taste. In social contexts the traditional usage of the word persists. Thus when the urban Yoruba of today talks of his 'equals' he is most probably referring to men of like age, his classmates in school; it is far less likely that he refers to persons of similar power or wealth. In the latter context he would refer descriptively to others as being of the same rank (in a bureaucratic hierarchy), having the same income, enjoying a similar style of life. Conversely when an educated Yoruba, cognisant of our Western concept, is asked to translate into his own language a sentence such as 'How much social (in)equality is there in Yoruba society?' he is in difficulty for the notion of equality so expressed is not embraced within the Yoruba concept.

The reasons for this seem obvious; as noted above most African societies are not passing from a structure of rigid hierarchical ranks. The Yoruba origin myths, tracing the descent of the people from Oduduwa, are still widely current and believed. Western-educated men will expunge from their own version of the myths those incidents which conflict with their scientific appreciation; but the Western observer, accepting that his own ethnic group is the product of countless migratory movements and cultural assimilations, is often surprised to find the African history teacher, or even university lecturer, believing a highly exclusive version of the origins of his own ethnic group; whilst a separate creation may not be claimed it is still frequently asserted that the tribe has maintained its peculiar identity in its migration to its present site over several centuries and thousands of miles. The Yoruba myths do not indicate any subsequent division of the Yoruba people in terms of social rank, but only of ethnic subdivisions. As the earlier chapters have indicated all men (and women, too, to some extent) participated in the political process according to their skills and personality, through their membership of their descent groups and eligibility for titled office. Polygyny furthermore rendered it impossible for sons, generally, to succeed to the status achieved by their fathers; indeed it was one of the most rigidly observed rules that a son should not directly assume his father's title (save of course where the father was the first holder of a newly created title intended to pass to his descendants). The recent patterns of mobility to new statuses in the modern sector have tended to reinforce, rather than negate, the traditional concept of social equality—as we would interpret it.

This does not mean that Yoruba are blind to differences of power or wealth. As will be described in more detail below (see Appendix, p. 228), when respondents were asked, as the opening question in a structured interview, 'What are the most important differences found among Yoruba people?', they answered largely in terms of ethnic differences—the differences between Oyo, Ekiti, Egba, Ijebu and so on. And when they were further asked to cite differences among people of their own town the ethnic theme persisted as they distinguished indigenes from strangers. But when subsequently asked, 'Are we all equal? How are we unequal?', responses relating directly or indirectly to differences of power and wealth were prominent. They were not however universal. Several answered in terms of personality: some of religion; one man referred to the incidence of witchcraft which benefited some at the expense of others. Nevertheless most answers were in terms of wealth. Said a young, illiterate farmer:

> God has created some people not to have a job and this makes them backward and to retrogress among the people of his town, while some have a job and progress in whatever they set their hands to. Some are farmers who cannot gain their profit until the end of the year; can you compare him with a trader who gets his money daily? Without money a farmer cannot meet his obligations and will remain backward.

A messenger in a government office with a secondary modern school-leaving certificate said:

> As we have those who are rich, so we know those who are poor. There are some who have no money but they manage in their

poverty—they carry on in life without many tears. There are differences in work—some are employed while others are jobless; from this many inequalities arise—differences in income and social life. Those who are neither rich or poor can loan money from others and pay back at the end of the month but the poor cannot get such a loan because people know that they have no salary from which to repay.

Education was often cited as a basic criterion from which derived differences in occupation and income. But taken in their totality, these responses indicate merely that, for the Yoruba, measurable differences in wealth are an obvious form of social differentiation. They say nothing of its cause or the legitimacy.

In fact one-third of all respondents (and a higher proportion of less-educated men) explicitly stated that inequality was a natural phenomenon and used the analogy of the fingers on the hand. (As with all the responses cited, the absence of a theme in any one response cannot be taken as meaning that the respondent would not subscribe to such an attitude—merely that he made some other point instead.) An even higher proportion said specifically that inequality was caused or ordained by God. 'God does not create us equally; the differences can be ascribed to what God has created. Some are born to be better off than others while some are not well off at all. There are some people who get angry quickly while some are gentle' (a semi-literate labourer). In these answers the traditional view of destiny prevails; a 'fate' given at their birth controls their lives and though by their own character they may modify this fate, this character itself is in part a product of one's destiny. 'According to my example of the five fingers, God created some to be wealthy but he did not create others to be poor; some are too lazy and do not work hard' (a factory worker with some post-primary schooling). Whilst the less-educated almost universally ascribed inequality to destiny, the better-educated were more agnostic in their responses and emphasised the constraints or advantages derived from the family into which one was born; some had wealthy parents, others poor; some had parents who educated their sons, while parents of others did not, in their ignorance, realise the importance of education. But the tenor of these responses is not that social origin determines one's success in life but merely that it can affect it—and not always in the obvious direction. As the opinions expressed in other contexts corroborate, a humble origin can encourage one to strive and, with this quality, enable one to succeed in all endeavours, whilst a childhood in an affluent and indulgent home can lead to sloth and subsequent failure. Many of the responses emphasised a third factor which will recur frequently in this chapter—the presence or absence of 'helpers' in one's life.

In the Yoruba view of social inequality as I have presented it, differences in wealth, seen usually as the corollary of education and/or occupation, are cited as one of the most salient forms of social differentiation within ethnic units. This inequality is seen as an inevitable feature of society, one's own position in the hierarchy being determined by a not altogether immutable destiny, by one's own character (and hence efforts) and by the good or evil intervention of others—helpers or witches, rivals and the like. At this point one might contrast this image with those so often presented to us as ideal (stereo-) types—types with which the Yoruba image might be expected to conform. On one hand 'traditional' societies are contrasted with 'modern' societies—the latter being societies of the contemporary industrialised West, the former all pre-industrial societies though the attributes cited seem far more appropriate to 'feudal' peasant societies of southern Europe or Latin America than to most 'tribal' societies of Africa. As I have written elsewhere (P. C. Lloyd, 1971b, p. 24):

Peasant societies the world over have been said to exhibit a number of functionally related characteristics, which inhabit their social and economic development. The elements of this culture include the strong subordination of personal aims to those of the family and a high degree of mutual distrust and suspicion between members of different families, resulting in a low level of co-operative activity. It is believed by peasants that social benefits are limited and that the gain of one member of a community can only be at the expense of another. Peasants have limited aspirations, a limited view of the world and generally lack any sense of deferred gratification; they are unable to conceive the content of roles with which they are, as yet, unfamiliar. Peasants have a strong dependence on, yet hostility towards, government authority. They are fatalistic towards the world and lack the innovating spirit. These characteristics are, it would appear, the mirror opposite of those attributed to the idealized men of western industrial societies.

On the other hand the dichotomy within the Western industrial societies is between the working and middle class images. As Goldthorpe *et al.* summarise them (1969, p. 118–19), the working class perspective divides society into 'them' and 'us', the former exercising authority over the latter, the division between the two being virtually unbridgable and immutable. Hence the working class individual accepts his position in society and aims to maintain a certain style of living rather than advance it. Emphasis is thus placed on current consumption rather than future planning. Fatalism, acceptance and an orientation to the present thus hold together as a mutually reinforcing set of attitudes. In contrast, the middle class conception is of an open society with hierarchically arranged strata differentiated in terms of life styles and prestige. The individual expects to improve his living style and also to rise in the hierarchy and his success depends on his own efforts. There is thus an orientation towards the future and emphasis on planning and deferred gratification. To cite Goldthorpe *et al.* (1969, pp. 120–1):

> The middle-class social ethic is thus an essentially individualistic one: the prime value is that set on individual achievement. Achievement is taken as the crucial indicator of the individual's moral worth. However, achievement is also regarded as a family concern: parents feel an obligation to try to give their children a 'better start in life' than they themselves enjoyed, and then anticipate that their offspring will in turn attain to a still higher level in the social scale. In other words, the expectation is again that advancement will be continuous—between generations as well as in the course of individual lifetimes. Indeed, through parental aspirations for children, it is possible for desires and hopes for the future to become virtually limitless.

Other Western writers have distinguished the working from the lower class. Thus Gans argues (1962, pp. 264–5) that the working class sub-culture is a satisfactory mode of adaptation to the opportunities offered by society, though it has negative features. Members of the working class are unable to participate in formal organisations; they fail to understand bureaucratic practice and so adopt a conspiracy theory in explaining the world, thus increasing the class gap; they reject social services; they emphasis group life, place low emphasis on privacy and penalise deviance. The lower class is characterised by a failure to cope with the world due to the intensity of deprivation; it cannot utilise the opportunities offered. In Western cities the lower class family is controlled by the mother; the male is marginal; life for the male is completely unpredictable. Banfield (1958, 1968) develops this image of the lower class: the individual has no control over events; he acts on impulse and is improvident; he suffers from self-contempt and inadequacy; he cannot form stable relationships. Far from being a small and extremely marginal category, the lower class as defined by Banfield embraces a large segment of the urban population of the United States—over half the non-whites in some estimates.

The values expressed by the Yoruba might be expected to approximate more to those of traditional than to modern society; and if one considers the urban workers, to those of the lower or working rather than to the middle class. In fact it is the modern and middle class values of achievement which are so salient among the Yoruba, whether one looks at pre-colonial or rural society, the modern urban workers or the educated and affluent élite.

To return to our structured interviews. Respondents were successively asked: 'Are you satisfied with your position in life or with what you have achieved?' 'If not, what would you have liked to have done or been?' 'What has hindered you from achieving this?' Without exception the respondents said that they wanted to be better placed, though several did preface their comments with a statement that they were satisfied inasmuch as they were adequately fed and clothed and not reduced to that absolute poverty which makes a man beg or steal. (This theme is taken up later in discussing self-rating as *mẹkunnu* or *talaka*.)

A grade II teacher responded:

In fact I am a little satisfied, yet sooner or later I hope to improve my present position. I have not built a house—I ought to have done this according to my age. I ought to have enough money to save me from having to borrow before the end of the month. I have a wife and children but I have not been able to help my brothers or sisters—in fact my salary is not enough for my own family. I have reached my present position through my own efforts; lack of money has been the main constraint. My hope is that soon I shall be better placed. I am doing private studies at home; I hope to improve my standard by taking professional courses which may lead me to achieve my aims.

A primary school–educated skilled electrician responded:

> As I am now I daily struggle for improvement. I always struggle
> hard in my workshop and I am progressing accordingly. Yet I shall
> have to do better to assure a better life for my children. I am
> satisfied because I eat and drink and have no problems facing
> me now. Had it been that my parents were able to educate me
> beyond the level at which I stopped, my present position would
> not have been as low as it is at present. I know that the more
> educated one is the more popular one becomes. At present one
> plans to educate children but this was not so in the time of my
> father—they reared children for their own prestige and for farming.
> Given education I would have been able to build a house, own a
> car and been more popular than I am. I did not get a helper who
> could finance further education; the little that I have achieved is
> through hard work. My belief is that one cannot hurry to do
> something because if one hurries one lands oneself in trouble;
> whatever God says one should be in this world, so shall it be. One
> can even get a good job; better still one can trade with a view to
> getting more money with which to fulfil one's aspirations. I am
> convinced that one should get whatever he wants from God,
> through prayer.

These are responses of *relatively* well-educated and affluent men.
But those of the illiterate are in a similar vein. Thus a drummer:

> The satisfaction that I have is merely from being able to get food
> and to sleep and wake in peace. If I am as God decrees I shall be
> happy in my present position but I am not satisfied. I want to get a
> good job. If I can become a labourer I shall build a house and buy
> a lorry. I shall add to my salary whatever I make from drumming
> and that will give me capital. The obstacle is lack of money. And
> when I am illiterate, if I seek a job which demands literacy, what
> can they give me?

A farmer/night watchman:

> I am a labourer, I am not satisfied at all. I do not know why—the
> reason is from God. I ought to have built a house; I ought to have
> adult children but mine are still small. I have no money. I had no
> parents who could send me to school or finance me in trading;
> those who did not send their children to school thought they

would become lazy and that the white people would take them away. If I had been sent to school I should have achieved the things I mentioned. It is God who knows why this has happened to me and to others—I am not the only one affected.

In these selected responses we see too the most commonly adduced reason for failure—lack of schooling due to the ignorance or poverty of one's parents, or their inability to establish one in trade. Such constraints have been detailed in earlier chapters. In some respects these responses would also be expected from a Western working class man, following the stereotype cited above—'I was born to poverty.' But there is a difference. For the Yoruba parental poverty is a handicap to be surmounted (as so many have done), not a determinant to be accepted. Furthermore to have poor parents is an element in one's luck or destiny; the destiny of all men is pre-ordained—and in this sense all men are equal, even though some may have better 'fates' than others; all have hurdles to surmount though these differ in number and severity; poor parents are one such hurdle. As Jahoda (1966) has described for Ghana, the characteristic response to failure is 'extra-puritive'—the responsibility is shifted to external agents, people who wish one ill, magical devices which fail. Only rarely are personal inadequacies invoked; some men said that they did not like school and so left in spite of their parents' pressure that they should stay. For others their lack of interest in school was reflected in their parents' unwillingness to pay further fees—a situation now ascribed by the informant to general family poverty, to the needs of siblings or to family crises. Very few traders or craftsmen attribute their failure to lack of entrepreneurial skill—the vagaries of the market provide too easy an alternative explanation.

To the extent that they ascribe their present status to their destiny the Yoruba might be described as fatalistic—and so in accord with the traditional or working class image of society. But the aspirations cited above are not those of men trying to maintain an established position in society—they are for positions in the upper ranks of society, as evinced by ownership of a house, car or lorry, by a large family, by great popularity. One expects men in modern bureaucratic or professional careers to aspire to promotion and social advancement; but Yoruba in this position are merely echoing the traditional aspirations to higher-ranking titles, to greater success in trade, to increased numbers of children. And of course these men are not only ambitious themselves, but even more so for their children. Only those at the very top expect their children to do as well but not necessarily better than themselves—everyone else wishes his children to become important, rich, widely known and respected, notwithstanding a recognition of the constraints which may well make success of this order virtually unobtainable. These too are traditional Yoruba attitudes, for in pre-colonial society the son of a poor man might well become a high-ranking chief, a very wealthy trader or a successful farmer; such attitudes have been confirmed and reinforced by the meteoric rise of well-known public figures from humble rural homes to the topmost positions in the modern sector—in politics, the civil service, business or the professions.

Goals

I have dealt with the Yoruba concept of equality and have emphasised their desire for achievement. But little has been said yet, beyond a few indirect remarks, about the specific goals of these men in terms of the occupations sought and preferred and the values attributed to these occupations. A conventional procedure to elucidate the prestige ranking of occupations was considered but a few trials suggested that this would yield little that one did not already know. Results seemed to be highly comparable with those obtained by Foster (1965) in Ghana, even though his sample was restricted to students; for not only did the ranking of occupations conform to that obtained in the USA and Japan but, to an even greater extent than in those two countries, it correlated closely with the perceived income of those occupations. For our own experiment we selected twelve occupations and sought the ranking and reasons for it, in each of four sets of three occupations. Thus respondents were asked: 'Now I want you to think about these different jobs. I shall give you the names of three of them. Tell me which you prefer most and the one you like next to that one. Assume that the money realised from each is the same. Why do you prefer the first and the second ones?' The reasons given for the occupations selected produced an interesting commentary on their perceived characteristics. The rank ordering of the choices is more difficult to interpret. It seems probable that some men rated an occupation higher because it carried more general prestige, others because it was the one to which they, given educational resources, could aspire to. Again some occupations seem to have been chosen because their holders constituted a highly valued local reference group, whilst other men selected an occupation of which they had little personal knowledge. Furthermore a slightly different ordering is obtained if one counts first choices only or if one scores all three occupations. In the following paragraphs I shall cite the results of ranking by the latter method, unless otherwise stated. In posing this set of questions we did not seek a negative reaction to any of the occupations, but some respondents did nevertheless provide these in their own answers.

The first triad of occupations were senior civil servant, transport owner and factory manager—selected thus to include one employee in the public sector, a self-employed man and an employee in the private sector.

In discussing the civil servant respondents overwhelmingly stressed his control over public affairs and saw him, in this context, as a highly important man. This control was exercised in a largely impersonal manner for they did not stress his authority over subordinates though a few did suggest that he could obtain jobs for junior relatives. The education of the civil servant was frequently cited in such terms as indicated that this of itself gave considerable prestige. Many said that the civil servant was well paid and that the occupation carried valued perquisites—a house and a car. The children of the civil servant would always be well provided for. Respondents frequently commented upon the relatively easy life of the civil servant (some who did not like the occupation referred to him as lazy); they said that he had the opportunity to mix with influential people. Some referred to the permanence and security of a civil service post, whilst others mentioned the early compulsory retiring age (now fifty-five again) and a few even suggested that the senior civil servant could be dismissed.

The most frequently cited attribute of the transporter was that he was very wealthy—much more so than men in the other two occupations here compared; this response dominated in spite of the instruction to presume that each of the three occupations carried an equivalent income. Second, men referred to the independence of the transporter, in terms which will be elaborated below. They said that he employed others—that is, on one hand he controlled the lives of his employees and on the other he was in a position to find work for relatives. He was described as a popular man, spending lavishly at social gatherings. Several respondents said that this was a good occupation for those who lacked education. Disadvantages cited were the high level of risk involved—lorries could easily break down on the road, or crash, and if the transporter were in the habit of travelling with his own lorries his life was daily in danger.

The factory manager was seen as a man of considerable skill and training—a feature for which he was admired. As a manager he was very well paid and enjoyed a safe and permanent job. But he could also leave salaried employment and set up on his own, and thus had an occupation for life. He employed others and could find jobs for relatives. Some respondents thought that he enjoyed better promotion prospects than the civil servant; others said that he enjoyed more 'rest of mind' than the civil servants who were always competing with each other for promotion.

Of these three occupations the transporter tended to rank lowest, scoring a high rating only among farmers, craftsmen and labourers in Agege—a town in which the transporters are dominant in social and political affairs (Peace, 1973). The factory manager was ranked highest, especially by traders and businessmen, by drivers and by the factory workers. The senior civil servant topped the ranking among the farmers and Ibadan labourers. Whilst teachers and clerks in Ibadan preferred the factory manager, those in Agege chose the civil servant—each group apparently selecting the occupation with which they had least contact, for Ibadan has many civil servants, few factory managers, while the reverse holds for Agege.

In the next triad a secondary school headmaster, a contractor and an accountant were compared, these occupations being slightly less prestigious than the first triad, but similarly contrasting salaried and self-employed occupations.

The principal response to the headmaster was that he is responsible for training the young—the future of the young rests with him. His position was seen as being well paid and the necessary high degree of learning was admired. Several cited the authority wielded, both over his staff and even more so over the pupils who feared him in consequence. He has to be a conciliator in settling disputes between his teachers and this quality is exploited beyond the school, in community affairs; he thus has to be a calm and gentle man, good at interpersonal relations. His position in the community makes him well known to all, and he has access to the government. Some respondents commented on the good salary and security of the post; others noted that the post was not particularly well paid, that promotion to higher positions was rare and that a pupil could often surpass his headmaster in wealth and power. Some saw the occupation as relatively easy and undemanding, whilst others commented on the taxing nature of student protests.

The attributes of the contractor were similar to those of the transporter—he is wealthy and, in particular, makes much more money than the teacher. He is independent and employs others. The occupation is open to those without education. But (unlike the transporter who at least owns his lorries) the contractor is heavily dependent upon others for his work; one needs not only capital but also 'long legs'; one is more susceptible to the vagaries of the market—one day there will be a boom in building, the next a slump (whereas cocoa and foodstuffs have to be transported whatever their price).

It was realised that the work of an accountant would not be well understood by most respondents, but the qualities which they imputed to the occupation are nevertheless significant. Dominant among the responses was the skill and training necessary; this not only commanded a high salary but could be used to an even greater advantage in self-employment. Many stated that the accountant had a perfect opportunity to use his own skills to become highly successful. A high number of respondents commented upon the role of the accountant in checking government, and other, accounts to uncover or prevent fraud; some however saw either a high degree of risk in that a man of insufficiently strong character would himself succumb to peculation, or a danger that one would make honest mistakes and be surcharged for the loss. To 'run to shortage' is the fear of every clerk handling money.

The accountant scored least in the ranking of the three occupations, falling far behind the other two, more probably because it was not a well known occupation rather than because of any weight attached to the disadvantages cited. Overall the headmaster ranked highest though the contractor did as well on first-choice occupations. The latter was preferred by traders and drivers, the former by farmers, craftsmen, labourers and factory workers. The clerks and teachers did not rank the headmaster above the other occupations but were divided approximately equally between the three jobs.

The next two triads of occupations were at the lower end of the scale of urban occupations. Comparison was first invited between a government clerk, a motor mechanic and a factory worker.

The clerk was seen as well paid though many Ibadan respondents

·thought that the factory worker earned more. The clerk's income was steady and his job secure—though several respondents said that he was liable to be sacked at any time, especially if he mishandled money. Teachers and clerks tended to be less sanguine about these risks. One of the major features of clerical work was its prospects: one either aimed for promotion or could study for shigher qualifications. The learning required for a clerical post, though light in comparison with some of the occupations discussed earlier, merited admiration. The work of the civil servant was seen as being easy, clean and 'neat'—one dressed in coat and tie for work. Value attached too to the involvement in affairs of government; one knew what was going on and could help others, as a broker, in filling forms, getting jobs and the like. One might even be in a position to influence an appointment if one were the chief clerk in charge of an office, or even if one could so arrange the files that one's own candidate was on the top of the heap, or the serious rivals deemed ineligible through the late arrival of their applications.

Most of these qualities were not shared by factory workers. This occupation was seen as better paid by Ibadan respondents; others distinguished between the skilled artisan and the unskilled labourer. The possibility of overtime work was mentioned by several men and the factory worker was seen as having an opportunity for pursuing a second occupation outside the factory. But factory work was seen as hard, fatiguing, dangerous and dirty; one was much more liable to summary dismissal; one had little time and even less inclination to study to pass exams. The great advantage of factory work was seen to lie in the acquisition or practice of a skill which could be exploited as soon as one left industrial employment—a skill which one would retain for the rest of one's life.

The mechanic's work too was dirty; but its greatest advantage lay in its being self-employment. One had a specific skill which could always be put to use, a use which was both socially advantageous— one mends lorries so that crops can be transported—and which had bright prospects—one can become a car owner. One had a chance of making much more money than either the clerk or the factory worker.

The factory worker was highly rated only by drivers, craftsmen and traders in Ibadan. Clerks and mechanics ranked equally as first choices, the former being the choice of the clerks and teachers themselves and of the wage labourers. The mechanics ranked high in Agege, which, being a commercial centre, provides plentiful and lucrative opportunities for such employment; this occupation was here chosen by farmers, craftsmen, drivers and factory workers.

The second triad of low-ranking occupations was primary school teacher, tailor and a shop assistant at Kingsway, the large department store of the United Africa Company.

Once again an overwhelming number of responses described the social importance of the primary school teacher in educating the young; no important man could have reached his present status save through the learning imparted in the early years. Respondents again referred to the prestige attached to learning; they mentioned the prospects of advancement through attendance at teacher training colleges or through passing examinations by private study. The regularity and permanence of the work were stressed. Some said that a teacher would always be highly respected by those of his pupils who became famous. Teachers were seen as having an opportunity for extra earnings, either by private coaching, taking evening classes, or in accepting gifts from parents.

The advantages of tailoring lie in self-employment and in the possession of a skill which, since clothes will always be needed, is bound to yield an income. Disadvantages lie in the seasonality of the work—many people buy new clothes at Christmas or other major festivals but there are weeks when little work is available; some men referred to tailoring as a form of concealed unemployment. The tailor, sitting in his shop facing a busy street, is a sociable person, he will meet many people, hearing all the gossip. Respondents did not mention the tailor's apprentices—these are apparently not seen as employees; the omission is significant inasmuch as the employment or training of others was cited so often in respect of other occupations.

Of all the occupations selected for this experiment that of shop assistant seemed to produce the widest range of answers. Respondents derided the work as being menial, 'like a house boy', being poorly paid and insecure, and involving one in a risk of 'running to shortage'. Yet others saw in the occupation an opportunity to learn to trade, or referred to chances of getting to know important people who came to the shop as customers. Some valued the regular wage and relative security of the work; furthermore it was a 'neat' job—one dressed well.

Each of these three occupations did well as first choices though in the overall scoring teachers were slightly ahead of, and the shop assistant a little behind, the tailor. Teachers were the choice of the clerks and teachers, and were rated highly by farmers and craftsmen in Ibadan, drivers and labourers in Agege. Ibadan traders preferred the tailor, those of Agege the shop assistant. Those who had chosen the mechanic in the previous triad were divided in their choice between tailor and shop assistant; they did not show a clear preference for self-employment by selecting tailor.

The above vignettes of the twelve selected occupations show that a wide variety of values are cited as attributes but that these are not directly comparable. There seems to be a fairly clear preference for clerks and teachers to select wage-earning or salaried occupations but elsewhere one finds little consistency. A more detailed analysis of the ranking of the responses would seem almost certain to produce not a greater clarity but a morass of conflicting detail. However, when we examine the reasons given for the choice of selected occupations a clear pattern quickly emerges.

Several themes run through all the answers. First and clearly predominant is the preference for self-employment—it is better to be one's own master. So strongly is this felt that wage employment is frequently equated with slavery. In wage employment one has to suffer the abuse of one's employer and one can be summarily dismissed. Whilst clerks realised the checks which existed against arbitrary actions in bureaucratic structures, many ill-educated men saw uncertainty even in the senior civil service. As a self-employed man one can work as one pleases, taking time to fulfil social obligations; one is not bound by the clock. One gets a little money each day, while the wage earner is paid monthly and usually has to beg for loans towards the end of the month. (This seems to the Yoruba to outweigh by far the uncertainty of the daily income when contrasted with the regularity of the pay packet.) The sum that one makes is directly related to one's own efforts—and so, if one works hard, one can make a lot of money; one's income is not determined by others. The taxi driver or shop assistant is perhaps in the most invidious position for the sum he takes each day is related to his own skills yet he has to hand over the takings to a master who returns a miserable proportion of it as a wage. (Though drivers often pay their taxi owner a fixed daily sum, retaining the 'profit' for themselves.) The self-employed man has a skill which he can exploit to the end of his days. He is better placed than the clerk who has learned routine techniques which are useless outside the office and leave him without gainful occupation upon compulsory retirement. (Soon after independence the official age of retirement in the civil service was raised from fifty-five years—an age to suit Englishmen who would by then have completed about thirty years' tropical service—to sixty years. But younger civil servants then complained that their promotion prospects were being reduced and the retirement age was lowered again. This embarrassed many men who relied on their salaries to repay house mortgages or pay secondary school fees.) In self-employment there is no ceiling to one's rewards; it is quite possible to make more money than one could in wage or salaried employment given one's educational resources or skills. The self-employed man has, in the words of English speakers, 'peace of mind'—he is not daily threatened by others. To an external observer the competitive nature of Yoruba entrepreneurship would seem to be most provoking of anxiety, in contrast to which a safe office job would be a haven of peace. But this is not how the Yoruba usually view the situation.

It is still widely felt that it is improper for a man to be in employment when his sons are old enough to start working—by this time a man should be self-supporting, and not in a state of dependency as a slave or a pawn. Furthermore there is every possibility that a son will rise above his father in bureaucratic rank and this too is felt to be highly undesirable. It is as if a son achieved a chieftaincy title whilst his father still lived untitled—or achieved a title higher than that held by the father. An elderly man who worked as an unskilled labourer in an Agege factory was frequently chided by his mates— he ought to retire home to trade or farm; but he valued his wage as a means of paying school fees.

When respondents were asked directly whether it was better to work for oneself than for another, nine-tenths answered 'for oneself'. Of those with no training in agriculture or a craft, that is to say clerks and teachers and wage earners who had entered employment straight from school, only a fifth said it was better to work for another. When subsequently asked whether one should work for another if thereby one received a greater income, half of the respondents opted for employment—a proportion which was rather higher among farmers, craftsmen and wage earners, but lower among traders, clerks and teachers. From the supplementary answers given it was clear that wage employment was seen as a means of saving and gaining the capital whereby one could establish oneself. Even among those senior civil servants whom a Western observer would consider well paid and doing interesting and satisfying work, though perhaps not likely to lead to further promotion, one hears a constantly reiterated desire to move into self-employment, into an occupation with possibilities of greater financial success (though perhaps with a slim chance of achieving it) and with this success more dependent upon one's ability to manipulate interpersonal relationships.

The advantages of wage or salaried employment are freely admitted —but most often in comparing jobs. One pays more than another, is cleaner or easier, has better security or provides greater prospect of advancement.

Second, while self-employment is so highly favoured, a man who does employ others has very high prestige, he is accorded deference. In traditional society there was no stigma to slave owning nor to being a creditor with many pawns—quite the reverse in fact. The employer is respected because he has jobs to give, a vital factor in an era of rising unemployment. The employer has a large number of 'followers', men who are either still dependent upon him for their livelihood or who have, perhaps through his generosity, set themselves up in business and continue to sing his praises.

A third recurrent theme is the amount of income yielded. In spite of being asked to exclude income in considering the occupations in each triad, many respondents said that the actual or potential reward from one or other occupation exceeded that of others. It is clear that occupations could be ranked in terms of income, though significantly the greater wealth of the transporter was not preferred to the high incomes of the senior civil servant or factory manager when other factors were also taken into consideration.

Fourth, many of the occupations were assessed in terms of the opportunities provided to exercise patronage or receive its benefits. Being able to mix with important people is a valued asset. The senior civil servant has access to men in the highest positions of power; the wealthy transporter goes to the lavish parties; the headmaster mediates between the government and his community. Teachers of all grades have successful pupils who will praise them and perhaps open opportunities to them. The tailor and Kingsway assistant see and meet notable people, whilst the office or factory worker is isolated with his files or his machine. A young civil servant who had served successively as an assistant divisional officer, helping to plan new services and to develop a division, and as a junior administrative officer in the Treasury, Establishment Branch, explained that the latter was by far the more satisfying job, for senior officials would seek his advice on the interpretation of civil service rules relating to leave, increments and other perquisites and (though he did not so express it) would so establish a relationship of indebtedness with him.

Fifth, value seems to be attached to learning and skill. The senior civil servant and secondary school headmaster were admired for their high education which, as will be elaborated later, is seen as the result of much hard work and suffering. The craftsman is admired for his skill and work of a high quality is praised. These achievements seem to be valued for their own sakes and not merely because of the power or reward which they undoubtedly yield. In similar vein service to the community is stressed; notably the social importance of the teacher and of the mechanics who keep the lorries on the roads, facilitating an expanding commercial activity.

Several writers, in describing the perceptions of social stratification held by industrial workers, have commented upon the apparent absence of the 'power model' (e.g. Goldthorpe *et al.*, 1969). The models elucidated by these surveys seem, however, to be those which I would associate with a cognitive map rather than the analytic structure. And, as I have argued earlier, the power dichotomy is not directly stressed in the cognitive map. Yet when one examines the reasons given by the Yoruba for preferring one occupation to another the concern with power is apparent. The senior civil servant was admired mostly for his control over the affairs of the country. Employers were highly regarded for they have a more direct and overt power over individuals. But very few men can exercise power in this manner. The task of the remainder is to free themselves from personal control—hence the desire to be an independent, self-employed man rather than an employee. For the Yoruba, power is closely correlated with wealth. Traditional rulers and chiefs were always the most affluent men of their communities and, today, a political leader is expected to be rich; if he is not flamboyantly extravagant he is suspected of tucking his money away in a Swiss bank account. Wealth is highly valued—and especially its overt display; though the highly educated man will ridicule the semi-literate trader who often quite literally showers currency notes at his parties, he too spends lavishly on house, car and dress. The highest incomes are to be gained only through self-employment, for the rewards here exceed even those of the few salaried posts at the summit of the civil service and large expatriate commercial firms. Thus the route to the top, in terms of rewards if not necessarily of power, lies through self-employment. Lesser occupations are viewed in terms of the opportunities provided for this mode of advancement. In a clerical post one can aspire for promotion to positions of greater power; the self-employed mechanic or tailor is already on the threshold of success—though he may never cross it; the factory worker and shop assistant, though in menial and often almost demeaning work, are acquiring skills which will enable them to work on their own. To get to the top one cannot, as we shall see later, rely on one's own efforts; one needs a helper. Those occupations which bring one into direct relationship with powerful people, which make one visible to them or involve one in a large network of personal relationships which one can exploit in other situations are preferable to those which isolate one from one's fellow men.

The specific routes to achieve these and other occupations have already been discussed above and are generally well known to the Yoruba. All appreciate the educational level to be attained for a job in the bureaucracy or a modern firm. Those who have not reached a desired level blame their parents' ignorance or poverty and, much less frequently, their own scholastic failings. All now send their children to primary school, but a distinction must be made between those, usually the semi-literate, who stress obedience to school rules, punctuality, payment of fees, having the right books, and those who spur their children to higher achievements by a greater interest in their progress, in home coaching and in advocating and facilitating home study. The career histories of successful craftsmen and traders are, since these men still live in their own communities, even better appreciated. Unskilled or semi-skilled wage employment is, to a large extent, regarded not as a goal, but as a transitory stage. It is entered by those who were trained as craftsmen but who have not been able to find the capital to start on their own or who found the local competition too severe; by those who left secondary modern school and felt it beneath their dignity to forgo a clerical career for manual work as craftsmen; by those who left primary school and whose parents were either unwilling or unable to apprentice them, or who hoped that employment would provide them with a skill.

As I have already emphasised, the desire for advancement is very strong and there is little suggestion that the methods used by some to reach the top have been immoral. The 'poor but honest' syndrome, in which one's honesty both explains and expiates one's poverty, is almost unknown to the Yoruba. The use of personal influence to gain appointments or contrasts is seen as legitimate and one is merely envious that the same opportunities were not presented to oneself.

Two great routes lead to the top—through education and the acquisition of higher levels of attainment and through self-employment and private business. But these are not alternatives in the sense that every parent makes a choice between them on behalf of his young son. The educational route is always preferred. One does not encounter a parent who argues that he is not going to bother about primary education because he intends to train his son as a trader. The attainment of a given education level promises a certain financial reward—or at least did so until the rapid expansion of primary education made it difficult for school leavers to find work. Qualifications required for specific posts have risen. The university graduate who is now engaged by a teacher training college may think this level of teaching beneath his dignity, he is nevertheless paid a graduate's salary. In contrast success in entrepreneurship is seen to be unpredictable by human means and impossible to inculcate into others. The enterprising educated man may, if he wishes, transfer his resources—his savings, his knowledge and skills, his personal contacts—into the field of independent business. The youth who drops out of the education system whilst still in parental care should be provided with the basic training in a skill through apprenticeship to a craftsmen or a trader and if possible, the initial capital subsequently to establish on his own. As the surveys of Harris (1971), Olakanpo (1968) and Callaway (1973) show the educated businessman stands *pari passu* a better chance of success than one who lacks education. Nevertheless the higher one rises on the educational ladder the less likely is one to move into business for the risks of entrepreneurship will outweigh a steady, regular if now static salary, though to an increasing extent such men are indulging in direct business activity (and not just investing in stocks and shares) as a second occupation. One might summarise the Yoruba attitude in saying that one tries to get as high up the educational ladder as possible before making a judicious jump onto the ladder of self-employment; some, as school drop-outs, have to make a very early transfer; and the longer one remains on the educational ladder the less likely is one to transfer—but the option remains open. There is of course no reverse option—the ill-educated transporter or contractor cannot become a teacher or civil servant. Even those politicians who were businessmen were comparatively well educated.

Means

The Yoruba man strives for power and wealth; he is cognisant of the importance of education and in his daily life he sees around him men who are accumulating capital. What are the qualities which are believed to promote success? In their life histories informants frequently stress the 'suffering' which they had to undergo in their youth; but prominent too are the references to a helper or patron. To a Western observer an emphasis on hard work seems to be the antithesis of dependence upon a helper, but to the Yoruba both are important; in fact many respondents when asked to choose between the two dodged the question and answered 'both'. Again one has the stereotype of the popular *gbajumo*—outgoing, generous with his time and money; the miser is universally despised. Yet one finds too an emphasis on saving and cautious investment. We considered asking in the questionnaire whether it was better for a man to invest a windfall in trade or spend it on luxuries and entertainment; it was soon clear that there would be an overwhelming response in favour of investment and the question was therefore discarded. In thinking of one's own future the emphasis must be on cautious investment; to try to buy friends who may be able one day to help one is a risky procedure. Nevertheless, if a young man is willing to be lavish, one praises and flatters him; one is expected to return the favour only if an opportunity is presented. The man who has already established his wealth is however expected to be generous to others; he should neither plough all his profits back into his business nor restrict his munificence to his own immediate family—to do so constitutes miserliness as the case of Chief Agbaje has already illustrated; but one does not usually accuse a young man of such a violation of the norms.

Respondents were asked: 'Some people say that hard work and suffering lead one to become important in the world; others say it is better to have a helper. Which do you say is the more important of the two?' The majority cited the helper. Hard work they said was not enough to get one anywhere; the extra that one would make from the increased effort would not be sufficient to constitute a worthwhile investment. How much, said some, could one expect to save from a monthly income of £15? Suffering itself does not make one rich and there is a good chance that it yields no reward at all. Those who answered in this vein argued that with a helper one would rise much more quickly and with less pain. But in contrast to this attitude, others stressed the virtues of hard work—in later life one would not spend extravagantly and unwisely as one would if the money had been too easily gained. Furthermore one sets an example to one's children in telling them of one's own efforts, perhaps countering the undesirable effects of childhood in an affluent family. The emphasis was on the future behaviour consequent upon suffering and the effect of this on future accumulation; respondents did not refer to any inner satisfaction or reward in heaven that present hard work and suffering might yield. However a man who had risen through suffering would be more likely to be appreciative of the efforts of other poor men still striving to rise. Too much reliance on a helper is unwise for he can let one down badly. And even if one does have a helper one still needs to work hard, for the helper is more likely to bestow his patronage on the most deserving and promising candidates; again one has to work hard to make the most of the opportunities presented to one. Nevertheless the response of most Yoruba was that hard work was a necessary but not a sufficient quality, while a helper was both sufficient and necessary: 'If one does not know an influential somebody one can get nowhere.'

In examining the distribution of responses one finds that hard work is emphasised more by craftsmen and traders—by their efforts they can increase their turnover; farmers, wage earners and labourers are most reliant on the helpers—their own increased efforts yield little extra return and they seek some external intervention to get them out of their present rut. The most highly educated (secondary school leavers) emphasised hard work but those with slightly less schooling were overwhelmingly in favour of a helper—they were seeking aid in getting work of the expected calibre, or indeed, any form of work at all. There was no difference in response between Christians and Muslims nor between those who came from relatively educated homes and those with illiterate parents. The difference in response thus seems to reflect the current economic position of the respondent more than his childhood socialisation; most of them were hoping for capital to start or further their businesses or seeking better jobs.

A slightly different emphasis was given by secondary school boys asked to write an essay, 'How easy is it today for a Yoruba boy with poor parents to rise to a high position in society?' Not unnaturally they all stressed that the route to the top lay through education. Most of the boys felt that a poor boy could rise through hard work—many felt that effort would certainly bring success, even though other factors gave advantages to boys from wealthy homes. They recognised that brilliant boys often come from poor homes and that the children of the rich may be dull—intellectual skills seem to be randomly distributed; but the rich can send their dull children to special fee-paying schools or gain admission to technical colleges and thus ensure that they get into a well-paid career, whereas the poor boy becomes a drop-out. Furthermore the rich parents can, through their influence, obtain good jobs for their children and also secure the available scholarships. But there are disadvantages in growing up in an affluent home; one obtains all that one seeks, and suffers no deprivation; one plays about at school believing that one's future is assured and then one fails the vital examinations. The poor but brilliant boy is dependent on others to pay his school fees, perhaps entering the benefactor's family.

'It is not easy today for a Yoruba boy with poor parents to rise to a high position in society; he must be wise and be able to move with those boys who are well bred.'

'He must leave the poor parents to live with a more civilised and experienced man who is either a relative or a friend to the family. Here the boy will see a new light and change his rustic ways. . . . During his life with the person he is depending on he will have to suffer in many ways. If he is unlucky, he will meet a harsh patron who will suffer him now and then on whatever mistakes he committed . . . he will undergo stages full of suffering and unrest and if he is not courageous will collapse and ruin his life in an attempt to mould it.'

'It is really very easy . . . if only the boy responds to the little education that his parents could afford. In the course of learning and by being honest in his dealings, he may by luck come across someone who may help him further in his learning or help him to seek for a job which will make him rich.'

To attract the favours of a benefactor one must be of good character —honest, hardworking, diligent and not too outspoken.

The Yoruba passionately desire children, sons above all. Childlessness is the worst plight which can afflict both men and, especially, women, for other forms of achievement—wealth or political office for instance—cannot compensate for it. Poor men express their need for sons in terms of care in their old age, of having someone to bury them; well-educated men today still stress their desire to found a noted lineage, to have descendants who will remember them. These desires are to some degree countered by those of their wives who see childbearing as a handicap to the prosecution of a successful career and who would be prepared to stop as soon as they had borne their husbands a few children.

Of the respondents to our questionnaire two-thirds replied that they thought that one should have one wife or should limit the number of one's children; only a little over half would both be monogamous and limit children. Those who preferred monogamy said that it obviated domestic strife and this contributed to the better upbringing of the children. Some referred to the costs of the polygynous household (though others said that one might have several wives if one could afford them). Some said that polygyny would increase the number of one's children. Those who preferred polygyny frequently said that they preferred from two to four wives. The tenets of Islam were cited. It was necessary to have several wives in order to have many children. Many referred to the risks of marriage—a wife might be barren, might die or might be personally incompatible; a second string was necessary. Thus some men who said that one should limit the number of children still advocated polygyny.

Monogamy was in fact advocated by almost all the better-educated men, by teachers, clerks and wage earners and younger men. Polygyny was the choice of half of the farmers and traders and of the illiterates. A far higher proportion of Christians (five-sixths) than Muslims (just over one-half) preferred monogamy; this discrepancy between religious groups was greater than that describing the limitation of children.

When men said that they thought that children should be limited they were thinking of numbers such as five or six. Few respondents were encountered who expressly fixed a lower number. (One such man educated in the USA said that he had to educate the sons of a deceased elder brother; not only did he feel that he was expected by his family to do this but he stated that if his nephews lacked education they could easily become petty criminals and so bring disgrace to the family, himself included.) The reason overwhelmingly cited for limitation was the cost of education and maintenance; one simply could not afford to train many children. And it was better to have a few children in good jobs to maintain one in one's old age than many in poverty. Nevertheless those who could afford many children had every right to have them. Well-educated men were apt to argue that the poor should limit their families whilst they produced a 'better stock' (they did not consider, apparently, that some of their many children could not thus be but downwardly mobile). None of those who urged family limitation did so on the grounds of national overpopulation. Those who advocated an unlimited family size gave the traditional responses—the prestige of a large household, the help given by sons on the farm, the greater chance of having one son who will be outstanding, and the risk of losing children by death when one is too old to procreate further.

The pattern of responses to the question on family limitation was similar to that on monogamy. Unlimited childbearing was accepted by farmers and traders, by the illiterate and older men. Family limitation was advocated by the literates, by salary and wage earners and the young.

Prominent among those who reject both monogamy and family limitation were the farmers, the most traditionally oriented group, and traders, businessmen and drivers, the wealthier self-employed. Craftsmen, struggling to save to buy tools, are less inclined to favour large households. The literate clerks and teachers hope to give their children a comparatively good education. The impression from the entirety of the responses is that restraint is accepted as a necessary means of attaining one's goals; but that once one is achieving those, a large polygynous family is, for all except the most highly educated, a valued symbol of one's success.

Yoruba career histories give a prominent place to the role of the patron; the necessity of a helper if one is to succeed in life is stressed; the patron is lavishly praised, as the following obituary notice (*Daily Sketch*, 27 July 1968) demonstrates:

People that I remember most fondly are those who use whatever they are endowed with by God to the benefit of their countrymen. What had Prince Ladejola not done to help his fellow men, particularly the Ijesha youngsters in Lagos? If one lost his job 'Prince' would beg the boss. If you wanted a job Prince was ready to go places and get you a job. When many highly placed Ijeshas built impenetrable hard shells and drew curtains around themselves it was Prince Ladejola and a few others who took on the younger generation of Ijeshas and 'helped' them, both morally and financially, to secure places in the dazzling life of Lagos. . . . When Prince Ladejola Oginni was wealthy . . . he spent his money to help the needy.

The spheres in which help is given fall into a few well-defined categories: the payment of school fees; introductions and support in obtaining a job; training and apprenticeship; the grant of a loan with which to start a business. But as the Yoruba tell their stories the observer begins to feel that the generous acts described were, in so many cases, either everyday acts of mutual assistance which one would encounter in any society, or acts which brought substantial benefits to the patron and which could not be construed as altruistic, bringing only inner satisfaction and no material benefit to the donor. The man who describes how his master over many years taught him to trade before giving him a small sum to start on his own, was, by another interpretation, being ruthlessly exploited in being paid so little during this period. The taxi owner who enables one of his drivers to buy a taxi, forfeiting a substantial part of his wage as instalment payments, is perhaps recognising his inability to control a larger fleet of taxis and in return for disposing of an old vehicle receives in return the grateful loyalty of a follower who may in turn rise to affluence. School fees are paid by the trader who has no issue of his own needing such help at this time and his generosity earns him popular approval. Thus these acts of generosity can be interpreted as behaviour calculated to win a popular following, being resorted to when investment in one's own family is impossible or less rewarding or when further investment in one's business is frustrated by one's inability to control a larger enterprise on one's own and one's reluctance to take on partners who would share the responsibility.

In so many of the situations described the Yoruba informant stresses the beneficence of a helper, when the Western observer feels that in a like situation *he* would emphasise individual achievement. Thus it is not that the Yoruba are more generous than others— merely that they interpret situations in a different manner. One cannot furthermore argue that this is associated more with traditional or rural spheres, for, as we have seen, patronage is strongly stressed by school leavers, and getting wage employment is seen as needing the assistance of a helper even more than is success in a craft or trade. Why should the Yoruba emphasise this relationship with the patron?

First, the Yoruba expect that all generosity should be acclaimed by the recipient; to fail to do so would be construed as a lack of gratitude and would mark one as lacking in manners and thus undeserving of further help. Second, one accepts one's fate or destiny but does not boast about it; to attribute one's success to one's individual genius would invite accusations of witchcraft against one. As Field (1960) has argued in respect of the Akan of Ghana, the poor attribute their own misfortunes to the machinations of others, but the successful are even more threatened by the suspected envy of others. Third, a relationship with a patron having been established, it is in one's interest to maintain this bond for future occasions. Furthermore in praising one's benefactor one is indicating to one's rivals and competitors the strength of one's support against possible victimisation, ultimately perhaps proclaiming allegiance to one of the major factions in the town.

For the patron too there are benefits. The manifestation of power most highly valued by the Yoruba is not so much an office of authority as a large personal following; the latter may of course derive directly from the former, as with a chieftaincy title, but as we have already indicated a bureaucratic post in which one manipulates people is better than one in which one deals only with plans or figures. In the performance of one's duties one may build up personal support; thus within a university the students describe individual members of the teaching faculty in terms of the help they give to individual students; in the civil service factional cleavages are openly admitted and discussed. This overt support gives personal satisfaction and enhances one's prestige in the sight of one's peers; and in so doing is thought likely to lead to further success. In the contest for a chieftaincy the support of the majority of one's descent group was a prerequisite for election; in the modern sector popularity is still felt to be an asset in swaying selection boards acting ostensibly according to criteria more specifically related to the post in question.

Whilst so many Yoruba are looking and hoping for a helper, relatively few are successful; this gives rise to envy and disillusion. The term 'long legs' is mildly pejorative in being used of the man who has access to powerful patrons. Most respondents when directly asked if they had anyone in mind who would pay their children's school fees or loan them the capital required for a business, stated that they had no such patron, they were trusting to some new chance encounter or to the re-establishment of a dormant relationship. Today, with more secondary school places available, wealthy men are financing the education only of their closer relatives. With technological advances they invest more heavily in their own businesses, buying expensive machines rather than creating quasi-subsidiary businesses for the benefit of loyal staff. In the urban situation the migrant is thrown into greater dependence upon distant kin or fellow villagers in seeking accommodation and work, but the help given is not of a substantial financial nature and costs little to the donor; in fact it enhances his own reputation as a broker. The local transporters, contractors and produce buyers, so often the popular *gbajumo* of the 1950s, today turn more to the government for licences and contracts, and need to rely less on their local image to maintain custom. The political parties are viewed as institutionalised organs of patronage with the local Member of Parliament being responsible for winning services for his entire community and favours for individual members. Many erstwhile political leaders are still active and some have offices as commissioners but they now depend not upon their electorate but on the military leadership. The high-ranking army officers and the senior civil servants are seen as unapproachable by the mass of the people. In the past any man felt that he could approach a member of the local élite or the local politician, for help; today these relationships are largely ineffectual. But the need for patronage remains and thus, in a competitive spirit, each individual exploits whatever links in his network are available to him. In this situation those closely connected to the already powerful and wealthy members of Yoruba society have an obvious advantage.

The divisions of society

From a discussion of individual achievement and patronage, themes more appropriate to the study of cognitive maps, we turn now to the perception of social groups and of their interrelationship, to the study of the analytic structure of society. But to link these two sections we might first examine the individual's image of his own position in society.

Much as one decries the question, 'To which class do you belong: upper, middle or lower?' one must at least admit that class terms are of everyday usage in Western industrial society. In Yoruba society they are not so used, nor are there alternative terms—either in English or in the vernacular—with wide currency. However, in order to avoid the wide range of responses which would result if we asked respondents, 'How do you see yourself (or your position) in society?' we selected three terms and asked them to identify with one of them, giving reasons for their choice which proved in fact to be more illuminating than the simple distribution of responses. The three terms were *olowo, mẹkunnu* and *talaka*. *Olowo* is a common word usually meaning 'rich man', the emphasis being on movable assets, perhaps transient in nature, rather than honour, deriving from property—land, or an established business. *Mẹkunnu* is defined in the dictionaries as 'a poor person' (Wakeman, 1950) or 'nincompoop, a person of no account' (Abraham, 1958), but it seems to be used nowadays, as the citations below indicate, to mean 'one of the common people'. *Talaka* is a word of Hausa origin, meaning in the emirates a 'commoner'—as opposed to the titled Fulani aristocracy; in Ilorin, a Yoruba emirate, it was similarly used, the Talaka Parapo being the 'commoner's' political party in opposition to the Northern Peoples' Congress associated with the Fulani. To Yoruba in Ibadan and elsewhere it seems to mean a poor person. But both *mẹkunnu* and *talaka* are somewhat differently used when informants refer to themselves or to others.

The majority of respondents described themselves as *mẹkunnu*—over four-fifths of most categories. In their answers they said: 'I have the power to work and I see that I am still in a position to become rich'; 'I can feed my wives and children'; 'I have no house or lorries but I can feed my family'; 'I can feed my family without looking for anybody's help'; 'I am average'. The emphasis is on sufficiency—one can meet the modest demands of feeding and clothing one's family, though one cannot afford to indulge in luxuries. Many of these respondents added that they were not *talaka* because they were not reduced to begging from others or worse still, to stealing—the expected correlates of an inability to provide enough for one's family.

Those who described themselves as *talaka* were clearly thinking of their lack of perceived necessities, not of their absolute poverty; they certainly did not refer to begging and stealing. One-quarter of those employed as labourers described themselves as *talaka*—but so did a tenth of the teachers and clerks. Again *talaka* responses were highest not only among the totally illiterate but also those with a little post-primary education. It is a statement of relative deprivation.

Not surprisingly traders were more likely to describe themselves as *olowo*—one-fifth did so. These men saw themselves as clearly better off than their neighbours and stated: 'I have my own house and a car, I can send my children to school.' But one-tenth of the farmers also said they were *olowo*, referring to their possession of a sufficiency of land, a large family and the like. Relatively few craftsmen or clerks and teachers thought they were rich and no factory workers did so. The questionnaire survey included very few persons with secondary or post-secondary education, but earlier interviews indicated that the well-educated and, by the standards of the craftsmen and wage earners, very affluent, thought of themselves as 'average' persons—neither rich nor poor.

Such perceptions of one's own position in society seem appropriate to one's cognitive map. Whatever one's status, the great majority of those with whom one interacts with frequency and intensity—the more proximate members of one's social network—are, like oneself, 'average people'. They share common values and normative expectations. Below are ranked those who are unable or unwilling to maintain these values—the outcasts, 'scum', ne'er-do-wells and such. Above are those whose styles of life clearly differ from one's own and entail somewhat different norms and values. In closed societies the cleavage between the rich and the masses is sharp and immutable; here one finds the dichotomy (in its various forms) between 'them' and 'us' widely stressed. But it is not so stressed by the Yoruba for the *olowo* are almost invariably men with quite humble origins, who still share the values of the majority of those around them. If the them/us distinction is made by the Yoruba it is usually with reference to the highly educated—the senior civil servant and the like, who are residentially separated from the mass of the people. But here too a blanket designation of such men as 'them' is countered by the recognition that individuals among them are from one's home area, and are either well known to oneself or else are persons with whom one would identify.

In earlier structured interviews informants were asked as the opening question: 'What are the most important differences found among Yoruba people?' One illiterate farmer answered that some had good health, some were bewitched; another said that some had work while others were jobless. In another context a well-educated man stated that society was divided into title holders—the *ọba* and chiefs —the mass of the people and those who because of physical or mental incapacity were unable to fulfil a citizen's role. But the great majority of the interviewees answered by describing ethnic differences, mentioning in particular peculiarities of speech or diet. There was however no suggestion that one ethnic group within the Yoruba was superior to another, beyond a natural feeling of preference for and identity with one's own group. When asked in a supplementary question to describe differences within their own ethnic group or within their own town they continued to refer to ethnic differences, citing in many cases the distinction between indigenes and strangers. Those whose answers were but weakly focused upon ethnic differences tended to be men whose life and work did not bring them into contact with persons other than from their own descent group and town, i.e. farmers, as cited above.

One reason for such ethnic responses is that the differentiation is still a very easy one to make. Dress, behavioural mannerisms, hair style, do not distinguish the urban migrants from the various kingdoms and provinces of Yoruba country. But many young men from humble homes (and still more older men) still bear facial marks which give strong clues as to their place of origin. Dialect differences, though becoming occluded through education, are still easily recognisable. The stereotypes cited earlier are a frequent topic of discussion and whatever their validity (I know of no psychological tests which have shown, or even attempted to show, behavioural differences among the Yoruba) they encourage men to believe that they can identify their acquaintances from different areas. Furthermore a man is known by the company he keeps; the patterns of friendship, home visits and the like serve to identify the individual. Thus it was with considerable ease that a civil servant listed for me the ethnic group—Egba, Ijebu, Ekiti, Oyo, etc.—of every one of his colleagues in the senior grades of the service. And similarly a university lecturer can cite the origins of most of the faculty, the exceptions being persons very little known to the informant and not persons who lack an ethnic identity, though doubt does sometimes arise as when a man is native of one area (i.e. his father belonged there) but was born and grew up in another area to which his parents had emigrated.

Ethnic differences are cited not only because they undoubtedly exist, but also because they are felt to be important. It is widely expected that those in power will use their positions to obtain benefits for members of their own kin and community. The politician was certainly judged by his electorate according to the new social services and amenities he won for his own constituency, especially in comparison with rival neighbours. Civil servants too are expected to exercise their discretion in favour of their own people. The upper ranks of the civil service were seen to be dominated by Egba and Ijebu—and not without good reason, for a survey of the senior administrative class in 1968 showed that each of these areas provided almost a quarter of the members, or approximately twice as many as their relative population. Ibadan, Oshun and Oyo were underrepresented. Egba with its long history of missionary contact and Ijebu, which avidly accepted education in the early years of this century, have in fact provided a high proportion of educated Yoruba prominent in government and the professions; they provided nearly one-half of the Yoruba faculty in the University of Ibadan. In the late 1960s however constant reference was being made to the increasing prominence of the Ekiti, whose enthusiasm for education in recent decades has already been mentioned. Several Ekiti had reached the rank of permanent secretary in the regional civil service; and they were disproportionately highly represented in the University of Ibadan faculty and that of the University of Ife. Quite fortuitously the first two military governors of the Western Region/State were respectively from Ado Ekiti and one of its nearby dependent towns.

Considerations such as these coloured the arguments relating to the possible creation of separate Yoruba states. The military regime, in an attempt to decentralise local political power, divided the Northern Region into six states, thus breaking the dominance of the Fulani aristocracy and the NPC for the Hausa Fulani emirates composed only three such states; the Eastern Region was similarly divided into three states—one for the Ibo alone and two for the non-Ibo minority groups. The Western Region, being almost completely Yoruba, was left intact though it thus became disproportionately larger than other states in the federation and subdivision was considered. Erstwhile Yoruba politicians were divided between those who saw themselves in power or positions of influence in a single Yoruba state and those who felt that they could only obtain dominance in a smaller unit. The Oyo and Ibadan tended to seek separation so that they could escape the domination of Egba, Ijebu and Ekiti, placing their own people in positions of power. Some Ekiti and Ondo men claimed to have calculated that their area provided two-fifths of the Western Region's revenue, largely from cocoa, but constituted only one-fifth of its population. Were they to become a separate state they would be twice as rich. But the several ethnic groups which one can distinguish in Yoruba country do not fall easily into two or three natural divisions and so endless bargaining results as each set of protagonists tries to create a viable state in which they would be the leading partners. Pressure from above, together with the absence of any obvious solution, have combined to date to prevent the sub-division of the State. But resentment in the underprivileged areas, notably Ibadan and Oyo, continues.

Finally patronage reinforces ethnic divisions and the concept of ethnicity. If one appeals to a man for help on the basis of common interest, he may argue that his own interests are in fact rather different from those of the supplicant. But a man to whom an appeal is made in terms of common origin—of membership of the same town or ethnic group—first of all can hardly deny the accuracy of the fact and, second will be under strong social pressure to accept the obli-gation placed upon him and not to claim that he does not recognise such obligations—a claim which would be tantamount to self-excommunication from the group. Thus a Yoruba man feels that he can approach a powerful or wealthy man from his home area with whom he has, hitherto, had little or no direct relationship; conversely he would perhaps be hesitant in seeking help from a person with whom he already has a rather more firmly established relationship, but who is from a different ethnic area. Thus the concepts of ethnicity remain strong in the urban context to the extent that patronage is seen as one of the prime modes of achieving one's goals. The fears of political domination are perhaps instigated by the highly educated who are in fact competing for the positions cited; but they are quickly transmitted to the masses, and can be used in stirring up local agitation (in the same manner in which Akintola, leading the Nigerian National Democratic Party, tried in the early 1960s to enhance his own support by appealing for Yoruba unity against the threat of Ibo political and economic domination). However it must be re-iterated that our interviewees cited ethnic differences in terms of speech, diet and the like, and not of power or wealth.

In neither the structured interviews and questionnaires nor in daily conversation did informants refer to factional divisions in their communities. Partly this may be the result of our questions which did not seek answers in these terms, partly because factions have a largely identical membership, partly because at the time of our enquiries political parties were banned. But factions undoubtedly exist. In the past the Yoruba town was often divided into two or more major blocks during an interregnum as the chiefs supported rival candidates for the throne, each hoping that benefits would accrue to them and their descent groups were their own candidate to be successful. From the 1950s the factions have usually borne the labels of the two contrasting political parties—the Action Group and NCNC in the 1950s, and the NNDP and Action Group in the first half of the 1960s (P. C. Lloyd, 1955a). In many instances the entrée of political parties into a town was occasioned by the support given by city-based lawyers to candidates in a title dispute. The preference of a town for one party was sometimes enhanced by the identification of a neighbouring rival or disputedly dependent town for the other party; thus Ile Ife identified with the Action Group, Ilesha with the NCNC. Again, where two rich men competed for local influence in a town, they usually became identified with rival political parties. The local government councils elected from 1953, consequent upon the Action Group law, had a party basis; in many of them the councillors conducted their business overtly citing British parliamentary rules of procedure. The councils controlled a wide range of local services and appointments, and membership of those committees with perquisites and benefices to allocate, i.e. establishment and education, was sought by all members of the dominant party and they were correspondingly reluctant to serve on others, equally necessary but giving no patronage. These councils became in effect the local branches of the party, for initial attempts to win mass membership and direct allegiance to the party quickly declined. Activity at the local level was thus a means of ensuring patronage from the regional government.

The leaders of the factions were therefore the members of the local élite identified with the political parties; those supporting the party in power were obviously in a position to obtain favours, while those supporting the rival set hoped that their day would come. The structure of leaders, brokers and followers enabled most members of the community to feel that they were participating in the political process.

At best the factions are peaceful rivals; but in the later years of the NNDP government and in the days following the first military coup victimisation and violence were common as prominent men had their houses or cars burned by gangs of the rival group.

For our purposes the most significant feature of these factions is that each is similarly constituted, containing educated and wealthy men as leaders, and followers from all occupations. They cannot be identified with any one socio-economic category. Furthermore, although factions are a permanent structural feature, their actual membership is fluid. The allegiance of many men to their leaders is seen as being determined by ascribed factors—membership of a descent group, affinal links, etc., though sibling rivalry can as easily throw half-brothers into opposite camps. But switching of allegiance is in fact common as men see a higher chance of winning favours from the rival leaders. The very size and success of a faction may limit the chances of the individual supplicant.

The inequality of wealth

There can be no question of the importance and significance which the Yoruba attach to wealth and power in their society. A rich vocabulary describes men possessing these, and the means by which they have achieved their positions. The traditional terms already described are still those most commonly used, though there are numerous others including many which are recent introductions, some being slang rather than accepted usage. But a feature of these terms is that they tend to describe one particular attribute of the person described and, by implication, point to the absence of others. Thus the *olowo* has money but may not have honour; the *ǫlǫlá* has the honour but may not be especially rich. Other terms have a specifically occupational referent: *ǫmǫwe* (literates); *oloye* (title holders); *ǫga* (master, in contrast to employee). 'Senior service' is now commonly used to describe a man with a car, for in the civil service men of this grade are granted loans to purchase, and monthly allowances to maintain, a car.

One is looking however for terms which embrace all members of the higher socio-economic categories and exclude all others. Terms such as oligarchy, used in some Latin American countries, have this connotation. Our own class terminology, of course, has just this quality. The very use of the term 'upper' implies the existence of a lower class; of middle, the existence of classes on either side. But such class terms are as yet little used in Nigeria; and when they are used the meanings may differ from those accepted in our own society. Thus I have heard the term 'working class' used to describe the senior civil servants who return to their offices in the late afternoon, distinguishing them from all lesser clerical staff who knock off promptly at 2.00 p.m. Factory employers refer to themselves as the workers (versus the management) rather than working class. One is reminded here of the use of 'working class' in early nineteenth-century England to refer to all those engaged in industry, both employee and employer, in contrast to the 'idle' landowner and renter —a use which excluded the relationship between factory owner and worker (Briggs, 1960). The term 'middle class', widely used by Western writers to describe the growing category of university-educated civil servants, teachers and professionals, was never current within Nigeria. The veritable 'upper class' of expatriates could always be referred to by Nigerians in terms of colour or race.

The terminology commonly used by the Yoruba, both in the vernacular and in English, is thus descriptive of a wide variety of aspects of social ranking, but it does not define socio-economic strata whether these be seen as juxtaposed and hierarchical groups or as opposed groups. Yet they certainly see some persons as being at the top of the social hierarchy, others near the bottom, and it is thus pertinent to ask how they see the relationship between these—the relationship in other words between the 'haves' and the 'have-nots'.

Asked whether it is fair that a labourer should earn £8 a month whilst a university graduate first earns £70 a month and can then rise to double or treble that sum, the majority of Yoruba respondents answered in the affirmative. In structured interviews held in 1968 a greater measure of assent was obtained than in the questionnaire survey of 1971; but this was probably due to the rapid inflation between the two periods, with the result that a greater number in the latter study said that £8 a month was insufficient to maintain a man and his family. The arguments used supporting or rejecting the statement were the same on both occasions. It was maintained by some that £8 was too low a wage. It was argued that labourers did hard manual work whereas the clerical work of graduates was physically easy. The predominant response of those who accepted the wide income disparity was in terms of the suffering endured by the graduate in obtaining his education, and of the expenditure incurred which merited substantial repayment. An illiterate shoemaker:

Very small children go to school, they are flogged and do not marry in time. If he earns £200 as a reward that is not too much because he has suffered for it.

A clerk with some secondary education:

If one buys some articles for trade, he must sell them and get the money back. The money already spent on them [the graduates] is very great. It is as if a man plants some grains of maize—he should expect to have thousands back and not the same number as he sowed.

A skilled artisan:

My opinion about this is that some of those who are labourers today curse themselves to be in such positions, because there are some who had the opportunity to go to school or take up an apprenticeship but failed to stay the course. Such people now find that they have no means of livelihood and they cannot get a helper and so become labourers. Those who are university graduates are big men, high-ups; but before they can become big men they have suffered a lot and they are now enjoying the fruit of their suffering. Let those who want a better position suffer now and they will do better.

Opinions were divided as to the cause of the labourers' plight—their laziness or their lack of opportunity, the former being stressed by those who accepted a wide income differential.

In the questionnaire survey of 1971 the fairness of the income differential was accepted by a higher proportion of teachers and clerks, of those with secondary education; it was rejected by a slightly higher proportion of labourers. Overall there was little correlation with education or occupation. Many of those who stated that the income difference was fair said when asked about the optimum wages of labourer and university graduate that the former should receive between £11 and £15 a month (46 per cent of such responses) or between £16 and £20 (30 per cent). Of those who said that the income difference was unfair, 20 per cent wanted £11–15 for the labourer, 28 per cent wanted £16–20, and 20 per cent wanted £21–25. The majority in both categories thought that the graduate ought to remain on his present salary, with the remainder of 'fair' respondents tending to a higher salary and of the 'unfair' respondents a slightly lower salary. Thus even those who think the present arrangement bad are still prepared to accept a starting point for university graduates three or four times the labourer's wage, in contrast with the nine-fold difference cited in the question.

A second question was contemplated asking similarly about the legitimacy of a trader's earnings, but it quickly became apparent that there would be an overwhelming acceptance of the rewards of entrepreneurship in the terms already illustrated. Traders expect a return on their investment and where the scale of these returns reflects their own skill and effort these returns are completely legitimate.

To what extent do the Yoruba see the wealth of some as deriving from the labour of others—in other words, do the rich exploit the poor? In a very simple subsistence agricultural economy there would be considerable differences in wealth. Some men are born to be strong and healthy, others weak and sick—the former will cultivate more land. Equally attributable to destiny is the laziness of some and the effort of others. Some marriages will be blessed with fertility, others prove barren; and in the former some parents will be lucky in seeing a majority of their children grow to maturity whilst others may lose them in infancy. It would require positive acts of co-operation to eliminate the inequalities produced by these natural differences. But a man's efforts may be negated by lack of resources. In pre-colonial Yoruba society a man never lacked land; today there is growing pressure on land in many areas but respondents who saw their future in farming referred only to the lack of capital to hire labour or to buy fertilisers, never to the lack of land. Capital for trade is scarce; but many successful traders have started with such small sums as would in fact be available to a great many people, had they the skill and enterprise to accept the challenge. Again education has in past decades been available to children from poor homes.

In pre-colonial society wealth could be seen to flow between four sets of persons. From unmarried sons to fathers, as the former worked on their father's land; but the father was responsible for providing his son's bridewealth and his own wealth would eventually pass to his sons. From pawn to creditor—a fair return on a loan or investment. From slave to master—the slave was not a full member of the society, being a member of another ethnic group. From subject to

PI — G

chief and *ọba*—but the amounts paid by the individual were very
small and the power and affluence of the chief both benefited the
entire descent group and reflected its status in the community. In
each case the flow of wealth was seen as legitimate—except perhaps
by the slaves but they too tolerated their plight as natural, for their
own natal societies were slave-owning, too.

Today one can cite more examples. The master craftsman exploits
labour of his apprentices; some may have cause for complaint that
their master is not teaching them his skills, but most masters do
impart whatever knowledge they have and many subsequently help
the trained apprentice to buy his tools. The shop assistant or taxi
driver may find it galling to hand over so much of his day's takings
to his employer; but he relies on him for help in establishing his own
business.

The profits of the trader are still viewed as resulting from his
abstinence (or suffering) in investing in business what he might have
consumed in food, clothing or in taking another wife, and from his
skill in manipulating the investment. With intense competition
between traders in any given commodity—the customer can haggle
over the price and go elsewhere—success lies in appreciation of the
market and in a large turnover. The price which the produce buyer
pays to the farmer for his cocoa is annually fixed by the government;
he cannot vary this though he may cheat the ignorant farmer in respect
either of the price or of the weight and quality of cocoa offered. Even
when a man becomes the owner of 'the means of production'—a
lorry, a printing press or even several sewing machines—he is still
perceived essentially as a trader—a man who invests his savings for
greater future gain. And in fact almost all such men have risen to
their present status as employers and businessmen by their own
efforts and not through inheritance. None of these remarks of course
applies to the large expatriate-owned or controlled companies.

Exploitation by the government

One mode by which wealth is transferred from one section of the
community to another is however widely recognised: 'government',
i.e. the civil service, is maintained by the mass of the people. It is
they who pay the salaries of most of the well-educated and affluent
élite. The means by which this transfer is made is somewhat obscured. For the local direct taxes collected, the rates, are for the most

part retained by the local government councils and used to pay for the services which they provide. The average farmer or craftsman pays only a small levy, the heir to the Capitation Tax of the early 1950s, to the State government. State revenues come directly from PAYE taxes on salary earners, from the Cocoa Marketing Board and indirectly from the federal government. Much of this last sum represents indirect taxes paid by consumers who are understandably ignorant of the proportion of the price they pay which is attributable to tax. Similarly, though they realise that the government (here including the Marketing Board) withholds part of the price of cocoa received on the world market, the farmers have little idea of the proportion so retained. The movements of the world price are rarely recorded in the daily press.

Furthermore there is, as we have already seen, a general acceptance of the high salaries received by educated men. These are seen primarily as a reward for their hard work and a due return on the sums of money expended. A substantial part of many of these salaries is known to be spent in educating poor relatives. It is recognised that the work of such men is both highly skilled and socially necessary. Nobody suggests that the structure of government should be dismantled.

Yet there is a growing disillusion with the government. When asked, 'Do you think that the government cares for the progress of all citizens or do you think it cares for only a few—whose progress do they care for?' a very large number of respondents answered 'a few'. These included four-fifths of the factory workers but a little over half of the clerks and teachers, craftsmen and traders. Religion and the level of education of either the respondent or of his parents seemed to have little or no effect on the answers; the most highly educated in the sample—those with full secondary schooling (all of whom were in fact clerks or teachers)—were markedly of the opinion that government worked for the progress of all. In Agege a higher proportion of respondents said that government cared for a few than in the traditional quarter of Ibadan.

Of those who stated that government cared for the progress of all, most gave as their reason the provision of social services—education and more especially health, mentioning specifically the hospitals, clinics and maternity centres. Several cited recent vaccination campaigns to control the outbreak of cholera. Many qualified their answers by saying that they recognised that the government could not

give everyone all the services they needed. Those who stated that
government cared for a few people only most frequently asserted
that it was the civil servants themselves who were benefiting: 'The
government looks after its own people.' Some said that 'government
helps the rich'; respondents did not specify other categories of
persons at the upper end of the social hierarchy, for instance, big
traders, industrialists and the like. The image presented was clearly
of a civil service using its power to benefit its own members—by
awarding scholarships to their own children, contracts to their near
kin and especially to their own wives. Their corporate loyalty to each
other in this respect was seen to be transcending their individual
loyalties to their own ethnic groups.

Is not such nepotism a common feature in Africa, one might argue?
Are the discontented Yoruba merely envious of the success of others?
Would they not do exactly the same had they the same opportunity?
Perhaps they would; but the civil servants are not conforming so
closely to traditional norms. In pre-colonial society a man's loyalties
lay to his descent group and to his community. However, as we have
already indicated, it was difficult for a man to perpetuate his own
achieved status in any or all of his sons. Not only did polygyny
dissipate wealth among a large number of heirs but rivalry between
co-wives and their issue also deterred a man from favouring one
son against others. There were strict and well-observed rules that a
son should not directly succeed his father in a titled office. The status
in the community of an adult woman depended as much on the
prestige of her own descent group and of her own wealth as a trader
as on her husband; with the exception of royal wives, one did not
find the wives of chiefs or wealthy traders deriving an importance in
the town from their husband's status; rich traders did not set up
their wives in business, their capital input or influence protecting
them against competition. But this is not what is happening today.
The rich are seen to be able to educate not only their bright children,
but also the dull ones; wives are oft-cited recipients of contracts
and quasi-monopolistic trading opportunities. The Yoruba norm of
assistance to a wide circle of kin has often been honoured in the
breach, as the story of the young Awolowo shows. Today, perhaps
because this norm is so threatened, it is hailed especially by educated
Yoruba who contrast their own values with those attributed to
Western society where each man looks after his own children leaving
his nephews to suffer for the inadequacies of their own parents. Yet

the actions of these same men often belie the values which they proclaim.

We must distinguish clearly between opposition to a structure of social inequality—a belief that the basic rules governing the allocation of power and rewards should be altered—and hostility towards those in power because they are not abiding by the generally accepted rules. Thus the well-worn dichotomy is made between revolutions which change the structure and rebellions by which a bad ruler, a tyrant, an oppressor, is replaced by the good ruler who fulfils the norms of his office. Today a degree of corruption is acknowledged by those in power. In Nigeria, as elsewhere in West Africa, one of the first acts of the military regime was to set up tribunals to enquire into the assets not only of the displaced politicians but also of civil servants and other public figures. Each incoming leader stresses his own opposition to corruption—thus Brigadier Rotimi, Military Governor of the Western State, who was on a meet-the-people tour, said that progress in the state was being retarded by 'vipers' in the civil service and government-owned corporations (*West Africa*, 11 August 1972, p. 1069):

> These people are sucking your blood. They are your enemies. They are the ones making things difficult for us in the state. These vipers are in every ministry, in government owned banks where they grant loans to their friends and family without any security or where they grant themselves loans for their own business.

But little has been achieved by these tribunals beyond creating a very few scapegoats and giving others investigated some sleepless nights (and perhaps obliging them to spend lavishly in winning support, as Chief Agbaje ought, in the eyes of the chiefs, to have done). The replacement of the bad king by the good is seen as a restoration of the *status quo ante*. The fulminations against corruption are designed to curb the worst excesses which arouse popular ire, but they facilitate the continuance of the process whereby the social divisions between rich and poor are being steadily hardened and perpetuated.

The ideal society

What kind of society do the Yoruba hope for? What might the government do to achieve this? Respondents were asked to choose between two pairs of alternative policies—raising the minimum wage of labourers or making secondary schooling free; raising wages or increasing the cocoa price. On the first pair opinions were fairly evenly divided. Nearly three-quarters of factory workers, for obvious reasons, opted for a wage increase. Free schooling was preferred by farmers. Correlations with age, education or religion could not be clearly established.

Justifications for increasing the labourers' wage fell into three categories. The labourers are so poor that they cannot maintain their families and are in danger of being obliged to resort to crime; if they receive more money they will in fact work harder. Increased wages will bring in more money to the whole community and all will benefit. If the labourers are better paid they will be able to afford the school fees—this was the most frequent response. Supporting these themes was a widely expressed distrust of free secondary education. The quality would be reduced as teachers grew lax; the school certificate would become worthless and there would be unemployment among secondary school leavers; the money already spent on such schooling would be wasted. One only appreciates what one pays for, said several men. Others argued that the rich would still dominate the secondary schools even if they were free and the labourer would not benefit; or that many of the children of labourers are dull and would not be able to enter secondary school—their parents would gain nothing, so a wage raise would be preferable. Some respondents were obviously thinking of an extension of secondary schooling, others of the abolition of fees in the existing schools. The analogy of free primary education was clearly in the minds of all. Those who advocated free education did so on the ground that opportunities would be available to all; even if one raised the minimum wage, a labourer would not be able to afford the existing fees and the wage increase would push up prices to the detriment of others.

A much larger proportion of respondents favoured the raising of the cocoa price over a wage increase, the farmers overwhelmingly preferring this, whilst a slight majority of manual wage earners preferred to see a wage increase. Agege craftsmen and traders tended to see their custom increasing with rising wages, Ibadan men with rising cocoa prices. Some of the justifications were in terms of greatest need; whilst some saw the farmers as the poorest category in the community, others argued that the farmer had a free house and cheap food whilst the wage earner had to pay for these at increasingly inflated prices. But the farmers could turn to no other occupation whilst wage earners could develop a second source of income. Some thought that farmers outnumbered wage earners and that an increased cocoa price would benefit more people; others saw wage earners in the majority. An increased cocoa price was seen as stimulating cocoa production, thus increasing the wealth of the farmers and also raising government revenues; the farmers would be able to hire more labour, buy fertiliser and so raise their output not only of cocoa but also of food crops; the price of local foodstuffs in the towns would thereby be reduced. (Low cocoa prices were seen as forcing farmers to increase their prices of food crops sold on the market in order to yield them a sufficient overall income.) A higher cocoa price would encourage young men to return to farming and this too would increase agricultural production. An increased cocoa price would result in more work for craftsmen, a greater turnover for traders; it would not, as seen by respondents, raise prices as would a wage increase. In the wide variety of economic arguments offered, none suggested that a low producer cocoa price would increase the revenue of the government, enabling it to invest in productive enterprises and so create new employment opportunities; nor did any argue that a wage increase, in resulting in higher food prices, would indirectly benefit the farmers—their own experience suggesting perhaps that it is the traders who are more likely to gain.

When asked what they felt the government should do to help people like themselves the answers were in terms of the creating of more opportunities. Those who still sought to further their education asked for scholarships; manual employees wanted more jobs; craftsmen, traders and farmers asked for loans with which to improve their businesses.

Thus, taken in their entirety, the responses of these Yoruba men indicate a general satisfaction with the pattern of the distribution of wealth in their society, save only that abject poverty should be alleviated. They seek for increased opportunities to rise in either of the two main employment hierarchies—that of clerical work, determined by educational attainment, or that of self-employed business, as farmer, craftsman or trader. But these opportunities are in fact being provided by those in power, who favour their own close kin; those who have no such close kin in high places feel that their chances of obtaining benefactions or of finding an effective 'helper' are steadily being reduced.

7 An overview

In attempting to portray the image which the Yoruba have of their own society, or even of a limited field such as the pattern of social inequality, our greatest difficulty lies in designing a framework. What should be included, what omitted? How should one present the data? One ought to use a framework adopted by the Yoruba themselves, even though the external observer is bound in some degree to introduce his own concepts? In the opening chapter I presented a set of heads under which I proposed to treat social inequality, claiming that these were as culturally neutral as I could make them. In giving importance to the concept of power I argued that the Yoruba too seemed to stress this as much as I would. Their comments on the attributes of different occupations, in the previous chapter, would seem to confirm this impression. In this same chapter I outlined the responses given by a stratified sample of informants in answering open-ended questions or providing explanations for their choice of simple alternatives. The choice of questions was of course mine; but the questionnaire was finally designed halfway through the fieldwork period when it was established that the questions would be meaningful to the Yoruba.

The explanation of these attitudes lies largely in the preceding chapters, each of which serves a double purpose. In describing the 'traditional' social and political structure of Yoruba society I both provided a base line for the study of change and outlined the concepts and propositions about inequality which were appropriate to traditional society and which continue to be used, substantially, by many Yoruba in their analysis of present-day society. Yet the introduction of the English language has brought few new terms into everyday Yoruba parlance. 'Class' for instance is still an alien term used (as it seems to us) in unusual ways; thus I have heard the senior civil servants described as the working class, i.e. those who work harder than others—and I have heard 'working class girls' used to refer to the salaried nurses, teachers, secretaries as contrasted with self-employed petty traders and craftsmen. In describing patterns of social mobility and interaction I presented my material as statements about events. Thus x per cent of those in school proceed to further education; the ys do interact with the zs. The choice of data is of course my own. But these statements do, after all, refer to actions by the Yoruba themselves and to the antecedent decisions made by them. The furtherance of education was one of a number of choices open to each individual.

In stressing the perception which the Yoruba have of their own society, I am consciously emphasising a viewpoint which is so often lacking in the sociological literature where descriptions of 'subjective' approaches to stratification are overwhelmed by 'objective' accounts, and where so many of these subjective descriptions are derived from the imposition by the researcher of his categories upon the often imprecise formulations of his subjects. My own approach is however simply that of the social anthropologist who explains the culture of the peoples whom he studies in the terms used by them, first, because he believes that this is his duty, and second, because his prime source of information is the statements made by the people, for in his limited fieldwork period he cannot observe a sufficient number of any but the most mundane events for him to form independent conclusions as to the statistical regularity of specific patterns. This approach seems too, at least to the anthropologist, to be a necessary antidote at the present time to the predominant analysis of African urban society in terms of concepts appropriate to Western industrial society—and especially the terminology of 'class'.

My own approach is paralleled in fact by new directions in anthropological and sociological theory though owing, I confess, little specifically to them. Thus the ethnomethodology of Garfinkel emphasises the importance of the study of native categories. Yet these studies, and those of cognitive anthropology in its various forms, lead to two rather different approaches (Tyler, 1969). One merely stresses the traditional anthropological task of presenting the 'world-view', 'cognitive map', normative structure of the people studied. The other, in searching for a deep or unconscious structure, has given us highly formalised analyses of very limited areas—of kinship or colour terminology, for instance—in a manner that seems to be of limited application in the study of the structure of inequality. Again, in these latter studies man himself once more becomes lost and we are presented with that mode of structural analysis of which Leach has said, 'To some extent the pleasure which can be derived from structural analysis is aesthetic' (1966, p. 70).

In sociology a revived interest in the writing of Alfred Schutz in developing Weberian theories of action has heralded the claims of phenomenological sociology to be the alternative to structural-functionalism with its Durkheimian heritage. Thus Schutz writes (1972, p. 6):

> All the complex phenomena of the social world retain their meaning but this meaning is precisely that which the individuals involved attach to their own acts. The action of the individual and its intended meaning alone are subject to interpretive understanding. Further, it is only by such understanding of individual action that social science can gain access to the meaning of each social relationship and structure, constituted as these are, in the last analysis, by the action of the individual in the social world. . . . The aim [of sociology], then, is to interpret the actions of individuals in the social world and the ways in which individuals give meaning to social phenomena.

This is in essence, the approach which I have adopted, albeit crudely, in this monograph; it gives nevertheless but a partial description of society.

To understand the action of an individual we must know the concepts and propositions which he uses together with his evaluation of the opportunities available to him and the constraints operating upon him, in terms of his own resources, the sanctions expected of others and so on; upon these are his decisions based. Similarly we may understand the common actions of a number of individuals within a given category. However, such understanding, whilst helpful, is not necessary for prediction; for we may know, statistically, that individuals in a certain category will in a given situation behave in a certain manner. This is the behavioural approach. We often postulate that the individual's view of his world is a consensual one—that it is shared by others. For ego to be able to predict a satisfactory outcome of his actions he must know the likely responses of alter and this is easiest if alter shares his own expectations. But man's actions so often do not lead to the desired ends. The assiduity with which the illiterate Yoruba father drives his own son to primary school does not ensure his successful entry to secondary school; revolts sometimes succeed but more often fail to achieve the goals sought. The reasons are obvious. Decisions may rest upon the inadequate ability of the individual to process information available to him (i.e. he is not very clever); upon the use of inadequate concepts and propositions (e.g. mere attendance at school is not a good predictor of scholastic success); upon false or insufficient information about his own resources or those of others; upon a misjudgment of the concepts being used by others which, together perhaps with a false estimate of their resources, results in a mistaken calculation of the sanctions to be expected. The sociologist cannot therefore explain the world simply in terms of man's intentions and decisions. But these must constitute a most important variable. For if we attempt to understand the world purely in structural terms, predicting events in terms of structural relationships rather than individual motivation, we deny the possibility that man can, by his own understanding of the pattern of events, himself influence their coure. The task of marrying these two approaches is the perennial problem of the social sciences. As Kingsley Garbett (1970, pp. 225–6) concluded his Malinowski lecture:

> When I began to work out this lecture I hoped to resolve the conflict between anthropologists focusing on institutions and those focusing on ego-centred interaction. I found that I could not do so. It may be my own weakness; or it may be that the subject is not yet ripe for a reconciliation. It may be even that no reconciliation is possible; and that this is a problem for philosophers and not for a field anthropologist.

I do not believe the problem to be insoluble, though a comprehension of the process of interaction between man and society may be an easier task than its explanation in written form.

The world of reality, the 'world out there', consists only of a sequence of events upon which each of us imposes a structure or pattern of his own creation whether he be an actor concerned to participate in successive events or an external observer *in extremis* creating structures solely for his own intellectual satisfaction. One structure is more valid than another only in so far as it enables its creator to predict more accurately the events of the future. The actions of men however depend upon the way in which they see the world around them.

With these simple statements I certainly do not wish to claim to make a contribution to the philosophical debate to which Garbett refers. In the introductory chapter of this monograph I framed my problem in rather specific terms and saw it as emergent from the Yoruba ethnography with which I was familiar. I did not set out to produce a contribution to or a justification of the phenomenological approach to sociology. But in this prologue to the concluding chapter I have tried, in a most simple manner, not only to indicate the theoretical position to which my descriptive studies have led me, but also to set it in the context of other descriptions of Yoruba social stratification and especially of those of my junior colleagues engaged in the research project.

In the following sections I shall attempt three tasks. First, a brief summary and recapitulation of the Yoruba perception of social inequality as I have described it. Second, a comment on the action which derives from this, stressing the manifestations of protest which have occurred in recent years. Third, an attempt to compare the Yoruba situation with that elsewhere in the world, elucidating, in the process, the concept of class consciousness.

The egalitarian though unequal society

To provide as a heuristic device a framework for description, I have suggested that we distinguish between the ego-oriented cognitive map and the externalised analytic structure—terms which are imprecise inasmuch as both constitute patterns or structures created by the individual. They differ, first, and by definition, in the location of the individual. But resulting from this the components of the two images differ substantially. The cognitive map delineates the goals available to the individual and the means by which these might be achieved. The means involve interaction with other individuals and so the map indicates the total social network of the individual, indicating not only the resources available to each person but ego's credit or debit balance in his relationships with them. The cognitive map is the individual's guide to immediate action. Hence my own concern in the previous pages with the attitude of Yoruba towards different types of occupation and the means which they see as appropriate to their achievement, rather than the comparative ranking of occupations with differently valued characteristics—a task so frequently undertaken in sociological research. For in practice the individual's choice, if any, between these similarly ranked jobs is usually determined by his resources—education, capital, skills—rather than any superior valuation of one over the other. The analytic structure is of a higher level of abstraction. In externalising himself from his society the individual is performing a task which some may rarely do, most find difficult. To create such a structure involves the ability to generalise. Furthermore the criticism of the structure as illegitimate involves the ability to postulate other different structures—that is to say alternative ways in which one's society might work, not alternative ways of seeing a legitimate structure in one's own existing society.

One postulates a high degree of congruence and compatibility between the concepts and propositions used in each of these two images. One would not expect a man whose cognitive map indicates the ease with which he or others could reach the positions of greatest power to construct an analytical structure of a rigidly stratified society with insurmountable barriers to mobility. But a certain degree of incongruence is both possible and likely. First, we may distinguish between long-term strategies and short-term aims. An analytic structure may indicate that the opportunities for workers or peasants radically to alter their relationship with employers or landowners respectively, are meagre and dependent for success on large-scale collective action. The cognitive map indicates the individual's own opportunities for personal advancement to a limited degree. Thus the analytic structure stresses opposition, the cognitive map patronage. Again one must reiterate the heuristic nature of the distinction made between analytic structures and cognitive maps; but one's questions may unwittingly (and unintentionally) predicate answers in terms of one image rather than the other.

Second, the ego-oriented cognitive map emphasises relationship within the local community—the 'us' category as opposed to 'them'. It may stress characteristics which are at variance with one's image of the total national or global society. Thus the local community in a peasant society may be seen as open though mobility out of its confines may be highly restricted. Intense competition for rank within the community is thus tempered both by a stress on equality and solidarity within the community and then by hostility towards those who not only succeed but who in so doing leave the community.

The cognitive map of the Yoruba stresses attainment of high-ranking positions; specifically, most Yoruba can point to men of their own home community, often closely related to them, who have done well. The same characteristic is stressed in their analytic structure; but here there is an ambivalence. The legitimacy of great differences in wealth and income was accepted by many men so long as they, or more realistically, their children could achieve high positions; but they are becoming increasingly unsure of their chances of success. The dichotomy and opposition between 'government' and ordinary folk become more commonly asserted. But the alternative structure which is postulated is a traditional one in which the benefits of power and wealth fall more widely upon the entire community, less exclusively upon the children of those in the eminent positions.

The sources of the concepts and propositions used in defining the situation, in creating a patterned order, have been summarised under three heads: the indigenous concepts appropriate to the traditional social structure to which the individual was socialised from infancy onwards; his own experience, and that of his peers and acquaintances, of social mobility; his present relationships in the social and occupational spheres.

In describing the traditional Yoruba social structure I particularly stressed its openness. A chieftaincy title could not pass directly to the son of a deceased incumbent; the wealth of a prosperous trader was not usually replicated in any one of his sons. Apart from rules designed to prohibit the perpetuation of status and to ensure the equality of siblings, the practice of polygyny effectively prevented a closed society, for the higher the status of the individual, in terms of power or wealth, the greater was the number of his children and the greater the likelihood that collectively they would in the next generation constitute a cross-section of the population, ranging from rich to poor, powerful to weak. Concomitant with such a structuring of society was a belief in innate individual differences, one's fate, tempered by the knowledge that, through appropriate rituals or good behaviour, this fate could be improved. Failure to succeed was ascribed either to a poor fate or to the machinations of others. Success as in attaining a chieftaincy title depended upon the patronage of others; those who succeeded were expected to help others to rise.

From such a society many Yoruba have moved into social economic or political fields dominated by institutions introduced from the West and thus alien to their traditional society. We have seen how youths were drawn into the educational system from all types of homes and how the present Western-educated élite has been drawn from a wide social base. For many the material benefits of urban migration are, to us, questionable. The migrant enjoys piped water—from a stand-pipe several houses away—and electricity—perhaps only in the street and not within the house; his diet is far less rich than that enjoyed in the village. But even if the material benefits do not seem to outweigh the losses, the migrant himself may feel that he has moved from a rural situation in which relatively few opportunities for advancement exist for him, to an urban one where the diversities and range of opportunities seem almost limitless. Again, whatever seem to be the merits or demerits of modern society, the rate of change has been in fact so rapid that the adult of today lives in a very different world from that in which his father grew up.

In examining the structure of present-day employment we distinguished between the self-employed (and their own apprentices or employees) and the wage earners employed largely by the state or by big expatriate-dominated companies—the informal and formal structures of the economy. Though the rewards of educational success are high, the wages of the unskilled or semi-skilled labourer are low and do not compare favourably with the incomes of farmers, especially when the cost of urban rents and food is considered. Only a very small proportion, the skilled manual workers, might be said to constitute a 'labour aristocracy'—though their incomes are well matched by traders. Wage earners generally enjoy a security of income but the value of this as perceived by the Yoruba may be compared with the opportunities open for advancement. Clerical posts, whether in the public or the private sector of large companies, are seen as careers; not only are there regular increments within salary grades but promotion to a higher grade is possible and may be achieved by educational success; and clerical work by its nature usually permits private study and the passing of further exams. Manual work, especially in a factory, offers neither the opportunity for promotion, nor the facility for study; it is thus seen as having no future, but in training the individual for a specific range of tasks it gives him a skill which he can then ply in the informal sector as a self-employed artisan. Even in the major industrial and administrative centres the numbers employed in the informal sector usually exceed those in the formal sector, and the attitudes appropriate to the former will tend to predominate, i.e. a stress on the virtue of self-employment, on the importance of patronage.

Each of the three sources of concepts and propositions relating to the structure of society thus stresses achievement. But one is led to ask whether any one of the sources has a predominant effect in determining prevalent Yoruba attitudes. Are the traditionally derived concepts irrelevant? Or would the Yoruba hold the same image if they were employed in a manner which gave little hope for advancement? How far will the attitudes of those a generation hence, who are born and reared in the modern towns, correspond to those of their parents? Only comparative studies can answer these questions. Touraine and Ragazzi (1961) for instance, in their study discussed below (p. 224), argue that the achievement orientation of factory workers of rural origin derives principally from their own experience of social mobility; their conceptualisation of the employers however is more similar to rural views of the provincial bourgeoisie than that of urbanised workers of bosses.

The choice of social inequality as a significant theme for study is my own; but in examining the Yoruba view of their social world one must first ask—in what way do they see themselves as unequal? Ranking by age was described as a dominant feature of social life with considerable deference shown by junior to senior persons of either sex. This continues to the present day with an added corollary that well-educated men, products of but a few prestigious secondary schools, retain close ties with their own classmates; and inasmuch as 'fagging' was a highly developed and conscious adoption from the English public schools, ranking in these schools is perpetuated in later social relationships. To the outside observer the overt display of wealth—gowns and horses in traditional society, dress, cars and houses in modern society—seems an obvious determinant of rank. In a society with a low level of technology and in which the rich continued to live in the compounds of their descent group, a covert accumulation and enjoyment of wealth would hardly be possible. But as we have seen it is not wealth *per se* which is most valued by the Yoruba, but power—demonstrated by the size of one's personal following, the praises sung of one's affluence and generosity. This is demonstrated in the greater prestige of the *ọlọlá* than the *olowo*, in the emphasis on power in the evaluation of occupations.

Power, by definition, implies an unequal social relationship, and relative overt wealth demonstrates the inequality; but the Yoruba traditionally did not see themselves as exploited by the powerful. The chief repaid gifts and tribute with his patronage and protection; the trader made a very small profit from cash customers, he could rarely monopolise any resources and was always vulnerable to competition. A chief held office for life and hence perhaps the tendency for a wealthy man to translate his wealth to political office when he reached the apparent peak of his trading career. Both chiefs and traders were expected to be generous—the ideal was the *gbajumọ* and miserliness was seen as most despicable. Chiefs could obviously protect their power from infringement or attack by their subordinates, and the wealth of traders could ensure their continued success. But in Yoruba history one encounters no reference to risings of the poor against the rich.

Access to positions of power was open; the chief was the democratic elected representative of his people; the superiority of the trader rested on his skill. At one extreme the social inequality of men may be seen to derive from innate abilities and personality characteristics, these being randomly distributed in the population; at the other it may be seen as rigidly ascribed by birth (the first-born son succeeds to political office), by inheritance of wealth or by a favoured upbringing (the children of the rich are clearly advantaged). The Yoruba stressed the former, emphasising the fate or destiny of the individual which could however be improved by hard work and good behaviour (reflected in one's success in attracting patronage) or impoverished by laziness. Skill in manipulating financial transactions or people clearly does not seem to pass from a man or a woman to all their children. Rules governing the rotation of political office prevented a son from succeeding directly to his father, however powerful a position the latter might have built up. An upbringing in an affluent home was seen as a disadvantage for it encouraged not achievement but laziness and arrogance. It is the poor boy who struggles, that gains the ultimate success. The epitome of this attitude was expressed in the rule, which operated in most kingdoms, that the eldest son of a reigning *ọba*, stereotyped as an arrogant playboy revelling in his father's power, could never succeed to the throne, even when it later became the turn of his segment.

Most of these attitudes continue to prevail at the present time. Scholastic success in particular is seen as a legitimate route to power and wealth. But the withdrawal of the educated élite from daily contact with the masses and the restriction of their generosity to their closer kin are seen as being contrary to traditional values.

Today a high proportion of the traditional chieftaincies are vacant as no specific duties have been allotted to the offices in the sphere of local government and justice; and the posts are thus not salaried.

Those which remain are—with the exception of the leading *ọba*—poorly remunerated. Traditional political office is no longer a prime objective of a young man. Two routes to success lie open to him—the scholastic one leading to civil service or professional posts and a career in a craft leading to trade. The resources and qualities seen as being necessary for success have already been described above.

In Western literature the middle classes are differentiated from the lower, modern societies from traditional, by their orientation towards the future rather than the present. Middle class persons and those of modern societies have a belief in their possible advancement, they can empathise other roles, they plan for their future and imagine that they can control events. The lower classes and men of traditional societies are present-oriented, things happen to them over which they have no control and in consequence they are apathetic, impulsive, lacking in self-respect. But this stereotype of the lower classes, often applied by writers indiscriminately to those in the slums of Western industrial cities and in the shanty towns of the Third World capitals, seems quite inapplicable to the Yoruba. At the very bottom of the social ranking one may find those who have ceased to strive for advancement; but for the majority the hope of self-improvement is dominant. Yet many specific attitudes do reflect those cited in Western literature. Thus the illiterate Yoruba father's emphasis on obedience and regularity of school attendance contrasts with the literate father's emphasis on helping his children with their lessons. Yet surely the difference here reflects not a difference in achievement motivation but in the resources available to the parent. The literate parent *can* help his children with their lessons; the illiterate cannot. The latter cannot be expected to understand the educational system and so to manipulate it to his advantage; he will feel shy of approaching his children's teachers. Again one may clearly plan one's career through schools into the bureaucracies; the qualifications and resources needed and the rewards obtained at each stage are clearly known. But the craftsman cannot similarly plan his future as a successful trader; he may work hard but capital availability and investment opportunities arising, for instance, from sudden changes in the prices of cocoa and imported goods, from the winning of a valuable contract through patronage, cannot be predicted, only hoped for. Family limitation is usually seen, in the West, as a planned activity in contrast to the unrestrained birth of children. Many Yoruba now realise that they cannot educate a large number of children and that family limitation is a prerequisite for assuring their children of at least a modest future. But equally a man may consciously increase the size of his family by taking more wives, in order to enhance his prestige and hence benefit his trade and ultimately bring advantage to his children. In other words one may aspire to powerful or prestigious positions through the manipulation of either modern or traditional values; and many Yoruba can be observed engaging in this process. Witness the manner in which a politician takes a chieftaincy title to enhance his status, or an unsuccessful trader takes one to compensate for failure. Thus an apparent orientation to present opportunities rather than to long-term planning, to traditional rather than modern values, may reflect not so much basic differences in personality or achievement motivation as a logical response to the opportunities and resources available to the individual. A change in the nature of the latter will not be nullified by apathy but may be expected to produce specific attitudes appropriate to the new situation.

In the traditional Yoruba town, chief and trader, craftsman and poor farmer all lived in close proximity in the compounds of their descent groups. Each descent group had certain cultural attributes; its interests rivalled those of other groups and similar conflicts of interest divided town from town, ethnic group from ethnic group. To the Yoruba therefore the primary division of his society was in terms of descent. Members of his own compound would obviously form the core of his personal network, and maternal and affinal relationships would tend to lie within the local community. These patterns continue to the present and there must be few Yoruba who cannot trace a fairly close relationship with a person of power or wealth, either in traditional or modern spheres of activity. Any distinctions which the Yoruba may now make corresponding to the us/them dichotomy thus tend to be along ethnic rather than socio-economic lines, for although their social networks are no longer bounded by the local community, in transcending it they embrace persons of predominantly local origin. Terms such as *mękunnu*, *talaka* and *olowo* are variously used to differentiate persons within the local community and in the social network. And as we have seen, the majority of persons see both themselves and most others as *mękunnu* —ordinary folk.

The view of Yoruba society as homogeneous is clearly unrealistic inasmuch as the educated élite is not only very wealthy, but lives in a style both very different and physically segregated from the rest of the population. The distinction is perceived by the latter though there is little consensus in the terms used to describe the former. They are seen as rich, powerful, big men. The stress is clearly on their occupancy of positions of political power rather than on their control of entrepreneurial activity. Crudely, the dichotomy is between government and ruled, and not between employers/capitalists/bourgeoisie and workers. For most larger business enterprises are either foreign or state-controlled. The government is certainly seen as parasitic upon the masses though the exact form and source of its revenues are not easily understood by the labourer or farmer. But attitudes towards the government are ambivalent. Collectively its members are responsible for the economic development in which all have shared. Individually they have gained their present position through ability and hard work. But those in the lower half of the social hierarchy have been increasingly experiencing a decline in living standards as inflation exceeds increases in wages or cocoa prices and they are growing more aware of the slight chances that their own children have of getting a secondary education and a commensurate job. The solution perceived lies in the increase of opportunities—the creation (by the government) of more jobs; the provision of loans to craftsmen and traders; the raising of wages or of the cocoa price paid to the farmers, with the resultant increase in the amount of money circulating and enabling more men to find secondary school fees. The opposition between government and masses is thus expressed in terms of the government's increasing restriction of the benefits of power to its members, their immediate families and clients, whilst the masses seek increased opportunities, analogous to those of traditional society, to participate in those benefits either through access to positions of power or through patronage. These themes will be expanded in the following section in discussing forms of protest.

In arguing that one should study the manner in which people see their own society rather than imposing a specific and rigid set of alien categories, one recognises that every individual has his own world-view, determined by his own peculiar experiences in childhood, in his past and present occupational history. And whilst social interaction tends to produce consensual attitudes and values one would expect marked differences to appear between classes, socio-economic categories, ethnic groups and the like. In fact one of the stated purposes of the research upon which this monograph is based was to discover changes in perception due to wage employment and urban migration. In the event I have generalised as though all Yoruba shared a common set of attitudes and beliefs. Four factors account for this stance. First, I have interpreted my contribution to the research project to be the provision of a generalised account of Yoruba stratification to act as a foil to the accounts of any two junior colleagues of the localities in which they worked. Second, the data on attitudes used in this monograph are in fact confined largely to the poorer urban workers; only a few farmers were included (and these were resident in or near the town) and no highly educated men were in the 1971 sample (though such men were included in my pilot study interviews of 1968). Third, within this limited category, systematic differences in attitude could not be discovered. On a number of items responses fell into two broad categories, often of a yes-no character. But no clear correlation between sets of attitudes emerged. A probable reason for this lies in our choice of questions. We avoided many questions where it seemed likely that every respondent would give the same answer, e.g. a question on the legitimacy of entrepreneurial profits. The question on the desirability of self-employment produced an overwhelming response in favour which was interesting in itself but unhelpful in discriminating between categories of persons. In selecting two values or attitudes each of which seemed likely to be supported, we sometimes chose pairs which were seen by my respondents not as alternatives but as complementary. Thus hard work and patronage are both necessary to success and in particular hard work without patronage is fruitless. The explanations given of the responses to the initial question do much to clarify the meaning of the response and constitute the more valued product of the questionnaire. Fourth, I believe it is highly likely that the lack of observed systematic differences, between for instance employees and self-employed, was due not so much to our faulty instruments as to the non-existence of such differences. The rural or traditional origin of respondents, the previous craft apprenticeship of so many factory workers, their aspiration to return to self-employment, the short period during which they have been wage earners, all militate against the emergence as yet of any clear distinction in attitudes. In an open society there will be far greater homogeneity than in a closed one. Nevertheless our data do indicate, as one would certainly expect them to, a growing disillusion and dissatisfaction among the poor with the government, whilst the more literate and the wealthier persons are satisfied with the existing structure of inequality.

Attitudes or actions; acquiescence or protest

I have described the attitudes of Yoruba towards social inequality and have shown their probable origin in traditional patterns of values and in the past and present experiences of individuals. But are these attitudes reflected accurately in men's actions? The distortion possible in the use of questionnaires is too well known to require elaboration. My own defence here is that the attitudes which I have cited from questionnaire responses recur frequently in informal daily conversations and interviews. But again, the attitudes cited are generalised statements; are they upheld in some situations more than in others? Are there occasions when behaviour seems to belie the values overtly stated? The brief examination below of modes of protest recently adopted by the Yoruba explores this possible discrepancy.

The descriptions of actions can be made at two different levels. One might adopt a case history approach, that of situational analysis; one would here present the actor's view of a given situation—for instance, an opportunity to send his son to secondary school—noting the information available to him and the perceived outcomes of various courses of action, given his resources, his access to patrons, the likely responses of others, and so on. One could amplify this picture by including the viewpoint of other actors involved in the same situation—the schoolboy himself, his mother and other relatives. One would note the arguments used to validate or justify each action. This I believe to be an extremely valuable approach which merits adoption in future studies. It does lay one open to a charge that the examples selected are not typical. The alternative is to generalise grossly about behaviour, as I have done here. Thus the statistical data showing the number of children in schools of varying types reflects the decision of countless parents; similarly the reasons given for these decisions—the lack of money, the values attached to education, the likelihood of a good job—have been summarised.

Actions may be categorised broadly by the degree to which they imply an acceptance or a rejection of the perceived structure; and in the latter case by the expression of rejection in protest against the structure or in withdrawal from the society. The ego-oriented cognitive map, as I have described it, describes to the individual actor the world as it is; he uses it to calculate and evaluate most of his everyday actions. He operates within the pattern of constraints which restricts his behaviour, rather than attempts to alter that pattern. To express it in another idiom, he plays according to the rules of the game rather than tries to change the rules. Most of the attitudes and values described in this monograph are those appropriate to the cognitive map.

Withdrawal

If one perceives one's society as a closed one with routes of social mobility barred and the distribution of rewards illegitimately favouring the superior groups, one's reaction is to attempt to change the system. If, however, one has an image of an open society one's own failure to achieve high status is the fault not of the system but of oneself and is reflected not in opposition to those ranked above one but in envy and jealousy. The continuing prevalent belief in witch-craft and sorcery even among educated Yoruba is evidence of this type of response. Thus Fadipe (1970) writes in his social anthro-pology doctorate thesis: 'Although I have not been a first hand witness, the circumstances in which some instances of the various forms of *oogun* (medicine) have been brought to my notice are such as to make one take the risk of describing them as well authenti-cated' (p. 286). Again an ordained Christian priest studying at the University of Ibadan asserted in a little pamphlet his belief in the forces of evil such as witchcraft; for him his Christian belief and practice were a surer protection against this evil than any traditional means (Omoyajowo, 1965). The various modes of extra punitive explanation of failure commonly adopted by the Yoruba—from the evil machinations of others to one's ill luck in not finding a patron—do not reflect on one's own personal inadequacy nor on the structure of society, both of which one could by one's effort attempt to change; they are the effects of chance or of other persons, neither of which one can control.

One mode of withdrawal is to live in a world of fantasy. One form of this is a belief that one will be rewarded in a future world beyond the grave where the rich may be humbled and the poor exalted. However, in the traditional Yoruba conception of 'heaven' men adopt the same statuses as they hold on earth—the chief continues to be a chief. Although much of Christian doctrine refutes this view, we have very little information about the teaching actually imparted from the pulpits of Yoruba churches. How far, for instance, do the relatively ill-educated priests and catechists tell their flock to endure hardship and frustration in this world in order to earn merit in the next? And how far does their congregation believe them? Alternatively one's fantasies may relate to changed conditions in the present life—a lucky break will suddenly change one's fortunes. The Yoruba craftsman and petty trader often sounds like Mr Micawber 'waiting for something to turn up'; a common motto on lorries reads 'No condition is permanent'. A poor Yoruba man who suddenly acquired thousands of pounds would have little difficulty in adopting the role and behaviour of a wealthy trader—he sees such men daily. (The butt of the satirists is the rich illiterate trader who attempts to imitate the Western styles of the educated élite.) But what we define as fantasy, inasmuch as the statistical chances of the changed situation ever occurring seem so remote, may to the Yoruba man seem quite a reasonable hope, for almost all the affluent and successful men around him *have* risen in this way. In anticipating that an opportunity will one day be presented to him, the Yoruba man maintains himself in a state of readiness by generally upholding the norms of his society, thus creating a favourable impression among others, and specifically by maintaining his relationship with those who might offer him the benefits of their patronage.

There are a few who do seem to withdraw from their society. These are the adherents of the numerous small *aladura* sects who follow usual occupations during their working hours but spend much of their leisure time congregated with their prophet. These small Yoruba sects have received little attention from sociologists, though some such congregations in Ghana have been vividly described (Baeta, 1962). But Soyinka's (1964) satirisation of Brother Jero gives a picture of one such prophet operating at Victoria Beach, Lagos, which contrasts with the description of the successful and highly organised Cherubim and Seraphim church given by Peel (1968). Members of these small sects usually wear simple white robes emphasising equality among them; many non-members have in conversation contrasted these little congregations with the established churches where Sunday services are merely an occasion for the rich and powerful to display their status—clad in their richest gowns, they arrive in big cars and occupy the front pews.

In 'class' societies, whether industrial or peasant, the 'poor but honest' syndrome is often encountered. A hierarchy of moral worth is constructed so that the poor—who have upheld the norms of their society—are at the top whilst the rich—who have gained their wealth by dishonest means—are ranked below them. In the extreme, one may substitute this ranking for that posed upon inequality of power or wealth, though those poor who claim to make this substitution continue to defer overtly to the powerful. Alternatively the two modes of ranking can be added so that the 'scores' of the corrupt rich are similar to those of the lowest poor; an impression of equality within the community is thus fostered, perhaps promoting its greater solidarity against other like communities or the outside world. This syndrome does not however seem prevalent among the Yoruba. Community cohesion is maintained by ethnicity rather than by a myth of equality. Gossips are quite willing to tell one how the rich achieve their position by rather shady moves—perhaps by bribing an official in order to obtain a contract—but these do not seem to be held by them to be too morally reprehensible. Again, the term 'long legs' is used to describe the man whose access to highly placed patrons yields its rewards; but though it is heard in pejorative contexts it describes rather than condemns the activity. One is envious of the man with 'long legs' rather than disapproving of his apparent moral standards or of the structure of society which gives him certain advantages denied to others. One condemns the present-day rich for restricting their benefits to their own families and friends; but it is quite fortuitous that a humble man is able to establish that chain of relationships which links him to the powerful patron who, by a single action, ensures his success.

Violent action

The foregoing pages have presented a picture of the Yoruba both accepting his society as highly competitive but legitimate and attempting to manipulate it to his own ends. Verbalised attitudes towards protest tend to confirm this. When asked, in structured interviews and questionnaires, how they would articulate their complaints against the government, literates tended to say that they would write to the newspapers. The amount of social criticism expressed in the Nigerian press is relatively limited though it has markedly increased in recent years; however the press has remained comparatively free throughout the post-independence period and under the military regime. The less-educated respondents say that they will approach powerful and well-placed men with their complaints. Absent from these responses is any suggestion that men might organise collectively to further their interests. One might argue that these responses were gained during the period of military rule when political parties were banned; but it is surprising that none even mentioned the possibility of such political activity. More plausible is the explanation that parties were seen not as collections of persons of like interests but as vast factions with ties of patronage maintaining the links between the leadership, the MPs, the local élite of wealthy traders, downwards to each humble citizen. The ban on party political activity and the increasing inability of local chiefs and traders to act as middlemen between the government and the masses contributed to a high rate of apathetic responses from the poorer respondents—there was nothing that they could do to bring their views before the government. Implicit in these attitudes is a belief that one's leaders are reasonable men who will listen and attend to the complaints of their people. This is probably a traditional attitude. In a period of unrest at the University of Ibadan, students marched to the Vice-Chancellor's house in the middle of the night; he dismissed them brusquely for disturbing his sleep and so raised the temperature of the crisis. (On the next day police broke up the student mob, killing one undergraduate.) Several Yoruba faculty members in conversation argued that the Vice-Chancellor ought to have behaved like an *ọba* who would understand that such a protest indicated deep discontent, and mollify the crowd with promises of full discussion as soon as day broke; he would not have chastised his people for troubling him but would have thanked them for their action. An *ọba* is described as a bad ruler if rioting breaks out during his reign; his role is to conciliate and violence represents failure. Thus planned violence is not seen by the Yoruba as a regular means by which one may coerce an opponent (Gurr, 1970).

Yet there have been countless outbreaks of violence in Yoruba towns during the present century. Some of these were confined to specific local communities whilst others, such as the Agbekoya movement and general strikes which will be discussed below, transcended community boundaries but involved specific social and economic categories.

British penetration of Yoruba country was substantially peacefu save for the armed resistance of the Ijebu in 1892. The imposition of tax in 1918, too, occasioned little violent protest. The outbreaks which did occur—the Ijemo rebellion among the Egba and the Iseyin riots—both seem to have been associated with a redefinition of the authority of local chiefs. In several Yoruba towns from the 1930s onwards, literate *ọba* had to flee hurriedly in face of the combined opposition of both their chiefs and the mass of the people who felt that they were departing too radically from the traditional role of the *ọba* and abrogating to themselves too much authority. But each such protest was confined to a single kingdom, though the pattern of events was widely replicated.

Self-employed craftsmen and traders have little opportunity for collective action. Their guild organisation is used to settle disputes among members but has no effective legal sanctions and thus relies on the consensus of its members. Members are competing with one another and, in increasing the number of apprentices taken for their own immediate profit, they merely intensify later competition. Combination between traders or craftsmen to facilitate a more rational use of resources is extremely rare. Ideally the complaints of an apprentice against his master should be heard in the guild meeting and probably are. Collective action by apprentice journeymen or even employers such as the drivers employed by taxi owners is not contemplated because the masters are seen as the patrons who will one day enable one to become self-employed. The apprentice hopes for a gift of tools; the taxi driver hopes that his loyalty will be repaid when his successful master will enable him to purchase over an extended period one of his poorer vehicles.

By a collective withdrawal of their services the self-employed can ventilate their grievances. Thus Ibadan taxi drivers have gone on strike against the oppressive actions of the police in demanding bribes and their rigid procedures devised to limit tax evasion. Owners and drivers are at one over these issues, though the punishments and hardships fall more heavily on the drivers. At times the resistance has led to bloodshed and death. The public inconvenience (Ibadan's bus service is poor)—to civil servants as much as to others—has led to the government acceding to some of the taxi men's demands. In other situations, however, traders have been unable to protest against pricing or licensing policies of government or manufacturers because of the internal differences in their scale of operations. The wealthier traders are likely to lead their guilds and the poorer ones are, in many cases, dependent upon them. The rich are better able to exploit monopolistic situations and to gain favoured access to the government or the supplying firms to the detriment of the small trader. Boycotting activity by the latter merely harms them whilst increasing the business of their bigger rivals (Williams, 1974).

Rural protest

Outbreaks of violence in the rural areas around Ibadan had occurred in the 1950s. Farmers had protested against the cutting out of their aged and diseased cocoa trees on the grounds that they continued to yield a crop and the compensation offered to them was too low. Again, when Adegoke Adelabu—the populist leader who supported the claims of the Ibadan against other Yoruba ethnic groups and appealed in particular to the artisans, small traders (the *mẹkunnu*) rather than to the wealthy and educated—was killed in a car accident in 1958 there was a sudden wave of rioting both in Ibadan town and in the rural area (Post and Jenkins, 1973). In the latter, local government tax collectors fled and their houses were burned. The Agbekoya (farmers shall not suffer) movement however was much more widespread and sustained than those earlier outbreaks, although the degree of co-ordination between activity in different areas is very unclear (Ayoola Report, 1969; Beer, 1971; Williams, 1974).

In October 1968 a large crowd in Oyo besieged the local government council offices and successfully demanded the release of tax defaulters; they later moved to the divisional office and protested to the sole administrator against the increased taxes and rates. In December a similar protest ensured the release of other detained tax defaulters. In October too some men petitioned the military government about tax increases which they felt were too heavy in view of the poor cocoa harvest; they received no reply to their petition. In the next month a large crowd marched on two occasions to the palace of the Olubadan to protest; in a clash with the army at Mapo Hall, the council offices, ten civilians were killed and eleven wounded. In December similar incidents occurred in several Yoruba towns. The Odemo of Ishara, a literate *ọba* and erstwhile politician who had frequently been assailed by his people during his reign, was attacked in his house and his car was destroyed; the mob alleged that he had gone to a neighbouring town to arrange for the army to enforce tax collection—he had in fact visited Chief Awolowo to seek advice on the mitigation of tax. In Egba Division, Ijebu Igbo and once again in Oyo there were like incidents. In spite of the common pattern—protests against the arrest of tax defaulters, attacks on chiefs and local government officials—there seems to have been little co-ordination between the several incidents; each was apparently locally spontaneous although the news of success in one area probably stimulated activity in the others. The government halted its tax collecting and appointed a commission of enquiry chaired by Mr Justice Ayoola. The violence subsided for several months, though in February 1969 the *ọba* of Ogbomosho was killed in his palace.

In April the commission reported, finding:

(1) That the disturbances referred to in the terms of reference occurred against a general background of tax agitation.

(2) That the Tax Agitation developed, when, against a background of economic depression and bad harvest, it came to the knowledge of the low income group that they were being asked by the State to pay some additional levies in one form or the other, all demanded together; namely, (*i*) increased water rates (in some places), (*ii*) the National Reconstruction Levy, (*iii*) the State Development contribution.

(3) That the Agitation was not inspired by anybody or group of persons, but was a spontaneous reaction by the low income group to the new measures aforementioned.

(4) That the Agitation quickly gained ground and subsequently resulted in the formation of various Tax Movements spread over the State, and that the Movements have similar objectives, hold regular meetings, and are now drifting towards a type of confederation.

(5) That the agitation has as its objectives demands for reforms in the spheres of Local Government and Taxation; the Movements make no secret of their existence and objectives.

(6) That there are general complaints practically all over the State concerning:

(*i*) The unsuitability of the Sole Administratory system as a means of running the affairs of Local Government.

(*ii*) The exclusion of the Obas, Chiefs and local men from participation in the running of local affairs, thereby shutting them off from knowledge as to how their taxes are spent.

(*iii*) Constant and rampant loss and theft of council funds, with no apparent punishment of offenders.

(*iv*) Corruption and high-handedness of some Tax Officials and other Council officials, which appear to go unpunished.

(*v*) Failure on the part of Local Government Councils to provide amenities for their respective areas.

(*vi*) Ignorance of local people as to how Local Government funds are spent.

(*vii*) The defects in Tax Structure and Administration with reference to:

    (*a*) Tax level

    (*b*) System of Assessment

    (*c*) System of collection.

(7) That the Nigeria Police, owing to shortage of personnel and insufficient equipment, had considerable difficulty in forestalling and checking mass lawlessness and riots, and that this facilitated the riots in some areas.

(8) That the Nigerian Army had to assist the Police in the maintenance of general law and order during the disturbances, although the Police is better suited for maintenance of civilian peace.

(9) That the general economic condition of the low income group needs improvement: this can be achieved *inter alia* by the provision of increased social amenities in rural areas, and deliberate efforts to raise their earning capacity.

(10) That if the economic condition of the farmers had been better, and particularly if the cocoa producers' prices for the current year had been higher than they were, the tax capacity of the masses would have readily borne the existing tax level and there would have been no mass agitation. A positive way out therefore is to increase the earnings of the masses as a means of rendering them able to fulfil their civic obligations.

(11) That the various attacks on council officials arose partly as a result of the poor image which many of them had cut in the eyes of the local public by their malpractices and partly because the agitation was aimed at refusing to pay the increased levies which the officials were out to collect. They suffered attacks in the process.

(12) That many areas, particularly the rural areas, have at present no adequate machinery for the maintenance of law and order: there are not sufficient police stations nor Police Posts: the gap

created by the abolition of the Local Government Police Force has not been filled, and this weakened the enforcement of Law and Order.

(13) That many roads in the rural areas are in poor condition, thereby reducing the economic activity of farmers, and rendering them poorer.

(14) That existing Tax Assessment Committees, due to their lack of knowledge of local people, have no adequate means of making fair assessments and they consequently resorted to arbitrary assessments, which annoy the people.

(15) That the present system of payment of tax and other levies among the low income group works hardship in that the various payments required of them are not staggered as to time of payment over different periods. This made the demands onerous and repulsive.

(16) That owing to the absence of adequate security measures, many council officials were unwilling to return to their desks in the remote areas and consequently the work in some council areas had come to a stand-still, and the uninformed took this as 'VICTORY FOR THE MASSES'.

(17) That there is a general feeling among the Ọbas and Chiefs that they have not been allowed to participate in the running of local affairs and that their traditional dignity had been reduced: some of them are therefore lukewarm towards administrative problems.

(18) That there is need for education of the masses in relation to civic obligations and rights. This can be undertaken by the Ministry of Information through the dissemination of vernacular literature and pictures.

The commission recommended the overhaul of the local government system, improvements in tax collection, and economic measures to raise incomes. The government accepted these general pleas and slightly reduced the water rate, but refused to lower the flat rate of income tax to the thirty shillings demanded by the farmers. Within a few weeks violence re-occurred as farmers again refused to pay taxes and attacked and ambushed police and army units sent to restore order. The climax of the movement came in September 1969 with an attack on Ibadan jail to release by force all tax detainees. At this point Tafa Adeoye, an illiterate and poor farmer, emerged as the leader of the Ibadan insurgents. It was apparent that a greater co-ordination existed within the Agbekoya movement. Paramilitary operations were led by the hunters and over wide areas committees were formed to administer the villages from which the *bale* and other local government officials had fled. In October Chief Awolowo, Federal Commissioner of Finance, dramatically intervened, walking for several miles through the bush to meet Tafa Adeoye. Nine months earlier he had been condemning the riots and urging people to pay their taxes, a viewpoint which the *Nigerian Tribune* had continued to uphold in its condemnation of the Agbekoya. In mid-October the Western State government reduced the flat rate of income tax to £2, pronounced an amnesty for all tax defaulters, and asserted that the rural population would not be taxed without their consent to provide amenities in which they could not share. The government also set up a farmers' society in which Adeoye and other Agbekoya leaders participated; previous farmers' organisations sponsored by the government had been dominated by the wealthy farmers and traders.

All the evidence points to a movement led and supported by the poorer farmers—those who held land but could not afford to hire labour and so expand their production. On such men the high level of taxes and rates bore heavily in times of poor cocoa harvests. From the outset the erstwhile politicians of Ibadan became involved, first as their support was sought by rural leaders and later as they saw in the insurrection an opportunity to revive their own flagging popularity. Awolowo's move was seen by the cynical as an attempt to win mass support, should the end of military rule again provide the opportunity for national leadership. The Ibadan politicians added to the farmers' demands a call for a separate state (corresponding to the former Oyo province) but the Agbekoya leaders asserted that this was of no concern to the farmers, only to the élite who sought the new positions of power thus created. In supporting the government Adeoye suddenly became rich—the owner of a three-storey house and an American car. Henceforth he seems to have become a pawn of the government and politicians, and eventually schisms among the farmers together with conflicts of interest between them and the political factions led to Adeoye renewing his opposition to the government in the villages and to his arrest and detention in September 1970.

Whilst the violence in Ibadan seems to have been centred in those areas most affected by the cutting out of diseased cocoa trees in the early 1950s, sporadic outbreaks occurred and continued to occur throughout Yoruba country; though in the relatively prosperous Ondo province the main demand was not tax reduction but a raising of the cocoa price.

Two features emerge from a study of the Agbekoya movement. First, the objectives of the farmers and their leaders were essentially limited—to issues of tax—and once their demands were met by the release of detainees and eventually by the lowering of income tax rates and the abolition of several other noxious levies, the violence subsided. Second, although the farmers were undoubtedly aware of their interests, their attitudes were conciliatory; they first petitioned the government and traditional chiefs and later, when the government seemed deaf to their protests and the chiefs allied to and dependent upon the government, they sought to coerce them in dramatic fashion. Their aims were not a revolutionary restructuring of Yoruba society. Nevertheless the farmers were substantially successful in their rebellion. Their taxes were reduced as an immediate consequence of their activity; the federal government in January 1973 announced an overhaul of the marketing board system to enable the farmers to receive a greater proportion of the proceeds of their crop.

Industrial action

Industrial protest in Nigeria has a long history; the first recorded strike was in 1886. In 1897 the governor, to effect economies in public spending, was preparing to cut wages and increase working hours. Three thousand artisans and labourers in the Public Works Department struck and within two days the salary cuts were abrogated and a rearrangement of the working week gave the strikers an extra half day's leisure. This action seems to have been a spontaneous outburst by threatened workers and with their success peace was restored (Hopkins, 1966). The civil service union was founded in 1912 and in the following decades others followed, notably the powerful unions of railwaymen and teachers. Many strikes are recorded (Hughes and Cohen, 1971).

After the Second World War the Labour government in Britain promoted the development of trade unions; expatriate officials of the colonial Labour Department were actively engaged in founding and establishing new unions (Ananaba, 1969; Yesufu, 1962). Some

PI—H

observers have interpreted these moves not merely as necessary steps towards industrial democracy but as an attempt to channel the protests of the poor into specifically industrial rather than political action. Many of the large expatriate companies resisted unionisation arguing that the joint consultative committees were quite effective in establishing a dialogue between management and workers. However these firms now have well-organised unions which have had considerable success in bargaining with the management according to well-established procedures; it is often the firms with Asian management which lack them, political activity among their semi- and un-skilled workers usually being punished by dismissal. Nigerian unions usually are 'house unions'. Members of some—railwaymen, civil servants and teachers for instance—are dispersed throughout the country though they have but a single effective employer, the government; in other cases all members of a firm belong to a single union irrespective of their trade or occupation. In the inter-war years some of the leadership of workers' movements was provided by the Western-educated intellectual élite though their attitudes towards militant action were usually highly ambivalent; some men, Wallace-Johnson for example, established links with European communist movements. A Trade Union Congress was formed which gained strength during the Second World War; in 1946 it became affiliated with the NCNC and in 1950 united with other large trade union bodies to constitute the Nigerian Labour Congress; a precipitately-called national strike ended disastrously for the workers. In the past two decades the Nigerian labour movement has been divided into two or more factions; some adhere to the western WFTU, others to the communist IFCTU. Much of the finance of the unions comes from overseas and not from the levies of the workers. Whilst many individual union branches are internally well organised, efficient and successful in winning benefits for their workers, the rank and file tend to have little respect for the higher echelons of union leadership; they see their leaders engaged in continual competition for external funds from which are financed not only their salaries and perquisites but also scholarships for study abroad which will lift them out of the labour movement; they are seen as career opportunists. Accounts of industrial unrest are thus apt to vary widely according to the degree to which they are based upon the reports of the union leadership or the workers on the shop floor.

A major national strike occurred in 1945; industrial violence was again precipitated in 1949 when police killed twenty-one striking Enugu coal miners and wounded fifty-one others. I describe here the two latest occasions of national industrial action—the strikes of 1964 and 1971. In September 1963 the factions of the trade union movement united, largely under the inspiration of the more radical United Labour Congress, to demand that the government institute an enquiry into wages, both in the public and private sectors. With the threat of a strike, a commission headed by Mr Justice Adeyinka Morgan was set up. In its own memorandum the Joint Action Committee recommended a minimum wage of £180 a year and an upper income scale varying between £500 and £960, thus doubling or trebling the wages of the lowest-paid and reducing by a third the salaries of those at the top. The Morgan Commission handed its report (1964) to the government in April—disclosing a recommendation of substantial wage increases—but it was a month before the latter published it without adding a white paper setting out its own proposals. The frustration caused by the expectancy and delay enabled the JAC to call for a general strike which was overwhelmingly supported. Pleas from the Prime Minister followed by threats of dismissal of all striking government workers produced no response; in fact the government's proposals to increase wages to levels well below those of the Morgan Commission intensified the workers' solidarity and increased support for the strike among all sections of the population. The strike was called off after two weeks when the government offered to hold negotiations with the trade unionists and private employers. As a result of these discussions the minimum wage rate for Lagos was fixed at £10 a month—compared with £12 recommended by the Morgan Commission and £9. 2s. 0d. originally offered in the government's eventual white paper (Melson, 1970; Woodis, 1972, pp. 152–7).

No general wage increases were awarded during the next six years though the demands made on the national economy by the Civil War and the rapid rise in the rate of inflation at the end of the decade were causing substantial hardship among the workers. The military government set up a commission headed by Chief Simeon Adebo, a senior civil servant with a widespread reputation for efficiency and integrity. With memories of the limited success of the Morgan Commission and of its castigation of the growing gap between rich and poor, expectations ran high. The united trade union leadership called for a minimum living wage of almost £120 a month but later reduced this to £48. 10*s*. 0*d*. It organised a public rally calling for an interim award; the Adebo Commission recommended in December an award of £2 a month for all workers earning less than £500 a year, backdated to April (Adebo Interim Report, 1970). This report too commented with asperity on the poverty of the workers when contrasted with the affluence of the rich. Coming in the Christmas season, the promise of an £18 bonus was joyfully received. Five days later the Commissioner of Labour, Chief Anthony Enahoro, announced that employers who had granted the cost of living awards in the past six years were not liable to pay the new award. Many firms—especially the Western expatriate-managed companies—had increased workers' wages but it was far from certain whether this has been ascribed to rising costs of living or increased productivity. Within each factory as Peace (1973, 1974b) describes, negotiations took place between management and workers' representatives. The Asian companies accepted the new award; but when the management of the more affluent firms refused to pay, the workers immediately went on strike, their local leaders being caught between loyalty towards their followers and a desire to retain the trust of the management. Officially strikes were still banned and police broke up many demonstrations; but they failed on other occasions to protect the management from rough treatment. Soon the loss of profits and possible damage to plant seemed far more costly than the new award and individually the managements capitulated, leaving the Enahoro ruling ineffectual. The strikes had spread from Lagos to other industrial centres and had received a wide measure of popular support. As the days passed the issue of the interim award broadened into a general attack on inequality and corruption in high places.

The final award of the Adebo Commission (Adebo Final Report, 1971) was disappointing to the workers; it gave them little further increase in wages and only minimally affected the 'colonial' income structure. Yet it was received without protest. Some workers argued that the Commission had succumbed to government pressure in muting its social criticism and confirming the existing patterns of inequality. Trade union branch leaders felt that further strike action might jeopardise the strong bargaining position in which they believed their earlier success had placed them.

In their different ways the Agbekoya movement and the strikes had immediate success—taxes were reduced, wage increases granted.

Both illustrate the vulnerability of government and of many employers; the former cannot contain the rural militancy; its activities are almost completely halted by a nationwide strike, though the indigenous economy continues as lorries bring food to the urban markets; highly capitalised expatriate companies find wage increases but a minimal addition to their overall costs. But equally, these protests have a high degree of spontaneity. The Agbekoya movement grew as tax collection started and when formal protests to the government and chiefs seemed to go unheeded. The government's maladroit handling of its commissions' recommendations   led in 1964 and 1970-1 to an explosive frustration which the national trade union leadership was probably powerless to control, though quite ready to support. As recent debate (Berg & Warren, 1969; Cohen, 1971; Kilby, 1967, 1968, 1971; Weeks, 1968, 1971) shows it is not easy to evaluate the effectiveness of the trade union movements in obtaining wage increases in recent decades; they have been active in situations of bargaining and protest, but the position of the urban employees has not markedly improved. The unrealistic demands made by the union leadership before the Adebo Commission is suggestive more of a sudden attempt to gain the popularity of the workers than of a process of continual bargaining with government and employers in which strike action is advocated when negotiations fail.

The initial demands of the rebellious farmers and the strikers were precise and limited, but with their success, their criticisms of government maladministration became far more general, embracing issues which all the poor could support. (In fact a wage increase was widely welcomed by traders and independent craftsmen for they saw this as directly contributing to their own prosperity; they did not always see themselves as contributing towards the increase. Similarly an increase in the price of cocoa received by the farmers benefits the remainder of the poor.) Again, ethnic differences seem to have had no effect upon the course of industrial strikes. But, as Melson (1970) reports, whilst some trade union leaders supported the idea of a 'labour party' in mid-1964, within a few months they had reaffirmed their allegiance to the existing national, though ethnically based, parties. Thus in certain contexts economic interests may unite men irrespective of their primordial relationship; in others the patronage network of the political party remains a dominant instrument both for one's own personal advancement and for that of one's ethnic community.

In these protest movements, as in the questionnaire responses, one sees the government portrayed as a patron, hopefully benevolent but frequently capricious or selfish. The farmers sought to beg for a reduction of the tax liability; the factory workers saw in Chief Adebo a man who would plead their cause before the government and obtain for them just and ameliorating benefits. Absent from their analysis of the situation was an appreciation of the interests served by the rejection of their demands; or in other words of any incompatibility in the interests of the rich and poor beyond those of individual self-interest, each man seeking to advance himself at the expense of his neighbour.

Class consciousness

To the question, 'How do urban Yoruba perceive social inequality?' our answers have been largely descriptive of attitudes and values; we have endeavoured to explain these in terms of the concepts and propositions derived both from traditional Yoruba society and from the recent experiences of men and their families. But ultimately we reach the point when we ask how the urban Yoruba differ from other people either in a similar or a different economic position. In attempting to measure differences cross-culturally we are often obliged to introduce concepts which are alien to the subjects studied. Thus throughout this monograph I have been sparing in my use of class terminology; but I now return to the ethnocentric formulation of the initial problem—how far are the urban Yoruba developing a class consciousness? First, however, we must define both 'class' and 'consciousness'.

Marx opens the *Communist Manifesto*: 'The history of all hitherto existing society is the history of class struggles.' Yet classes really emerge only in the period of capitalism when they acquire a consciousness of themselves as such. Hobsbawm (1971) has outlined the classlessness of pre-capitalist society; legal and status distinctions between men overlie their economic stratification, the lower ranks are on one hand fragmented into groups with separate interests and on the other see themselves united as the 'common people' against the rich. Only with capitalism do economic interests become predominant. Historically the use of class terminology in the West developed only in the nineteenth century and the 'working class' or the 'dangerous classes' were used as much by the more affluent who feared the poverty of the urban masses as by the latter themselves

(Chevalier, 1973). As Briggs (1960) describes, the distinction between lower and middle class was cross-cut by another dividing the workers or industrial classes—all those engaged in manufacturing—from the idle, unproductive landowners. The concept of 'unemployment' developed in England towards the end of the century in respect of the industrial workers in textile factories and mines in the north, not of the casual labour of London.

The application of class terminology to a modern African society raises many difficulties. With the wide range of incomes and the association of affluence with education, an élite/mass distinction is relatively easy to draw. But within the former—often termed the national bourgeoisie—one may discern different interest groups. In the field of entrepreneurial activity one distinguishes on the one hand those who are directly employed by expatriate companies or who have their own business subsidiary to foreign firms and, on the other, the indigenous businessman who is competing against the foreign firms and seeks the protection of his government, readily espousing nationalist slogans. This entrepreneurial or true bourgeoisie is further distinguished from the much larger and more powerful 'comprador bourgeoisie' of civil servants and political leaders who may either bend their energies towards the maintenance of the dominance of expatriate commercial enterprise or may seek a more direct control of the economy of their country. Within this category one may also differentiate civil servants, members of the armed forces and police, and so on, each having their own sectional interests.

Opposed to the bourgeoisie, in radical discussion, are the peasants and workers, two categories which again seem unambiguous until we attempt to use them in Africa. Among the Yoruba farmers there are, as we have seen, few men completely without rights to land though many perform casual labour to earn some ready cash. A sizeable proportion grow cocoa and most market part of their food crops. A few farmers have substantial holdings of cocoa and these constitute a segment of the local élite of the provincial towns. 'Peasant' is no more precise a term in this context than is 'farmer'. Again, many writers assume that the working class is coextensive with wage earners and cite the number of persons so employed, i.e. half a million persons in Nigeria. But only a small proportion of these are employed in industry (and of these some are in white-collar jobs). Many are in fact employed in the public service as unskilled workers and can see little opportunity of raising their status; but the statistics include a large number of teachers, and clerks with career aspirations. (Included, too, are the higher civil servants!) Allen has recently argued (1972) that peasants and wage earners ought to be joined within the working class; for both categories are subject to capitalist forces and pressures, and with the continual migration between the rural area and modern towns many individuals pass successively from one category to the other. From his working class Allen excludes farmers who employ non-family labour (a distinction which does not seem very meaningful in the Yoruba situation) and he adds both petty traders who employ no labour and the lumpen-proletariat—persons without fixed occupation, beggars and criminals.

From this rather rigid classification a substantial category is excluded—the self-employed artisan or the trader with his apprentices, journeymen and few employees; the very category to which most Yoruba aspire to belong. A Soviet writer (Iskenderov, 1972) has recently termed these 'urban middle strata', including within them the intellectuals and some civil servants. He argues that the social heterogeneity of these groups leads to a variety of political positions, ranging from reaction to revolution. He notes that members of these middle strata are as poor as—or even poorer than—the proletariat of skilled and semi-skilled workers and can be expected to ally themselves with the workers. He concludes (p. 62):

> In many African countries, class formation is still in progress and distinctions between the classes and social groups are varied and changeable. But the recognition of this fact gives no ground to say that the Marxist–Leninist theory of classes and class struggle is inapplicable to the newly free African countries.

Given the difficulty which external observers experience in delineating significant social categories, it can hardly be wondered that these have on so many occasions little meaning to the members of them.

Marx, in his own writing, distinguished the 'class in itself', an observers' category, from the 'class for itself'—the subjective recognition of class. Miliband (1971, pp. 22–3) however has outlined four levels of class consciousness:

> A fairly accurate perception of class membership on the part of a particular individual; . . . a certain perception of the immediate interests of the class of which one is conscious of being a member; . . . a *will* to advance the interests of the class; and . . . a particular

perception of what their advancement requires, not simply in immediate but in more general, global terms.

The Yoruba, as we have seen above, are fully conscious of certain economic interests, lower taxes or higher wages for example, and these might be embraced within Miliband's second level. However, apropos of the third level, Miliband notes 'a worker who, though conscious of belonging to the working class, and of its interests, is primarily concerned to 'rise' above it, is not in this sense class conscious' (p. 23). This stricture would seem to bar almost all Yoruba urban workers from this level. The distinction made in the fourth level of class consciousness between 'immediate' and 'more general global' terms reiterates the Leninist distinction between 'trade union consciousness' emphasising bargaining within the existing structure of society, and the higher socialist consciousness which envisages a total transformation of society. Such class consciousness as might be ascribed to the Yoruba is clearly of the former type.

Lukács, says Hobsbawm (1971, p. 6) distinguished, further

> between the actual ideas which men form about class and which are the subject matter of historical study and what he calls 'ascribed' class consciousness. This consists of 'the ideas, sentiments, etc., which men in a given situation in life *would* have, *if they were able to grasp in its entirety* this situation, and the interests deriving from it, both as regards immediate action and as regards the structure of society which [would] correspond to those interests.'

Here the actor's interpretation of his situation is set against that of the external observer which is assumed, in terms of prediction, to be of greater validity. (See also Portes, 1971.)

Thus three problems are posed for us: first, the degree to which the interests of the Yoruba are expressed in terms of class, rather than of individual or narrow occupational interests; second, the level of consciousness displayed, ranging from an awareness of the interests to a planned intention to promote them; third, an evaluation against the judgment of outside observers. The answers to each of these will depend upon one's own definition and one's theoretical viewpoint in evaluating long-term strategies.

Marxists assert that true class consciousness can only develop within the proletariat. But as many have argued it is the upper strata which first develop a mode of class consciousness for they are not only aware of their privileged position but fear the violence of the deprived categories. However, rather than divide their society in class terms, they seek to unite it under vague ideological banners in which classlessness is asserted. They require no separate organisation to protect their privileges for they are defined in terms of power holding. The lower strata however must organise through new associations in order to further their own class interests—existing associations reflecting primordial unities are inadequate. Any ideology promoting the restructuring of the society is articulated through this organisation. But, ask the political activists, can such an organisation spontaneously develop among peasants and workers, or must it be introduced from without? (In practical terms, must one wait for the development of class leadership and class consciousness among peasants and workers before sparking off the revolution?) The social relationship between employer and employee is far more conducive to the establishment of collective organisation among the latter than are the relationships encountered in peasant society. Furthermore in an established industrial society it is conceivable that many members of the working class will be quite well educated, though in many cases self-taught. In peasant societies, both past and present, it is most unlikely that a man of great ability and leadership would remain a poor farmer; he may become a wealthy one. Again the African unskilled urban worker usually owes his status to his lack of education and his inability to succeed as a small entrepreneur. As the Agbekoya movement suggests, protest among poor farmers can arise with a high degree of local spontaneity, but the calibre of the local leadership is insufficient to maintain the integrity of the movement in face of attempts by rival political leaders to absorb and manipulate it. But in asserting that peasant and workers' movements depend upon middle-class leadership, a distinction is rarely made between the present occupation of the political leader and his social origins. He may be a lawyer, but he may yet come from a peasant, rather than an urban professional, home. Though occupationally mobile he strives for the interests of his natal group rather than escaping from it into the ranks of middle class society.

Finally, in spite of the fact that class consciousness may be poorly developed among the lower strata and that effective leadership within these strata is not likely to emerge, it nevertheless remains possible for a high degree of discontent to exist and for this to be exploited by leaders of other groups primarily for their own ends, with partial satisfaction of the demands of the poor, expressed in their own terms, being a recompense for their support.

Comparisons

There are obvious difficulties in measuring attitudes when the concepts employed in one's yardstick are alien to one's subjects. Thus it is not easy to give a precise answer to our question, 'How class-conscious are the urban Yoruba?' In general terms, however, the answer would seem to be 'not very'. They are aware of course of great differences in power and wealth; but the individual sees his own attainment of an enhanced status as lying in his own efforts rather than in collective action. An opposition of interests between the privileged and the masses is feebly articulated. No radical alternative structure of Yoruba society is postulated; and hence no one social category or group sees its mission in bringing about the changes. Are these attitudes peculiar to the Yoruba, deriving perhaps mostly from the concepts appropriate to their traditional society or are they encountered elsewhere in societies undergoing similar social and economic transformations? I believe that they are fairly general especially in those cities which are rapidly growing and have a high population of rural migrants and in those cities in which a high proportion are working as self-employed artisans or traders or in small enterprises—in the informal economy. In such cities we might make a further distinction between the old, decaying slums of the centre and the newly developed suburbs, albeit poverty-stricken shanty towns, though the patterns of urban growth appear to differ widely, as for instance between Latin America and Africa. Our criteria of recent immigration and informal economy do however embrace most of the large urban centres of the Third World, excepting only the industrial concentrations. They would embrace, too, many of the new industrialised Western nations as they existed a century ago. Thus Jones writes (1971, p. 327):

Nineteenth century London was a city of clerks and shopkeepers, of small masters and skilled artisans, of a growing number of semi-skilled and sweated outworkers, of soldiers and servants, of casual labourers, street sellers and beggars. But with the exception of some isolated communities on its periphery, it was a city virtually without a factory proletariat.

(In fact in 1851 only twelve factories employed more than 300 persons (p. 19).) These very words are equally applicable to mid-twentieth-century Lagos.

We are presented with apparently irreconcilable images of life in these so-called slums. Whilst some writers describe the apathy of their population, others refer to their achievement orientation; so the former stress the social disorganisation which prevails—men are incapable of forming organisations or even of maintaining stable marital unions; the counter view argues that these people do plan rationally, at least within the constraints placed upon their actions. Apathy and disorganisation have as their corollary aggression and unstructured violence; but others aver that it is safer to walk at night through these slums than it is in many American cities. Mangin (1967) argues that both images are correct, expressing different aspects of reality. He shows from answers to a questionnaire which he administered in a Lima *barriada* that individuals are capable of seemingly contradictory opinions; whilst four-fifths of the respondents agreed that 'the future looks blacker every day', an even greater majority accepted that 'a young man of today can have much hope for the future.' Again whilst one may accept that the attributes of apathy, disorganisation and violence characterise the most poverty-stricken areas of urban society, it is not always clear from the literature just what proportion of the population is so described. Thus Lewis (1968) differentiates between 'poverty'—measurable in any society in terms of income with corollaries of poor housing and sickness—and the 'culture of poverty', relating to a feeling of relative deprivation; he believes that the 'culture of poverty' embraces only that one-fifth of the urban population of the USA which is deemed statistically to be below the poverty line (p. 57). However, many authors would make the culture of poverty coterminous with poverty itself thus embracing almost the entire semi- or unskilled working population. Poverty however is defined by the more affluent members of the society—it is they who decide what is the minimum standard. (And such standards vary enormously across nations—poverty in the USA would equal moderate affluence in Lagos.) The depressing image of slum life comes from 'middle class' observers and reflects their guilt about the disparity of income and their fear of the latent violence which they see exists. It is they who coin such terms as 'lumpenproletariat', the 'dangerous classes'. They are terrified of the unstructured violence of the urban mob whether they see this as likely to spark off more general revolutionary movements or as an outcome of more organised forms of protest by skilled workers or artisans. Contrasting descriptions of the rationality of the actions of the poor, or their hopes and plans for achieving a better life, tend to come from social anthropologists and sociologists who have lived for substantial periods in the slums.

The dichotomy presented in the images of slum life has polarised inasmuch as each supports a rival political ideology and programme. At one extreme the characteristics of apathy, disorganisation and violence are attributed either to the moral weakness of individuals who have fallen to such levels or to the culture into which the young have been socialised. In either case, the 'cure' lies in altering those values either by individually uplifting reform or by education; when these people have learned to achieve, then they will be able to seize the opportunities presented to them; the poor will become integrated into 'middle class' society. On the other hand, if one portrays the poor as rational and achievement-oriented, then their hope for improvement lies in providing them with more opportunities; in other words in restructuring the pattern of distribution of rewards in the society and removing many of the existing constraints on social mobility, the affluent are asked to forgo some of their privileges. The image which one holds of slum society is thus inextricably interwoven with one's own political ideology.

Some descriptions of attitudes attributed to the poor have already been cited as a foil to the presentation of Yoruba values. More pertinent perhaps to our argument is the elaboration of the subculture of poverty by Oscar Lewis (1968, pp. 47–59). His original anthropological fieldwork in India and his later and highly popular descriptions of life in the slums of Mexico City, Puerto Rico and New York have earned for their author not only a widespread acceptance of his formulations but also a considerable distortion. Lewis argues that the culture of poverty can be traced across continents and in a variety of historical contexts. He associates it with a cash economy, with high rates of unemployment and under-employment of unskilled labour, with low wages, with a failure to provide social, economic or political organisation for the poor, with a bilateral kinship system and with a set of values in the dominant class stressing the accumulation of wealth and upward mobility whilst poverty is attributed to personal inadequacy and inferiority. He adds that it tends to develop in periods of rapid social change as when feudal structures are replaced by capitalist ones or in situations of colonialism and 'detribalization'. He specifically excludes from his culture the well-integrated tribal societies with subsistence economies (though desperately poor by our standards), Indian caste societies, Jewish communities because of their traditions of literacy and voluntary association, and perhaps socialist societies. However this would seem to leave most of the urban populations of Third World nations within his orbit. The culture of poverty 'represents an effort to cope with the feelings of hopelessness and despair which develop from the realization of the improbability of achieving success in terms of the values and goals of the larger society' (p. 49).

Its features are listed (pp. 51–3) as:

> The lack of effective participation and integration of the poor in the major institutions of the larger society . . . a minimum of organization beyond the level of the extended family . . . free unions or consensual marriages . . . a strong predisposition to authoritarianism . . . verbal emphasis upon family solidarity which is only rarely achieved because of sibling rivalry . . . a strong feeling of marginality, of helplessness, of dependence and of inferiority.

But Lewis emphasises that this refers to 'a sub-culture with its own structure and rationale, a way of life which is passed down from generation to generation along family lines' (p. 48). And he states (p. 50):

> There is a striking contrast between Latin America where the rural population long ago made the transition from a tribal to a peasant society, and Africa, which is still close to its tribal heritage. The more corporate nature of many of the African tribal societies, in contrast to Latin American rural communities, and the persistence of village ties tend to inhibit or delay the formation of a full-blown culture of poverty in many of the African towns and cities.

Two variables are cited in the latter quotation—the social characteristics of rural society and the ties between the urban migrant and his home; a third is raised in the earlier sentence—the recentness of urban migration. Of these Lewis places greatest stress upon the difference between the rural communities from which the migrants come. Other evidence to be cited below stresses the importance of migration.

Lewis's formulation of the culture of poverty has a number of elements which accord to a considerable degree with the more 'conservative' of political ideologies; and he has consequently been attacked by the 'liberals'. Thus Mangin (1967) argues that the poor share more values with the more affluent members of their own society than with the poor of culturally different societies. And from his own considerable knowledge of Lima and similar Latin American cities he catalogues the degree of organisation required to found the squatter settlements, and the subsequent associational activity within them, the degree of participation in national life and the low incidence of radical political activity. In discussing the same areas Portes (1972, p. 272) sets out three hypotheses which he finds supported by the data:

1. Inhabitants of these areas are, to a large extent, members of upwardly mobile sectors of the urban lower class. As such, they will recurrently engage in behaviour patterns that provide the fastest and most efficient way of securing socioeconomic rewards;

2. Though coming from lower educational levels, the general orientation of these people to life, and their interests and values, do not differ significantly from those of the more established urban middle classes;

3. Desperate political action, in the form of radicalism, is to a large extent absent; though frustrations of slum life are numerous, the strength and flexibility of individuals in these areas have often been underestimated.

He demonstrates (pp. 283–4) that where associational activity seems likely to lead to the desired results it is strongly developed.

The phenomenal world of immigrants and migrants alike shares three fundamental characteristics:

1. There is an individualistic ethic of promotion through personal effort. The crucial concern is not the collective progress for the poorer classes, but individual advancement *away* from them. As Mangin appropriately states, the dominant ideology of peripheral slum dwellers is very similar to the petty capitalism of nineteenth century small businessmen in England or the United States: work hard, save your money, outwit the state and vote conservatively if possible, but always in your own interest.

2. Such an ideology tends to place the blame for economic failure on the individual or on accidental circumstances rather than on the broader socioeconomic structure. The revolutionary

potential of frustrations is deflected to the extent that the focus of
blame is non structural. . . .

3. The absence of structural blame is closely linked with the
fact that the lower class migrant . . . does not feel himself entitled
to anything. Phenomenally, he perceives his presence in the city as
the single opportunity in life to improve his lot. . . The city which
offers the opportunity of upward ascent also sets its own hard
rules. The migrant's decision to come to the city . . . implies a tacit
acceptance of these rules.

Such attitudes are not peculiar to Third World slums. In a study of
workers in two Parisian automobile factories, Touraine and Ragazzi
(1961) distinguished the attitudes of men from rural areas, predominantly Bretons, and those who had grown up in the city and were
skilled workers, apprentices or professionals. They cite three possible
modes of adaptation to factory life: the passive adaptation to but
not identification with the new structure; the acquisition of working
class values; the desire for upward mobility with industrial work seen
as a means to an end. The questionnaire responses showed (pp.
109ff.) that the workers from the rural area saw their employment,
albeit unskilled, as a measure of their success, though they had
failed in not rising higher. They did not adopt the attitudes of those
workers who identified with the work situation. They were not blind
to the constraints on their upward mobility but they believed, more
than did the urbanised workers, that these could be surmounted; they
were more concerned with their personal advancement than with an
analysis of the total situation; they gave greater weight to personal
and chance factors likely to lead to their success. The rural workers
were more optimistic about the future of their children—a smaller
proportion felt that they would have the same occupation or life
style as themselves. The authors attributed this optimism not to the
comparative ignorance of the migrants but to their already established success in entering the urban economy. The 'rural workers'
seemed less concerned than 'urbanised workers' with job satisfaction; they sought higher salaries rather than improved conditions
of work. Most wanted to leave industrial employment to set up their
own business. They did not see their society as founded upon social
antagonism; they stressed socio-economic differences but not dichotomies as between boss and employee; they included within the
'working class' such men as civil servants, apparently defining it in

terms of income level rather than relationship to the means of production. When they went on strike it was simply for more pay and
not to enhance working class solidarity. These responses seem to
replicate almost exactly those of Lagos factory workers, and indicate
an adaptation to factory life of the third type—a desire for upward
mobility, corresponding to the values cited by Portes in respect of
Latin American shanty towns.

The historian of nineteenth-century London is less able to present
us with the image of society held by its 'outcasts'; the middle classes
were so much more literate. But Jones, too, emphasises the lack of
political radicalism among the poor (1971). In many of the London
suburbs a majority of the inhabitants were city born; and generally
these were poorer than the more recent immigrants. He stresses the
growing divide between rich and poor, as entrepreneurs no longer
lived over their workshops and maintained close ties of patronage
with their employees, but moved to new suburbs. The dominant
characteristic of London slum society was, however, the dependence
of the poor on casual labour—low paid and highly seasonal. And
because men relied so exclusively upon credit, they were restrained
from moving from their existing abode where they had an established network of relatives and friends, patrons and helpers, to other
areas where the economic opportunities might have been more
favourable. Jones stresses, too, the social distance between the artisan
and the unskilled labourer, the former ever striving for advancement
and fearful of slipping into the ranks of the latter. Thus the poor of
London lacked that 'working class-consciousness' which was developing among the factory workers of northern industrial towns; nor
had they memories of violent revolutionary action such as spurred
the poor of Paris to further activity. Outbreaks of violence there
were but these were ill-articulated protests and quickly subsided,
perhaps with the attainment of the most immediate goals. As Jones
notes, the poor saw their society divided vertically in terms of trade
rather than horizontally in terms of class.

The perception which the urban Yoruba have of their society
thus seems far from unique. From Latin America and Paris is
reported a similar emphasis on individual achievement, on the possibility of rising to heights of wealth and power; wage employment is a
means to this end and the migrant, in finding urban work, has surmounted his first obstacle. Rather than identify with wage employment, the migrant aspires to be his own master; he sees society as a

P I—H**

ladder up which individuals have risen to various levels of success;
he does not see an irreconcilable antagonism between rich and poor.
These are over-generalisations of course, because we have stressed
the growing hostility among urban Yoruba towards their govern-
ment. In the present study and those just cited a significant factor
is the rural origin of the town dweller; but the point made by
Touraine and Ragazzi is that it is success in settling into urban life
which is important—not the characteristics of rural life and values.
This would not seem to be at variance with the present findings, and
Portes makes the same implications. Thus the distinction which
Lewis draws between peasant society of Latin America and tribal
African society would seem to be irrelevant. Instead I would emphasise his statement that the culture of poverty is transmitted from
generation to generation; one would therefore expect to find it in the
older slums of the long-extablished cities and among the more stable
populations. One would least expect it in the recently created suburbs
of the rapidly growing Third World cities where a very high proportion of the population was born in the rural area. This does not mean
that, in the next generation when these slums are peopled by men
and women who were born and raised in them, many of the attitudes
of hope and achievement will not be replaced by those of frustration
and despair. But for the moment these cities are overwhelmingly
peopled by recent immigrants.

A second important factor is the nature of the economy. Figures
which stress the increase in wage earning, the rapid growth of the
manufacturing sector, obscure the fact that this growth is usually
exceeded by that of the urban population. That is to say, save in
industrial or mining centres, it is the proportion of the population
engaged in small-scale crafts, in petty trade, in services, which is
increasing. The dominant sphere of economic activity is this one
in which entrepreneurship and individual achievement are valued
and seen as a means to wealth and power. Wage employment is
viewed by the manual workers as providing a stepping-stone towards
this end; it is not perceived as dividing the population into antagonis-
tic classes.

Should one therefore view the description of traditional concepts
as irrelevant? This we must not do; for though current perspectives
may depend more on the present work situation and recent experiences, these are expressed largely in the idiom of traditional concepts.

Finally, this book stresses throughout the importance of studying the way in which the urban Yoruba see their own society—as against our own interpretation of their situation. But in emphasising the importance placed on individual advancement, the significance of the ego-centred cognitive map is demonstrated. The distinction made between this and the externalised analytical structure was described as a heuristic one. So many studies of social stratification in all parts of the world focus upon those elements which we have included within the analytic structure to the exclusion of those proper to the cognitive map. In the process some major themes in the perception of social inequality have been omitted.

Appendix

Interview schedule—pilot study 1968

Administered in Ibadan to 5 illiterate farmers, 10 illiterate or semi-literate artisans, craftsmen or petty traders, 5 wage labourers, 5 teachers and clerks, 5 university graduates.

1 (a) What are the most important differences found among Yoruba people?

Kini awọn iyato pataki ti o wa lerin awọn Yoruba?

(b) Are we all equal? How are we unequal?

Njẹ gbogbo wa dọgba? Ki lo fa aidọgba?

2 How would you describe yourself? To what group of people do you belong?

Bawo ni e ṣele ṣe apajuwe ara yin? Iru ọna wo ni ẹ wa?

3 What are the characteristics of the group you describe? What enables a man to belong?

Kini awọn nkan pataki ti ẹ mọ nipa awọn ọna ti ẹ ti ṣe apajuwe wọn? Kini ẹ mọ to le mu ki enia kan bọ sinu awọn ọna ti ẹ ti ṣe apajuwe?

4 Which group do you admire most; which do you despise most?

Ọna wo ni ẹ feran ju; ọna wo ni ẹ ko feran tabi ti ẹ fi oju tẹmbẹlu?

5 Are you satisfied with your position in life?

Njẹ ẹ ni itẹlọrun ninu ipo ti ẹ wa bayi?

6. What would you have liked to have been?

Kini nkan ti iwọ ibati da laye yi tabi ti iwọ iba ti ṣe?

7 What has hindered you from achieving this?

Kini awọn nkan ti o di yin lọwọ lati le da bi ẹ ti nfẹ?

8 Do you still hope to achieve your aims? How or by what means?

Njẹ ẹ ṣi ni ireti lati le da bi ẹ ti nfẹ? Ọna wo ni ẹ ro pe ẹlegba ki ẹ to le dabi ẹti nfẹ?

9 What would you like your children to be?

Kini ẹ nfẹ ki awọn ọmọ yin da?

10 What do you think that your children must do to achieve these aims?

Kini awọn nkan ti awọn ọmọ yin ni lati ṣe ki wọn to le da bi ẹ ti nfẹ?

11 Do you think that your children will be able to achieve these aims?

Njẹ ẹ ro pe awọn ọmọ yin le de awọn ipo wonyi ti ẹ ti sọ?

12 Do you want your child to be a farmer, tailor, labourer, primary school teacher?

Njẹ ẹ fẹ ki awọn ọmọ yin je agbe, tailọ, lebura, oluko ile-iwe alakọbẹrẹ?

13 Do you think it fair that a labourer should earn £8 a month and a graduate teacher earn between £60 and £200 a month?

Njẹ ẹ ro pe o dara ki awọn legura ma gba £8 l'ọsu ki awon ti o jade ni Unifasiti ma gba bi £60 tabi £200 l'ọsu?

14 What are the most important things that should be done to improve Yoruba society?

Kini awọn nkan pataki ti o yẹ lati ṣe ti yio mu ilọsi waju wa si ilẹ Yoruba?

15 What ought the government to do?

Njẹ o si awọn nkan ti o yẹ ki joọba o ṣe?

16 How can you make your views known to the government?

Bawo ni ẹ ṣe le mu ki ijọba o mọ ero ọkan yin lati le ṣe gbogbo awọn nkan ti ẹ ti ṣọ?

Questionnaire 1971 (abridged)

Administered to stratified samples in Ibadan and Agege, each containing 20 farmers, 20 craftsmen, 20 traders, 20 labourers, 20 factory workers (Agege only), 20 teachers and clerks.

1–7 Personal data: name, age, present residence, home town, years in Agege (for Agege respondents only), religion, present occupation.

8 Schooling: schools attended, levels/certificates obtained; why school not attended; why schooling terminated; who paid for schooling.

9–10 Parental data: number of wives of father; status of own mother; schooling, occupation, religion of father; number and education of respondent's siblings.

11–15 Occupational history: occupations followed; training received; help given in finding work.

16 Do you think you will continue this work until you retire or die?

Njẹ ẹ ro wipe ẹnyin yio maa ṣe iṣẹ yi lọ titi ẹ o fi simi iṣẹ di ọjọ iku nyin?

If 'yes' to 16.1.; if 'no' to 16.2.

16.1 Is there any other work you would like if you could get it? If so, what?

Njẹ nkan miran wa ti ẹ fẹ ti ẹ ba le ṣe?
Kini nkan naa?

16.2 What other work would you like?

Iṣẹ wo ni o tun wu nyin?

16.3 What would you need before you could start this job?

Kini ẹ nilo ki ẹ to le bẹrẹ iṣẹ yi?

16.31 Do you think that this work would bring you more money, or do you choose it because of some other satisfaction?

Njẹ ẹ ro wipe iṣẹ yi yio mu owo t'o pọ wọle tabi ẹni awọn itẹlọrun miran ti o mu nyin yan iṣẹ yi?

17 Is there any way in which you can get more money from your present job? How?

Njẹ ọna miran wa ti ẹ fi le ri owo t'o pọ si ninu iṣẹ nyin yi?
Ọna wo ni?

18 Children's education: age, education and occupation of each child; why did education terminate?

19 I expect that you would like your child(ren) to go to secondary school; will you be able to pay the fees yourself?

Mo ro wipe ẹo fẹ ki (awọn) ọmọ nyin lọ si ile ẹkọ giga. Njẹ ẹnyin yio le san owo ile-ẹkọ rẹ fun rara nyin?

If 'yes' to 19.1; if 'no' to 19.2.

19.1 Is there anyone else who can help you to pay them? Who?

Njẹ ẹnikẹni wa ti o le ran nyin l'ọwọ lati san owo naa?
Tani eni naa?

19.2 Where will the money come from?

Nibo ni owo na yio ti wa?

20 What can you do to help your children to do well in their education?

Kini nkan ti ẹ le fi ran awọn ọmọ nyin l'owo lati maa ṣe dada ni ile ẹkọ nwọn? Njẹ awọn nkan miran wa ti ẹ fun le ṣe?

21 If a boy does not finish his secondary school course, what other opportunities does he have to become an important person?

Bi ọmọ kunrin ko ba pari ẹkọ rẹ ni ile ẹkọ giga, kini awọn ọna ti o le gbe di enia pataki l'aiye yi?

22 Is it better for a man to have one wife than to have many?
Njẹ o dara fun ọkunrin lati ni iyawo kan jupe ki o ni iyawo pupọ lọ?

23 Some people say that it is better for one to have as many children as he can and to hope that one or two will do well in life; some say that it is good to limit the number so that he can educate each child at school. Which do you think is better?
Awọn enia miran sọ wipe odaraju ki enia bi ọmọ de ibi ti enia nbi ọmọ de ki enia fi ọkan si ikan tabi meji ti yio sẹ daradara l'aiye nwọn. Awọn miran sọ wipe o ye ki enia fi iwọn si ọmọ bibi ki o ba le fun ikọkan ninu awọn ọmọ rẹ ni ẹkọ to dara. Ewo ni ẹnyin ro wipe odara ju?

24 Now, I want to ask you what you think about these different jobs. I shall give you the names of three of them. Tell me the one you prefer most and the one you like next to that one. Assume that the money gained from each of them is the same. Why do you prefer the first and second jobs?
Ni isisiyi, mo fẹ beere nkan ti ẹ ro nipa awọn isẹ t'o yato siru wọnyi. Emi yio fun nyin ni ọruko mẹta ninu nwọn. Sọ fun mi ewo ni ẹ fẹ ju ninu nwọn, ewo ni ẹ fẹ s'ẹkeji. Ki ẹ fi oju inu wo wipe owo ti nwọn nri ninu awọn isẹ yi jẹ bakanna. Kini idi rẹ ti ẹ fẹ ti akọkọ? Kini idi rẹ ti ẹ fi fẹ ti ẹkrji ju ti igbẹhin lọ?

24.1 Senior civil servant—*Akọwe agba ni ile isẹ ijọba.*
Transporter   —*Eniti o ni ọkọ ero pupọ.*
Factory manager   —*Oludari ile isẹ ero.*

24.2 Secondary school headmaster—*Ọga ile-iwe giga.*
Contractor   —*Kọnitrakitọ.*
Accountant   —*Akọwe isiro owo.*

24.3 Clerk in secretariat—*Akowe ni ile isẹ ijọba.*
Motor mechanic   —*Mekaniki mọto.*
Factory worker   —*Osisẹ ni ile isẹ ero.*

24.4 Primary school teacher   —*Oluko ile-iwe alakọbẹrẹ.*
Tailor   —*Telọ.*
Kingsway shop assistant—*Olutaja ni ile-itaja bi Kingsway.*

25 Is it better for someone to work for himself or to work under someone else?
Njẹ odara ju ki enia maa sisẹ fun arare ju pe ki o maa sisẹ labẹ ẹlomiran?

25.1 But suppose you can earn more money by working for someone else?

Ṣugbọn, bi enia ba le ri owo gba lọdọ ẹlomiran julọ nkọ?

26 Some people say that hard work and suffering leads one to
become important in the world; others say that it is better to
have a helper. Which do you think is the more important?

*Awọn enia miran sọ wipe iṣẹ aṣe kara ati iya jijẹ ni o maa
nmu enia di ẹni pataki l'aiye. Awọn miran sọ wipe o yẹ ki enia
ni oluranlọwọ. Ewo ni ẹnyin ro wipe o jẹ pataki ju ninu mejeji?*

27 In Nigeria a labourer earns about £8 a month whilst a
university graduate earns £70 and can earn twice or thrice
that sum. Is this fair?

*Ni ile Nigeria, lebura ngba nkan bi pọun mẹjọ l'oṣu, nibiti eni
ti o kawe jade ni Unifasiti ngba nkan bi adọrin pọun l'oṣu ti o
de tun ni anfani ati gbai ilọpọ meji tabi mẹta eleyi. Njẹ eto yi
bojumu?*

27.1 How much should a labourer earn?

Elo lo tọ ki awọn lebura maa gba?

27.2 How much should a university graduate earn?

Elo lo tọ ki awọn ti o kawe jade ni Unifasiti maa gba?

28 Some people say that if the government has more money it
should increase the wages of the labourer; some say that it
should make secondary schooling free. What do you think?

*Awọn miran sọ wipe bi ijọba ba ni owo ko fi owo kun owo awọn
oṣiṣẹ lebura awọn kan sọ wipe ki ijọba fi owo sile ki wọn fi sọ
ile ẹkọ giga di ọfẹ. Kini ẹrọ rẹ si eleyi?*

29 If the government had more money which of these two things
should it spend it on—increased wages for workers or a
higher cocoa price for farmers?

*Bi ijọba ba ni owo pupọ sii ewo ninu nkan meji yi lo yẹ ki nwọn
na owo na sii. Ninu pe ki ijọba fi owo kun owo awọn oṣiṣẹ tabi
ki nwọn fi kun owo koko fun awọn agbe ki nwon le ni owo sii?*

30 Do you think that the Nigerian government cares for the
progress of all citizens or of a few? Whose progress does it
care for?

*Njẹ ẹ ro wipe ijọba ile Nigeria nbojuto ilọsiwaju gbogbo awọn
ọmọ ile yi tabi awọn enia diẹ ni ẹ lero pe nwọn bojuto? Awọn
enia wo ni ẹ ro wipe ijọba ni ifẹ lati mo nipa ilọsiwaju nwọn?*

31 What is the most important thing that the government can do
to help people like yourself?

Kini nkan pataki julọ ti ẹ ni ẹ ro wipe ijọba le ṣe lati fi ran enia be iru nyin l'ọwọ.

31.1 How can people like yourself get the government to help you?

Ọna wo ni awọn bii re le gba lati mu ijọba ṣe iranlọwọ yi fun nyin?

32 In which of these categories would you place yourself—rich man, common man or poor man?

Ipo wo ni e ka ara nyin kun ninu awọn ipo wọnyi—olowo, mẹkunnu, tabi talaka?

THE ASSISTANCE OF DR A. A. AKIWOWO IN DESIGNING AND TRANSLATING THIS QUESTIONNAIRE IS GRATEFULLY ACKNOWLEDGED.

Bibliography

ABERNETHY, D. B. (1969), *The Political Dilemma of Popular Education: an African Case*, Stanford University Press.

ABOYADE, O. (1969), 'The Economy of Nigeria', in *The Economics of Africa* (ed. P. Robson and D. A. Lury), Allen & Unwin, London.

ABRAHAM, R. C. (1958), *Dictionary of Modern Yoruba*, University of London Press.

ACHEBE, C. (1966), *A Man of the People*, Heinemann, London.

ADEBO (INTERIM) REPORT (1970), *First Report of the Wages and Salaries Review Commission 1970*, Federal Ministry of Information, Printing Division, Lagos.

ADEBO (FINAL) REPORT (1971), *Second and Final Report of the Wages and Salaries Review Commission*, Federal Ministry of Information, Lagos.

ADEDEJI, A. (ed.) (n.d.), *An Introduction to Western Nigeria: Its People, Culture and System of Government*, Institute of Administration, University of Ife, Nigeria.

AJAYI, J. F. A. (1965), *Christian Missions in Nigeria 1841–1891: The Making of a New Elite*, Longmans, London.

AJAYI REPORT (1963), *Report of Commission of Inquiry into the Fees charged by Public Secondary Grammar Schools and Teacher Training Colleges in Western Nigeria*, Western Nigeria Official Document No. 11 of 1963, Government Printer, Ibadan.

AKEREDOLU-ALE, E. O. (1972), 'Environmental, organizational and group factors in the evolution of private indigenous entrepreneurship in Nigeria', *Nigerian Journal of Economic and Social Studies*, 14 (2), pp. 237–56.

ALLEN, V. L. (1972), 'The meaning of the working class in Africa', *Journal of Modern African Studies*, 10 (2).

ALUKO, T. M. (1959), *One Man, One Matchet*, Heinemann, London.

ALUKO, T. M. (1965), *One Man, One Wife*, Heinemann, London.

ALUKO, T. M. (1966), *Kinsman and Foreman*, Heinemann, London.

ALUKO, T. M. (1970), *Chief the Honourable Minister*, Heinemann, London.

ALUKO, T. M. (1973), *His Worshipful Majesty*, Heinemann, London.

[AMIN, S.] (1964), 'The class struggle in Africa', *Revolution*, 1 (9), reprinted by African Research Group, Cambridge, Mass.

ANANABA, W. (1969), *The Trade Union Movement in Nigeria*, Hurst, London.

ASHBY REPORT (1960), *Investment in Education: The Report of the Commis-*

sion of Post-school Certificate and Higher Education in Nigeria, Federal Ministry of Education, Lagos.

AWE, B. (1967), 'Ibadan, its Early Beginnings' in *The City of Ibadan* (ed. P. C. Lloyd, A. L. Mabogunje and B. Awe), Cambridge University Press.

AWOLOWO, O. (1947), *Path to Nigerian Freedom*, Faber & Faber, London.

AWOLOWO, O. (1960), *Awo*, Cambridge University Press.

AWOLOWO, O. (1968), *The People's Republic*, Oxford University Press, Ibadan.

AWOLOWO, O. (1970), *The Strategy and Tactics of the People's Republic of Nigeria*, Macmillan, London.

AYOOLA REPORT (1969), *Report of a Commission of Enquiry into the Civil Disturbances which occurred in Certain Parts of the Western State of Nigeria in the Month of December 1968*, Government Printer, Ibadan.

BAETA, C. G. (1962), *Prophetism in Ghana: A Study of some Spiritual Churches*, SCM Press, London.

BANFIELD, E. C. (1958), *The Moral Basis of a Backward Society*, Free Press, Chicago.

BANFIELD, E. C. (1968), *The Unheavenly City*, Little-Brown, Boston.

BANJO REPORT (1961), *Report of the Commission Appointed to Review the Educational System of Western Nigeria*, Government Printer, Ibadan.

BEER, C. E. F. (1971), 'The Farmer and the State in Western Nigeria', Unpub. PhD thesis, University of Ibadan.

BERG, E. and WARREN, W. M. (1969), 'Urban real wages and the Nigerian trade union movement: a comment', *Economic Development and Cultural Change*, 17, pp. 607–8.

BERGHE, P. L. VAN DEN (1973), *Power and Privilege at an African University*, Routledge & Kegan Paul, London.

BERGHE, P. L. VAN DEN, and NUTTNEY, C. M. (1969), 'Some social characteristics of University of Ibadan students', *Nigerian Journal of Economic and Social Studies*, 11 (3), pp. 355–77.

BERRY, S. S. (1967), 'Cocoa in Western Nigeria 1890–1940', Unpub. PhD thesis, University of Michigan.

BOHANNAN, P. J. (1957), *Justice and Judgement among the Tiv*, Oxford University Press for International African Institute, London.

BOTTOMORE, T. B. (1965), *Classes in Modern Society*, Allen & Unwin, London.

BRIGGS, A. (1960), 'The Language of Class in Early Nineteenth Century England', in *Essays in Labour History* (ed. A. Briggs and J. Saville), Macmillan, London.

BUTCHER REPORT (1951), *Report of the Committee of Inquiry into the Allegations of Misconduct made against Chief Salami Agbaje, the Otun Balogun of Ibadan, and Allegations of inefficiency and maladministration on the part of the Ibadan and District Native Authority*, Government Printer, Lagos.

CALLAWAY, A. (1963), 'Unemployment among African school leavers', *Journal of Modern African Studies*, 1 (3), pp. 351–71.

CALLAWAY, A. (1967a) 'Education Expansion and the Rise of Youth Unemployment', in *The City of Ibadan* (ed. P. C. Lloyd, A. L. Mabogunje and B. Awe), Cambridge University Press.

CALLAWAY, A. (1967b), 'From Traditional Crafts to Modern Industries', in *The City of Ibadan* (ed. P. C. Lloyd, A. L. Mabogunje and B. Awe), Cambridge University Press.

CALLAWAY, A. (1973), *Nigerian Enterprise and the Employment of Youth: Study of 225 Businesses in Ibadan*, Nigerian Institute of Social and Economic Research, Monograph Series 2, Ibadan.

CHEVALIER, L. (1973), *Labouring Classes and Dangerous Classes*, Routledge & Kegan Paul, London.

COHEN, R. (1971), 'Further comments on the Kilby-Weeks debate', *Journal of Developing Areas*, 5, pp. 155–64.

COHEN, R. (1972), 'Class in Africa: Analytical Problems and Perspectives' in *The Socialist Register 1972* (ed. R. Miliband and J. Saville), Merlin Press, London.

COLEMAN, J. S. (1960), *Nigeria: Background to Nationalism*, University of California Press.

EKUNDARE, R. O. (1972), 'The political economy of private enterprise in Nigeria', *Journal of Modern African Studies*, 10 (1), pp. 37–56.

FADIPE, N. A. (1970), *The Sociology of the Yoruba*, Ibadan University Press.

FIELD, M. J. (1960), *Search for Security*, Faber & Faber, London.

FOSTER, P. (1965), *Education and Social Change in Ghana*, Routledge & Kegan Paul, London.

GALLETTI, R., BALDWIN, K. D. S. and DINA, I. O. (1956), *Nigerian Cocoa Farmers*, Oxford University Press, London.

GANS, H. (1962), *The Urban Villagers*, Free Press, New York.

GARBETT, C. K. (1970), 'The analysis of social situations', *Man*, (n.s.) 5 (2), pp. 214–27.

GLUCKMAN, M. (1955), *The Judicial Process among the Barotse of Northern Rhodesia*, Manchester University Press for Rhodes-Livingstone Institute.

GOLDTHORPE, J. H., LOCKWOOD, D., BECHHOFER, F. and PLATT, J. (1969), *The Affluent Worker in the Class Structure*, Cambridge University Press.

GRUNDY, K. W. (1964), 'The "class struggle" in Africa: an examination of conflicting theories', *Journal of Modern African Studies*, 2 (3), pp. 379–93.

GURR, T. R. (1970), *Why Men Rebel*, Princeton University Press.

GUTKIND, P. C. W. (1967), 'The energy of despair: social organization of the unemployed in two African cities: Lagos and Nairobi', *Civilisations*, 17 (3) and (4), pp. 186–215, 380–405.

GUTKIND, P. C. W. (1973), 'From the energy of despair to the anger of despair', *Canadian Journal of African Studies*, 7 (2), pp. 179–98.

HARRIS, J. R. (1968), 'Nigerian enterprise in the printing industry', *Nigerian Journal of Economic and Social Studies*, 10 (2), pp. 215–27.

HARRIS, J. R. (1971), 'Nigerian Entrepreneurship in Industry', in *Entrepreneurship and Economic Development* (ed. P. Kilby), Free Press, New York.

HARRIS, J. R. and ROWE, M. P. (1966), 'Entrepreneurial patterns in the Nigerian sawmilling industry', *Nigerian Journal of Economic and Social Studies*, 8 (1), pp. 67–95.

HEISLER, H. (1970), 'A class of target-proletarians', *Journal of Asian and African Studies*, 5 (3), pp. 161–75.

HELLEINER, G. K. (1966), *Peasant Agriculture, Government and Economic Growth in Nigeria*, Irwin, Homewood, Illinois.

HOBSBAWM, E. J. (1971), 'Class Consciousness in History', in *Aspects of History and Class Consciousness* (ed. I. Mészáros), Routledge & Kegan Paul, London.

HOPKINS, A. G. (1966), 'The Lagos strike of 1897: an exploration in Nigerian labour history', *Past and Present*, 35, pp. 133–55.

HOPKINS, A. G. (1973), *An Economic History of West Africa*, Longmans, London.

HUGHES, A. and COHEN, R. (1971), *Towards the Emergence of a Nigerian Working Class*, Occasional Paper, Series D, No. 7, Faculty of Commerce and Social Science, University of Birmingham.

IDOWU, E. B. (1962), *Olodumare: God in Yoruba Belief*, Longmans, London.

ISKENDEROV, A. (1972), *Africa: Politics, Economy, Ideology*, Progress Publishers, Moscow.

IWAJOMO, T. A. (n.d.), 'The Western Nigeria Economy', in *An Introduction to Western Nigeria* (ed. A. Adedeji), Institute of Administration, University of Ife, Ibadan.

JAHODA, G. (1966), 'Social aspirations, magic and witchcraft in Ghana: a social psychological interpretation', in *The New Elites of Tropical Africa* (ed. P. C. Lloyd), Oxford University Press for International African Institute, London.

JONES, G. S. (1971), *Outcast London*, Clarendon Press, Oxford.

KELVIN, P. (1970), *The Bases of Social Behaviour*, Holt, Rinehart & Winston, London.

KILBY, P. (1965), *African Enterprise: The Nigerian Bread Industry*, Stanford University Press.

KILBY, P. (1967), 'Industrial relations and wage determination: failure of the Anglo Saxon model', *Journal of Developing Areas*, 1, pp. 489–520.

KILBY, P. (1968), 'A reply to John F. Weeks' comment', *Journal of Developing Areas*, 3, pp. 19–25.

KILBY, P. (1969), *Industrialization in an Open Economy: Nigeria 1945–1966*, Cambridge University Press.

KILBY, P. (1971), 'Further comment on the Kilby-Weeks debate: final observations', *Journal of Developing Areas*, 5, pp. 175–6.

KOPYTOFF, J. H. (1965), *A Preface to Modern Nigeria*, University of Wisconsin Press, Madison.

LEACH, E. R. (1966), 'The legitimacy of Solomon: some structural aspects of Old Testament History', *European Journal of Sociology*, 7, pp. 58–101.

LERNER, D. (1958), *The Passing of Traditional Society*, Free Press, Chicago.

LEWIS, O. (1968), *La Vida*, Panther, London.

LITTLE, K. L. (1965), *West African Urbanization*, Cambridge University Press.

LLOYD, B. B. (1966), 'Education and Family Life in the Development of Class Identification among the Yoruba', in *The New Elites of Tropical Africa* (ed. P. C. Lloyd), Oxford University Press for International African Institute, London.

LLOYD, B. B. (1967), 'Indigenous Ibadan', in *The City of Ibadan* (ed. P. C. Lloyd, A. L. Mabogunje and B. Awe), Cambridge University Press.

LLOYD, B. B. (1968), 'Choice behaviour and social structure: a comparison of two African societies', *Journal of Social Psychology*, 74, pp. 3–12.

LLOYD, P. C. (1953), 'Craft organisation in Yoruba towns', *Africa*, 33 (1), pp. 30–44.

LLOYD, P. C. (1955a), 'The development of political parties in Western Nigeria', *American Political Science Review*, 49, pp. 693–707.

LLOYD, P. C. (1955b), 'The Yoruba lineage', *Africa*, 25 (3), pp. 235–51.

LLOYD, P. C. (1960), 'Sacred kingship and government among the Yoruba', *Africa*, 30 (3), pp. 221–37.

LLOYD, P. C. (1962), *Yoruba Land Law*, Oxford University Press for Nigerian Institute of Social and Economic Research, London.

LLOYD, P. C. (1963), 'The status of the Yoruba wife', *Sudan Society*, 2, pp. 35–42.

LLOYD, P. C. (1964), 'Traditional Rulers', in *Political Parties and National Integration in Tropical Africa* (ed. J. S. Coleman and C. Rosberg), University of California Press.

LLOYD, P. C. (1965a), 'The Yoruba of Nigeria', in *Peoples of Africa* (ed. J. L. Gibbs), Holt, Rinehart & Winston, New York.

LLOYD, P. C. (1965b), 'The Political Structure of African Kingdoms: an Exploratory Model', in *Political Systems and the Distribution of Power* (ed. M. Banton), A.S.A. Monograph 2, Tavistock, London.

LLOYD, P. C. (1966a), 'Agnatic and cognatic descent among the Yoruba', *Man*, (n.s.) 1 (4), pp. 484–500.

LLOYD, P. C. (1966b), 'Class Consciousness among the Yoruba', in *The New Elites of Tropical Africa* (ed. P. C. Lloyd), Oxford University Press for International African Institute, London.

LLOYD, P. C. (1967a), *Africa in Social Change*, Penguin, Harmondsworth.

LLOYD, P. C. (1967b), 'The Elite', in *The City of Ibadan* (ed. P. C. Lloyd, A. L. Mabogunje and B. Awe), Cambridge University Press.

LLOYD, P. C. (1968a), 'Divorce among the Yoruba', *American Anthropologist*, 70 (1), pp. 67–81.

LLOYD, P. C. (1968b), 'Conflict Theory and Yoruba Kingdoms', in *History and Social Anthropology* (ed. I. M. Lewis), A.S.A. Monograph 7, Tavistock Publications, London.

LLOYD, P. C. (1971a), *The political development of Yoruba kingdoms in the eighteenth and nineteenth centuries*, Occasional Paper 31, Royal Anthropological Institute, London.

LLOYD, P. C. (1971b) *Classes, Crises and Coups*, MacGibbon & Kee, London.

LLOYD, P. C. (1974), 'Ijebu', in *African Kingdoms Today* (ed. R. Le-Marchand), Cass, London.

LLOYD, P. C., MABOGUNJE, A. L. and AWE, B. (eds) (1967), *The City of Ibadan*, Cambridge University Press.

LUCKHAM, R. (1971), *The Nigerian Military*, Cambridge University Press.

MABOGUNJE, A. L. (1962), *Yoruba Towns*, Ibadan University Press.

MABOGUNJE, A. L. (1967), 'The Morphology of Ibadan', in *The City of*

Ibadan (ed. P. C. Lloyd, A. L. Mabogunje and B. Awe), Cambridge University Press.

MABOGUNJE, A. L. (1968), *Urbanization in Nigeria*, University of London Press.

MCHUGH, P. (1968), *Defining the Situation*, Bobbs-Merrill, Indianapolis.

MANGIN, W. (1967), 'Latin American squatter settlements: a problem and a solution', *Latin American Research Review*, 2 (3), pp. 65–98.

MELLANBY, K. (1958), *The Birth of Nigeria's University*, Methuen, London.

MELSON, R. (1970), 'Nigerian Politics and the General Strike of 1964', in *Protest and Power in Black Africa* (ed. R. I. Rotberg and A. A. Mazrui), Oxford University Press, New York.

MILIBAND, R. (1971), 'Barnave: a case of bourgeois class consciousness' in *Aspects of History and Class Consciousness* (ed. I. Mészáros), Routledge & Kegan Paul, London.

MITCHELL, J. C. (ed.) (1969), *Social Networks in Urban Situations*, Manchester University Press.

MORGAN REPORT (1964), *Report of the Commission on the Review of Wages, Salary and Conditions of Service of the Junior Employees of the Governments of the Federation and in Private Establishments 1963–64*, Federal Ministry of Information, Printing Division, Lagos.

OLAKANPO, O. (1968), 'A statistical analysis of some determinants of entrepreneurial success: a Nigerian case study', *Nigerian Journal of Economic and Social Studies*, 10 (2), pp. 137–52.

OMOYAJOWO, J. A. (1965), *Witches?*, Abiodun Printing Works Ltd, Ibadan.

OREWA, G. O. (1962), *Taxation in Western Nigeria*, Oxford University Press for Nigerian Institute of Social and Economic Research, London.

OSSOWSKI, S. (1963), *Class Structure in the Social Consciousness*, Routledge & Kegan Paul, London.

PANTER-BRICK, S. K. (ed.) (1970), *Nigerian Politics and Military Rule: Prelude to the Civil War*, Athlone Press, London.

PEACE, A. J. (1973), 'Social Change at Agege: Tribe, Status and Class in a Nigerian Township', Unpub. DPhil thesis, University of Sussex.

PEACE, A. J. (1974), 'Industrial Protest in Nigeria' in *Sociology and Development* (ed. E. de Kadt and G. Williams), Tavistock Publications, London.

PEACE, A. J. (forthcoming), 'The Lagos Proletariat: Labour Aristocrats or Populist Militants', in *The Development of an African Working Class* (ed. K. R. J. Sandbrook and R. Cohen), Longmans, London.

PEEL, J. D. Y. (1968), *Aladura: A Religious Movement among the Yorubas*, Oxford University Press, London.

PERISTIANY, J. G. (ed.) (1965), *Honour and Shame: The Values of Mediterranean Society*, Weidenfeld & Nicolson, London.

PORTES, A. (1971), 'On the interpretation of class consciousness', *American Journal of Sociology*, 77 (2) pp. 228–44.

PORTES, A. (1972), 'Rationality in the slum: an essay on interpretive sociology', *Comparative Studies in Society and History*, 14 (3), pp. 268–86.

POST, K. W. J. and JENKINS, G. D. (1973), *The Price of Liberty: Personality and Politics in Colonial Nigeria*, Cambridge University Press.

POST, K. and VICKERS, M. (1973), *Structure and Conflict in Nigeria 1960–1966*, Heinemann, London.

PRINCE, R. (1961), 'The Yoruba image of the witch', *Journal of Mental Science*, 107.

REES, J. (1971), *Equality*, Pall Mall Press, London.

RUNCIMAN, W. G. (1966), *Relative Deprivation and Social Justice*, Routledge & Kegan Paul, London.

SAUNDERS, J. T. (1960), *University College Ibadan*, Cambridge University Press.

SCHUTZ, A. (1972), *The Phenomenology of the Social World*, Heinemann, London.

SCHWARZ, W. (1968), *Nigeria*, Pall Mall Press, London.

SKLAR, R. L. (1963), *Nigerian Political Parties*, Princeton University Press.

SOYINKA, W. (1964), *Five Plays*, Oxford University Press, London.

STRICKON, A. (1967), 'Folk Models of Stratification', in *Latin American Sociological Studies* (ed. P. Halmos), *Sociological Review* Monograph 11.

TAIWO REPORT (1968), *Report of the Committee on the Review of the Primary Education System in the Western State of Nigeria*, Government Printer, Ibadan.

TERIBA, O. and PHILLIPS, A. O. (1971), 'Income distribution and national integration', *Nigerian Journal of Economic and Social Studies*, 13 (1), pp. 77–122.

TOURAINE, A. and RAGAZZI, O. (1961), *Ouvriers d'origine agricole*, Laboratoire de Sociologie Industrielle de l'École Pratique des Hautes Études, Paris.

TOYO, E. (n.d.), *The Working Class and the Nigerian Crisis*, Sketch Publishing Co. Ltd, Ibadan.

TYLER, S. A. (ed.) (1969), *Cognitive Anthropology*, Holt, Rinehart & Winston, New York.

(UCCLO) UNITED COMMITTEE OF CENTRAL LABOUR ORGANISATIONS (1970), *Equitable Demand for Economic Growth and National Prosperity*, Government Printer, Ibadan.

WAKEMAN, C. W. (1950), *A Dictionary of the Yoruba Language*, Oxford University Press, London.

WALLACE, A. F. C. (1961), *Culture and Personality*, Random House, New York.

WALLACE, A. F. C. (1965), 'Driving to Work', in *Context and Meaning in Cultural Anthropology* (ed. M. Spiro), Free Press, New York.

WEBSTER, J. B. (1964), *The African Churches among the Yoruba 1888–1922*, Clarendon Press, Oxford.

WEEKS, J. F. (1968), 'A comment on Peter Kilby: industrial relations and wage determination', *Journal of Developing Areas*, 3, pp. 7–17.

WEEKS, J. F. (1971), 'Further comment on the Weeks-Kilby debate', *Journal of Developing Areas*, 5, pp. 165–74.

WILLIAMS, G. P. (1970), 'The Social Stratification of a Neo-colonial

Economy: Western Nigeria', in *African Perspectives* (ed. C. Allen and R. W. Johnson), Cambridge University Press.

WILLIAMS, G. P. (1974), 'Political Consciousness among the Ibadan Poor', in *Sociology and Development* (ed. E. de Kadt and G. Williams), Tavistock Publications, London.

WOODIS, J. (1972), *New Theories of Revolution*, Lawrence & Wishart, London.

WORSLEY, P. (1972), 'Frantz Fanon and the "Lumpenproletariat" ', in *The Socialist Register 1972* (ed. R. Miliband and J. Saville), Merlin Press, London.

YESUFU, T. M. (1962), *An Introduction to Industrial Relations in Nigeria*, Oxford University Press, London.

Statistical sources

FEDERATION OF NIGERIA (1963), *Manpower Situation in Nigeria*, National Manpower Board, Manpower Studies No. 1, Federal Ministry of Information, Printing Division, Lagos.

FEDERATION OF NIGERIA (1968), *Management in Nigerian Industries*, National Manpower Board, Manpower Studies No. 8 by T. M. Yesufu, Federal Ministry of Information, Printing Division, Lagos.

WESTERN STATE OF NIGERIA (1966–), *Report of a sample survey of unemployment among school leavers*, 1 December 1966, 2 December 1967, 3 1968, 4 1969, Ministry of Economic and Social Development, Statistics Division, Ibadan.

WESTERN STATE OF NIGERIA (1970, 1971), *Digest of Income Tax Statistics*, Ministry of Economic Planning and Reconstruction, Statistics Division, Ibadan.

WESTERN STATE OF NIGERIA (1971), *Industrial Statistics of Western Nigeria, December 1970, Vol. 3, No. 1*, Ministry of Economic Planning and Reconstruction, Statistics Division, Ibadan.

WESTERN STATE OF NIGERIA (1970), *Staff List, Revised to 1st April 1969*, Government Printer, Ibadan.

WESTERN STATE OF NIGERIA (1960–), *Statistical Bulletin*, Ministry of Economic Planning and Reconstruction, Statistics Division, Ibadan.

WESTERN STATE OF NIGERIA (1971), *Western State Development Plan 1970–74*, Ministry of Economic Planning and Reconstruction, Ibadan.

WESTERN STATE OF NIGERIA (1960–), *Digest of Local Government Statistics*, Ministry of Economic Planning and Reconstruction, Statistics Division, Ibadan.

WESTERN REGION OF NIGERIA (1959), *Triennial Report on Education, 1st April 1955 to 31st March 1958*, Sessional Paper No. 11 of 1959, Government Printer, Ibadan.

WESTERN REGION/STATE OF NIGERIA (1960–), *Annual Abstract/Digest of Education Statistics*, Government Printer, Ibadan.

Index